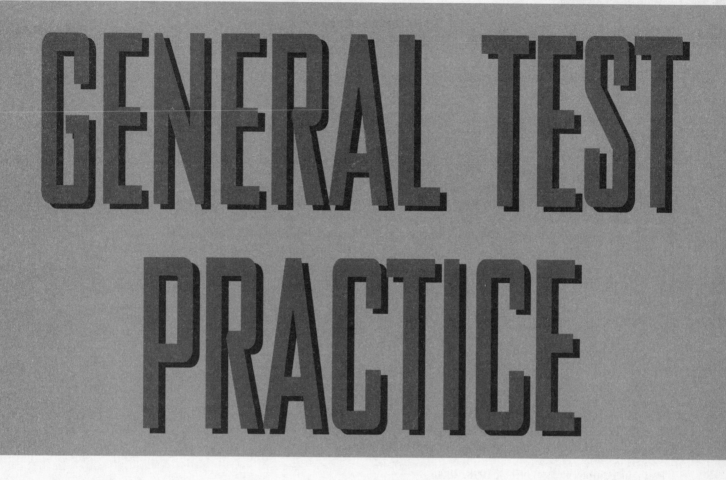

GENERAL TEST PRACTICE

FOR 101 U.S. JOBS
5TH EDITION

Hy Hammer

**Revised by
Kim Munzert**

THOMSON

PETERSON'S ™

Australia • Canada • Mexico • Singapore • Spain • United Kingdom • United States

About Thomson Peterson's

Thomson Peterson's (www.petersons.com) is a leading provider of education information and advice, with books and online resources focusing on education search, test preparation, and financial aid. Its Web site offers searchable databases and interactive tools for contacting educational institutions, online practice tests and instruction, and planning tools for securing financial aid. Peterson's serves 110 million education consumers annually.

Petersons.com/publishing

Check out our Web site at www.petersons.com/publishing to see if there are any revisions or corrections to the content of this book. We've made sure the information in this book is accurate and up-to-date; however, content may have changed since the time of publication.

For more information, contact Peterson's, 2000 Lenox Drive, Lawrenceville, NJ 08648; 800-338-3282; or find us on the World Wide Web at www.petersons.com/about.

ISBN 0-7645-6103-0

Printed in the United States of America

10 9 8 7 6 5 4   05 04

CONTENTS

PART THREE
Arithmetic Ability

PART 4
Appendices

INTRODUCTION

The Idea Behind General Test Practice

Hundreds of federal civil service tests are based in whole or in part on the so-called *General Test*. *General Test* questions probe your overall level of intelligence and your ability to work in many different government jobs. If you acquire the knack of scoring high on these *General Test* questions, you can practically name your job.

This book provides extensive practice in *General Test* subjects, among them word meaning, grammar, reading comprehension, spelling, and arithmetic. When prepared in these subjects, you will have a competitive edge over other candidates. You will learn by a proven question and answer method carefully presented to bring out the best in you.

The U.S. Office of Personnel Management frequently employs *General Test* questions in making up its exams and in testing candidates for jobs. In this way, OPM gets an indication of the candidate's general intelligence and ability to succeed in a variety of government jobs.

This book is based on a study of the kinds of questions that the OPM has employed on its tests in past years. New question types may be developed and used in the future, but the tried-and-true *General Test* standbys are not likely to be abandoned.

There is no *General Test* as such, although there are intelligence (I.Q.) tests that are composed solely on the basis of *General Test* subjects.

This book prepares you for the question types given most frequently on federal examinations. Therefore, it prepares you most efficiently for a good part of any federal civil service exam that you might want to take. Although state, county, and municipal civil service exams utilize *General Test* questions, we concentrate on federal exams in this book.

For some exams, this book may be all you need. But for other jobs, in which the examinations are more specialized, you should also study the Arco text prepared especially for that exam.

How General Test Subjects Are Used

In addition to appearing on federal, state, county, and municipal civil service examinations, *General Test* questions are quite frequently used on intelligence (I.Q.) tests, scholastic aptitude tests, military placement exams, and employment tests for jobs in industry. *General Test* subjects may be broken down into clerical, verbal, and arithmetic areas.

CLERICAL ABILITIES

Alphabetizing and Filing. General Test Practice explains the basic rules for alphabetic filing and makes helpful suggestions for mastering this *General Test* question category.

Clerical Speed and Accuracy. This section gives helpful hints and practice with the clerical portion of the General Test. Clerical questions often must be answered under time pressure, and you may face penalties for inaccuracies.

Typing. Typing is another *General Test* subject. Typing may enter into the competitive score or may be included as a pass/fail topic.

VERBAL ABILITIES

English Grammar and Usage. General Test Practice explains the simple rules of grammar and provides abundant practice for correct usage. This is the first step to scoring high on any exam.

Spelling. This section explains the basic rules of this essential job tool and provides practice with sample tests.

Synonyms. General Test Practice not only shows how to choose the word that means the same as the one given in a test question, but it also shows how to choose the word whose meaning is closest to that word.

Sentence Completions. This is one of the most difficult areas of federal exams because sentence completions are often tricky in their wording. This section shows how to supply the missing word that best completes the meaning of the sentence.

Reading Comprehension. This type of *General Test* question might be used on readings in a variety of fields, such as clerical, administrative, and business. *General Test Practice* prepares you for a broad spectrum of reading comprehension questions.

Effective Expression. This section not only sums up what you have learned in the previous verbal sections, but it also provides the training to make your writing on the job clear and effective.

Verbal Analogies. This section explains and illustrates this rather difficult type of verbal question, which is based on the relationship of words.

ARITHMETIC ABILITIES

Fractions, Decimals, and Percents. General Test Practice simply and clearly explains the principles behind these three arithmetic categories. As in the rest of the book, each test problem is explained afterward.

Graphs. Graph problems can be conquered when you grasp the principles explained in this section. A graph is a picture; this section prepares you to see the "complete picture" and to supply the correct answers.

Ratio and Proportion. Long a popular type of question given on exams, ratio and proportion questions are clearly illustrated here so that you will feel confident when you have to tackle them.

Work and Rank Problems. Work and rank problems have become increasingly popular because they pose the sort of problems that must be solved on the job. *General Test Practice* shows you how to score high.

Tabular Completion. This is the newest type of arithmetic question to appear in federal *General Tests.* The explanations clarify the method for answering these questions.

Arithmetic Reasoning. A wrap-up including typical arithmetic questions.

Aptitude and Ability Tests

When using *General Test Practice,* it is helpful to understand the distinction between *aptitude* tests and *ability* (or *achievement*) tests.

Aptitude tests are used to estimate overall level of intellectual function, apart from schooling. The general intelligence (or I.Q.) test seeks to measure a candidate's *aptitude* for learning. *Aptitude* tests are used to predict success in some occupation, such as engineering, stenography, music, police work, and so on. In form, these tests are not distinctly different from other types. A clerical aptitude test might include sections measuring general mental ability, clerical knowledge, and possibly even spatial reasoning. The test is referred to as an *ability* test when it is used primarily to examine a person's success in past study, and as an *aptitude* test when it is used to forecast success in some future assignment.

Ability (or *achievement*) tests are designed to assess the effects of a specified course of training. Any standardized examination on a school course is an *achievement test*. Trade tests, for use in screening and selecting industrial, business, and civil service employees, constitute another type of achievement test. As in educational achievement tests, such trade tests assume that the testtakers have had a specific course of instruction, job apprenticeship, or other relatively uniform experience.

Obviously, some schooling is necessary in order to answer questions in the *General Test* subjects of reading, spelling, grammar, English usage, and arithmetic. But they demand less schooling than most other subjects that are employed in testing candidates for particular jobs. Consequently the *General Test* subjects are regarded as reasonably good measures of a candidate's *aptitude* for learning.

General Test subjects are favored by the U.S. Office of Personnel Management because they tend to probe a candidate's native intelligence and *aptitude* for learning how to do a job and to succeed in it. The Commission does not want to handicap those candidates who have been deprived of a complete education.

Because *aptitude* and *ability* tests overlap each other, it clearly behooves all candidates for U.S. civil service positions to study the subject matter and to learn how to achieve the highest scores on *General Test* questions. Our experience has shown that it is possible to improve your scores, and thus to demonstrate your *aptitude* for a job.

Government Job Search: Acquiring an Overview

Most portions of text in this section, and the appendices provided in the back of this book, are excerpts from the recently released 14th edition of the *Civil Service Handbook*. Those portions have been included here to help you get a better overview of the government job market and to develop your government job search.

The nature of government employment is unique. Anyone seriously seeking a career with the government should also get the 14th edition of the *Civil Service Handbook*, in addition to this *General Test Practice* publication. The entire 14th edition of the *Civil Service Handbook* is an invaluable tool and is a good companion text to the *General Test Practice* publication.

While this book has the primary goal to provide practice tests, the *Civil Service Handbook* is a guide to the employment search itself. The *Civil Service Handbook* includes many employment topics not covered here, including local and state government employment and U.S. Postal Service jobs. It also includes specific postal employment tests.

DECIDING ON THE BEST JOB FOR YOU

There is no easy formula for comparing civil service jobs to those in the private sector. There are no numbers that result in a right or wrong answer to the question of where you should work. You have only advantages and disadvantages to consider, each of which has its own importance to your particular situation. Many of the advantages are practical: salary, healthcare, vacation, and pension benefits. Conversely, many of the disadvantages are more a matter of atmosphere, context, and your own personality.

The smart way to make the decision is to be absolutely honest about your needs, your family's needs, what motivates you, and even what drives you crazy. Ask yourself these tough questions:

- How much money is "enough"?
- How much job risk is tolerable?
- How much money does your family need?
- How much risk can your family tolerate?
- What are the health benefit needs of you and your family?
- How well do you handle change?
- Do you require constant change?
- What type of work environment do you prefer? (slow-paced vs. fast-paced, and so on)
- How well do you work with other people?
- Can you be a team player, or must you be the "star"?
- How much frustration can you tolerate, in exchange for how much security?

You will have to choose which factors make the most sense for you and your personal situation. You'll also have to rely on a certain level of instinct and decide which feels right to you—or at least feels better.

Launching Your Federal Government Job Search

The federal government is so huge and complicated that it may be difficult to envision yourself as a federal employee. You're familiar with civil service on the local area: You know your town or city's police and fire personnel, at least by sight, and you've probably had dealings with local officials. You may even be somewhat familiar with civil service on the county level; perhaps you've had jury duty and have toured the county's court and jail system.

But what about the *federal* government? We seldom think of our local letter carrier as a federal employee, so trying to "break into Washington" may summon up the picture of ourselves knocking on the door of the White House.

But the federal government has innumerable offices throughout the country. Look in your county phone book for the government listings. The Veterans Administration, Social Security Administration, various divisions of the Armed Forces, the Justice Department, the Internal Revenue Service, the Small Business Department, the Department of Transportation, and others all likely have offices surprisingly close to where you live right now. And everyone in those offices is a federal employee. You could be, too.

General Job Categories and Programs Available at the Federal Level

The federal government is the country's largest employer. That means it has room for almost every imaginable occupation. It also has an enormous variety of special programs to encompass many different hiring situations. A quick look will show you just how many:

- **Professional occupations** require knowledge of a field that is usually gained through education or training equivalent to a bachelor's degree or higher, with major study in or pertinent to the specialized field—for example, engineer, accountant, biologist, chemist.
- **Administrative occupations** usually require progressively responsible experience. More than a college education is required, although professional training and study may be involved—for example, personnel specialist, administrative officer.

- **Technical occupations** involve training and experience—for example, computer programmer, telecommunications specialist, or electronics technician.
- **Clerical occupations** generally involve structured work in support of office, business, or fiscal operations—for example, clerk-typist, mail and file clerk.
- **Skilled trades** involve manual work that usually requires a "journeyman" status in fields—for example, plumber, HVAC technician, electrician, carpenter, and machinist.

PART-TIME PROGRAMS

Part-time positions—that is, positions involving 16 to 32 hours per week—are available in agencies throughout the federal government. Flex time, job sharing, and nontraditional workday and workweek scheduling is also available in some positions. Inquire at personnel offices in agencies where you feel that you may want to apply.

STUDENT PROGRAMS

The Federal government has a number of programs in place specifically designed to provide employment for students. These programs include:

- **Summer employment** is available for high school, college, law, medical, and dental students. Applications are accepted for summer employment from December through April 15, and the jobs usually run from mid-May through September 30. Hiring is done by individual agencies. Some restrictions limit summer employment in the same agency where the applicant's parent may be employed.
- **The federal student career program** is a work/study option for high school, vocational or technical school, and college students enrolled in school at least half-time. This program offers employment in positions directly related to the student's course of study. Positions in this program can lead to permanent employment upon a student's graduation. Students interested in this option should contact their high school counselors or college employment coordinators, or the agency where they would like to work.
- **Student temporary employment** offers a part-time opportunity for students. These positions are not necessarily related to the professional careers for which these students are preparing themselves. This employment must end when a student is no longer enrolled in school at least half-time. The procedure for identifying and qualifying for this program is similar to the federal student career experience.
- **The Presidential Management Interns (PMI) program** is targeted at graduate students in the last year of their advanced studies who intend to make a career in public service. Only graduate students who expect to receive their degrees by the following June should apply. These students enter the two-year PMI program at the GS-9 level and perform high-level work in their chosen fields. At the end of the two years, PMIs may continue in regular federal employment at the GS-12 level. Students interested in this program must be nominated by the dean of the college or university, or by the chairman of their department or graduate program.

VETERAN PROGRAMS

U.S. Military veterans are entitled to special consideration in federal hiring. In some cases, veterans are entitled to positions that are not open to the general public. In other cases, extra points are added to their exam scores, giving them a competitive advantage. The Veterans Employment Coordinator at the agency where you apply can give you additional information.

PROGRAMS FOR PERSONS WITH DISABILITIES

Persons with disabilities should contact the Selective Placement Coordinator at the agency of interest to explore special placement assistance that is available to candidates with physical, cognitive, or emotional disabilities. By law, the federal government—just as the private sector must—will make "reasonable workplace accommodations" for persons with disabilities; this means that the employer may adjust the duties of the job, the location where it's performed, or the methods in which it's performed.

PROGRAMS FOR RESIDENTS OUTSIDE THE CONTINENTAL UNITED STATES

Alaska, Guam, Hawaii, Puerto Rico, and the Virgin Islands offer very limited federal employment possibilities. Local residents will receive first consideration for employment in these areas. Other candidates will be considered only when no qualified residents are available.

How to Find Federal Jobs That Are Right for You

Matching your experience and background to a federal job is perhaps one of the most difficult aspects of getting federal work. Part of this difficulty results from the fact that you have to find the vacancies yourself. You can't simply send in a resume or application and say, "Hey, Washington—here's what I can do. Who wants to hire me?"

There's no centralized personnel department for the federal government. Years ago, the Office of Personnel Management (OPM) used to serve that function. However, with so many agencies and so many applicants, OPM would take months to identify candidates and send their applications to the agency with the opening. Agencies complained that it was almost impossible to hire the people they needed *when* they needed them. Finally, OPM gave up its authority in this area, and now each federal agency does its own hiring. The result, however, doesn't make it easier for applicants, for a number of reasons, many of which are discussed here.

YOU MUST LOOK BEYOND THE TITLE

Say you want to become a federal employee. You're open to a number of position types, but because of your background, you look for jobs with titles similar to your current title. If you limit yourself to that, you might miss other openings for which you qualify. Instead of looking at a title and thinking, "I don't have the experience to do that," pick titles that make you think, "Gee, that sounds interesting." Then read the qualifications. You just might be eligible.

Some titles also can be very deceptive. When looking for a federal position, for example, an administrative assistant rightfully may think that the position of "secretary" could be appropriate, and then may discover that it's for a high-ranking executive (think Secretary of State). Or, a recent graduate might see impressive-sounding titles such as Agriculture Science Research Technician or Airway Transportation Systems Specialist and immediately assume that these are higher-ranked jobs for people with years of experience. A look at the salary, however, shows that these jobs start at under $22,000— obviously positions for the newer employee. A few extra seconds of investigation can help you decipher the title to get a closer look at the job.

Additionally, don't dismiss federal work in general because you think government wouldn't hire "someone like you." The government needs more than just accountants, soldiers, mechanics, clerks, nuclear scientists, and so on. On a single recent day, there were openings for a graphic illustrator, a sports specialist, an archaeologist, a horticulturist, a manager for a community club, an outdoor-recreation planner, a leisure-travel arranger, and a religious education specialist. What's even more surprising than the variety is that all these jobs were for the same agency—the Army!

KEEP CHECKING THE ANNOUNCEMENTS

You must apply for a particular position in a particular agency because you're really applying for a specific vacancy, not just a job title. Most agencies don't refer to past applications. They don't "keep your resume on file," like many private-sector companies do. Think of it like this: You're not just applying for, say, an accounting position. When accountant Pat Smith retires, it's Pat Smith's vacancy that you're applying for. What this means in terms of legwork is a constant monitoring of openings.

For every opening, agencies must publish an announcement of the vacancy, if they're going to fill it. This means that you must constantly watch the job vacancy announcements for the agency you're interested in—or keep track of vacancies for several agencies, if you're focused more on the kind of job rather than the agency where you perform it.

APPLY SEPARATELY FOR EACH VACANCY

Each time you spot an appropriate vacancy, you usually must fill out an application form. You can't ask Agency X to refer to the application you sent in last month to Agency Y, even though that application might have taken days to fill out and was two dozen pages long. Except for a few closely related jobs that might be open within the same agency, each position requires its own application.

TAILOR YOUR APPLICATION OR RESUME TO THE JOB

While you would do this in the private sector as well, there is simply no comparison to the depth of "tailoring" that's needed to get federal employment. The two-dozen page application mentioned previously is not an exaggeration. Your application should mirror the language of the vacancy announcement and then provide details that prove you have the knowledge, skills, and abilities (abbreviated KSAs) to fill the opening. You'll learn more about KSAs in the next section.

WATCH OUT FOR CIVIL SERVICE JOB-HELP SCAMS

About now you may be asking yourself, "Can't anyone help me? Aren't there federal employment agencies?" And the answer is—beware! The government does not sign itself up with employment agencies the way a private-sector company might, so avoid any "employment agency" promising that the government or a particular agency is its client and that it can help you get the job you want—for a hefty fee.

Everything you need to get federal work can be had directly from the government, and it's readily available if you're willing to spend the time and do the legwork to find it. All the information is free, the forms and directions are free, and the process of applying is free. A person or agency that suggests otherwise is stealing from you as directly as a pickpocket. Also beware a person or agency that guarantees you a job, guarantees you a higher score, or says that there are "hidden" vacancies not listed in the announcements, but which *they* can reveal to you.

REMEMBER, YOU *CAN* DO IT YOURSELF

What's *legitimate* help? Your *Civil Service Handbook* and other guides to the topic are not only legitimate, but they're often your best buy because they give you the most bang for your buck. These guides can save you time and effort, plus give you valuable proven tips that you might not have discovered otherwise.

There are also personal coaches who will hold your hand step by step through the search-and-application process. They, too, are legitimate, but sometimes they provide simply the same information that's in a guide like this, only at higher cost because of the personalized, one-on-one nature of the service.

With the advent of the Internet also comes brand new legitimate help—search engines that automatically match up keywords in your experience or education with keywords in current vacancies. Some of the free government sites will do this, and some private sites provide this matching, as well as a range of other services, for varying prices—a monthly subscription cost in some cases, or a flat fee per each service in others.

If you're interested in this type of help, however, try to stay with sites that appear as links on official government Web pages. These will be the most reputable. And check carefully. Some online sites have names implying that they're "official government sites" by tagging "U.S." or "American" or the like onto the site title—and then they bury the fee down where the information you want most is located. A reputable private site should say right up front that it's a private source of information.

Speaking of sources of information, we're up to the next question on any job seeker's list: If you can apply only for a specific opening, where do you find announcements about actual job vacancies?

Making Contact: How and Where to Track Down Actual Job Vacancies

Although the difficulty involved may convince you otherwise, the federal government *wants* you to work for it. It has many avenues through which you can find out what openings are available in what agencies. The following sections discuss the many sources for federal employment information and job bank listings.

DIRECT CONTACT

If you know which agency or agencies you want to work for, you may contact them directly to learn what vacancies exist and how to apply for them. At some agencies, you may be able to prepare an application that will be kept on file for future vacancies. Other agencies accept applications only for current or projected openings. Ask so that you'll know whether the agency's openings need constant monitoring.

If a federal agency has an office in your area, you may find its telephone number under "U.S. Government" in the blue pages of the phone book. If the agency has no office in your area, place a call to information in the District of Columbia, 202-555-1212, and ask for the telephone number of the personnel office or employment office of the agency you want to reach. Calls to government offices must be made during business hours, so prepare your questions ahead of time to hold down your phone bill.

To get you started, Appendix A, "Important Civil Service Employment Contacts," lists phone numbers, addresses, and Web sites for the major federal agencies.

AUTOMATED PHONE CONTACT

Under the blue-page listing for "U.S. Government," you also should find numbers for the U.S. Office of Personnel Management or the nearest Federal Job Information Center. This number can give you automated job information about your own area, or may direct you to a location where you can pick up printed materials or conduct a detailed search on a computer touch screen. Automated telephone systems can be accessed 24 hours a day by touch-tone phone. Because you may be on for quite a while searching job categories and geographical areas, you may want to place your call when less-expensive evening, night, or weekend phone rates apply. A complete listing of local numbers for Automated Telephone Systems appears in Appendix A.

Another source of automated telephone information is the *Career America Connection*. This system provides current worldwide federal job announcements, salary and benefits information, special recruitment messages, and so on. The system also can record your name and mailing address so that you can be sent vacancy announcements and forms through the mail. This service can be contacted using the following telephone number:

Career America Connection
912-757-3000
TDD service: 912-744-2299

FAX ON DEMAND

Yet another way to receive information is through *FEDFAX*. This fax-on-demand service allows you to receive information on a variety of employment-related topics, as well as forms, by fax. The automated service may be accessed 24 hours a day, 7 days a week, by calling any of the following telephone numbers from a touch-tone phone or a fax machine:

Atlanta: 404-331-5267
Denver: 303-969-7764
Detroit: 313-226-2593
San Francisco: 415-744-7002
Washington, D.C.: 202-606-2600

STATE EMPLOYMENT OFFICES

Some state employment offices carry federal job listings in print or on microfiche. Others maintain touch-screen computers, which maintain the listings of available federal jobs within those states. To see what services *your* state employment office offers, call directly or check with your public library.

TOUCH-SCREEN COMPUTER KIOSKS

Federal Job Information Touch-Screen Computers are located throughout the United States. These kiosks (small, open-sided buildings, like a newsstand) provide current federal job opportunities available worldwide, in addition to online information and more. The kiosks are generally open during normal business hours, Monday through Friday. Appendix A contains a complete listing of locations for these kiosks across the United States.

THE INTERNET

The Internet is perhaps the single most valuable source of federal job information. Information on federal jobs available in your neighborhood is as easily accessed as information on jobs across the country—or around the world. You also can download application forms, check salaries and benefits, and even research the geographic areas where particular jobs are located.

In Appendix B, "Webliography of Federal Employment Web Sites," you'll find listings of sites that are enormously useful in getting federal employment. Not all of them are official government sites, but even the private ones contain much helpful information and practical tips—for free.

The Anatomy of a Federal Job Announcement: What to Look For and How to Use It

Job announcements in the private sector are short and simple. A classified ad, whether in the paper or online, states that ABC company wants to hire someone for XYZ position. The requirements are summed up in a few words or, at most, a few sentences. An address or phone number is given for you to mail, e-mail, or fax your resume. You send in your cover letter and a one- or two-page resume, and that's it—you've successfully applied for the job. Your resume generally goes to ABC's Human Resources Department, and if it passes the initial screening, it is forwarded to the actual department with the opening.

In the federal government, however, this process is more complicated. Most federal vacancy announcements are between four and eight pages in length, single-spaced. That's just the job *announcement,* not the application document that you submit for the job. The announcement may include descriptions of the position's duties and responsibilities, qualifications, experience desired, KSAs desired (knowledge, skills, and abilities), whether competitive testing is required, and so on.

The key to surviving the application process and to being seriously considered (and thus, hired) begins with you understanding the job vacancy announcement. The vacancy announcement is filled with details that *MUST* be on your application or instructions that *MUST* be followed to keep your resume out of the trash bin. The announcement is also filled with clues that, if found and understood, tell you what *SHOULD* be on your application to get you called in for an interview.

THE "MUSTS"

You must make absolutely certain that you include each of the following items on your application:

- **The job vacancy announcement number.** You already know that to qualify for a federal job, you must apply for an announced vacancy: a *specific* position with its own vacancy announcement number. This number must be put on your application; otherwise, the screening panel won't know which position you want to be considered for. Without this number—whether you apply by form or resume—your application is likely to be thrown out. The screening panel will *not* sift through all the available jobs to match up other hints from your application to the current vacancies: "Oh, he must have meant Job #XXXX." It won't happen.
- **The job title, job classification series, and grade-level number**. When you refer to the vacancy in your application or in any correspondence or communication (even in a phone conversation), you must refer to the position you want by its official job title, job classification series, and grade-level number. For example, *Computer Specialist, GS-334-11,* means that the job title is computer

specialist, its classification series is 334, and its pay-grade level is GS-11. "GS" refers to positions covered by the General Schedule; they go all the way up to GS-13, 14, and 15 management positions; SES in this number refers to the higher-rated Senior Executive Service positions, which range from SES-1 to SES-5 in terms of the salaries they pay.

- **The application deadline.** While the deadline date does not have to be entered on your application, it absolutely must be met. Check the announcement for the date. Some federal jobs are "open until filled" and some are "continuously open," but this usually isn't the case. Most federal announcements will have a two- to four-week application period. In addition, how you go about meeting the deadline differs from announcement to announcement. Some state that the deadline date is the *postmark date*; others state that the deadline date is when applications must be *received*. Read carefully. Most announcements look the same, but they don't all read the same. If you submit your application after the closing date, it will not be considered.

- **The application procedure.** Most federal vacancies can be applied for by one of several methods: Form SF-171, Form OF-612, resume, or computer-scannable resume. However, some vacancies must be applied for in only one way, or a page limit will be given for the usually longer-is-better form or resume. Again, read carefully. Each announcement is explicit about what is required.

THE "SHOULDS"

When you have the mandatory details straight, also check the announcement for hints on what *should* be on your form or resume. Here's a list of strong possibilities:

- **Language that mirrors the job announcement language.** The federal announcements are lengthy and detailed. Agencies know what they're looking for. Your application should echo the job announcement's language to show the agency that *you* are *exactly* what they're looking for. Obviously, this doesn't mean either to quote directly from the announcement or to falsify background, experience, or abilities, but do keep the announcement at hand when crafting your application or resume. Focus on what's important to the hiring agency.

- **KSAs or "ranking factors."** An application or resume sometimes is not required to include a description of the applicant's KSAs (knowledge, skills, and abilities) to be considered for a job, but it really should. If more than one applicant passes the initial screening, the KSAs are used to rank the qualified applicants. An application with no KSAs or inadequate KSAs will drop to the bottom of the list.

Putting Together Your Federal Job Application

Finding the right job with the federal government is a big step—but it's only the first of many. The federal government application and hiring procedures are very different from those of the private sector. You need to know how to "read" the federal job announcement to pull out all the information you'll need in order to craft the best application. Then you must find and correctly complete the right application form.

The federal job application is the "make or break point" of aspiring federal employees, the place where dreams either *remain* dreams or become reality. Some people never even get past the forms and give up before they apply; others don't put enough effort into their applications and never get called.

There's no getting around it: The process is difficult, but it is *not* impossible. It may just take more time and patience than you had anticipated.

Giving Yourself the Edge in the Federal Hiring Process

Remember that you can't approach the federal employment hiring process the same way you would in the private sector. To begin, you have to hustle more in the beginning—to track down job openings, to apply separately for each one, and to tailor your application or resume to the listed requirements. In a way, it's not like applying to one employer, but to dozens—as many agencies and departments as you are interested in.

Above all, you must follow procedure, no matter how brilliant or qualified you may be. In other words, even though you haven't yet been hired, it's time to start thinking like a bureaucrat: Fill out the entire application, answer all the questions, and recognize that *more* paperwork is *better* paperwork.

If you approach your federal job search the same way that you approach the job search in the private sector, you can be hurt by several different points of ignorance. For example, you might assume—because it's true elsewhere—that brevity is the heart of a good presentation. When searching for a job with the government, however, this is the not the case. You also might assume that if anything crucial were missing from your application package, the hiring agency would call and ask for it. That's another wrong assumption. If an agency does not have the required information to process your application, you could be taken out of consideration—without knowing it. In other words, what you don't know *can* hurt you.

Information is key to your success. Find out as much as you can beforehand about the particular job, the agency, the application process, and other considerations. Then give the agency as much information as you can in return. It's really a very influential factor. In your search, patience and persistence are as important as any of the special qualifications that you may bring to the job.

Finally, think of the application as an example of the kind of work that you normally do, a way to show the screening panel the neatness, accuracy, and thoroughness that you normally bring to the job every day.

Federal Application Forms

With your selected job vacancy announcement in hand, you now begin the process of filling out an application form. A wide variety of applications exist that you may use to apply for a job with the federal government. So, which do you use?

Basically, you need only two forms: First, you will need what is called an entry document, which can be an SF-171, an OF-612, a Federal Resume, *or* a computer-scannable resume. Second, you will need a set of KSAs.

Let's look at each of these in turn.

SF-171

This is the Everest of federal employment forms, the one that has traditionally intimidated applicants on a regular basis. A completed SF-171 form can be quite long; a good one can run anywhere from 7 to 15 pages (an example of one follows), the form is tedious to fill out. You must provide details about your academic and professional career that you may not have thought about for years. But if you don't provide these details, or at least respond to these questions in some way, chances are that a personnel clerk may review your SF-171, see that items are left blank, and throw it out. Then, no matter how qualified you may be, your application will receive no further consideration.

As a result, you should fill in *all* the blanks. If you don't know the answer to a question on the form, write "N/A." But make sure that you write *something* in every blank.

One final piece of advice: Remember to sign the form. In fact, federal personnel specialists advise that you sign it in *blue* ink rather than black. On a quick glance, black ink may look like a photocopy. Because your application must contain an *original* signature, it could get thrown out by mistake.

OF-612

This form, developed during the mid–1990s, was part of a well-intended effort by the U.S. Office of Personnel Management to simplify the federal hiring process by having an alternative form. The OF-612 is less cluttered visually and doesn't squeeze in two columns of questions on the very first page the way the SF-171 does. It also skips a few of the SF-171's questions, such as availability, military service, and others. Simply put, OF-612 looks less intimidating and more user-friendly, which is probably what the OPM wanted in an alternative form.

Unfortunately, in trying to simplify the federal hiring process, officials wound up making it more complicated because they did not drop the old form when they instituted the new one. Instead of just having one simpler form, OPM gave people a choice, and choices are always confusing. Which form should applicants fill out? Is one form better than the other? Do two forms mean that both should be filled out? Finally, many applicants think that because the OF-612 form is only two pages long and looks easier to write and to read, their responses should be shorter.

That makes sense, but it's not true. When the OF-612 comes to the questions on describing your past work duties and describing your other qualifications, you should provide the same detail as you would on an SF-171. Don't hesitate to attach your own sheets of paper to the application so that you have room to explain in full. As with all federal job application documents, you'll do better if you write more rather than less. Invariably, federal screening panels choose the strongest set of paperwork. As far as these screening panels are concerned, a good candidate equals a good set of paperwork. If you keep this in mind, you'll think more like the people who actually have a vote about your application, and that's a useful thing to do. Their vote is your ticket to a federal job. Try to put yourself in their shoes.

FEDERAL RESUME

Yet another way of applying, the Federal Resume is probably the least understood because it often gets confused with a private-sector resume. Unlike a private-sector resume, which is usually no more than one or two pages, a Federal Resume can be as long or short as you want it to be. Some Federal Resumes are as long as an SF-171.

In fact, the only significant difference between this type of resume and an SF-171 is that the Federal Resume is generated by you and therefore doesn't have the form's printed lines and boxes all over the page. In addition, some of the personal information requested on the SF-171 isn't needed on a Federal Resume: your date and place of birth, questions about whether you've ever been arrested, how many hours a week you're willing to work, and more. In short, a good Federal Resume provides as much information about the details of your work history as an SF-171 does. The higher level the position you are applying for, the more detailed your Federal Resume should probably be. Federal Resumes that run 6 to 12 pages are acceptable. In the private sector, job candidates would never turn in a 12-page resume unless they were applying for an upper-level academic or research position and had dozens of publications to their credit.

Warning: Don't be misled by the word *resume* on the vacancy announcement. The "resume" you're being asked to submit is a Federal Resume.

If the "How to Apply" section of a vacancy announcement states that you can submit "a resume, SF-171, or OF-612," the kind of resume that you should submit is the Federal Resume. If you read the vacancy announcement carefully, you often will see a list of details that your resume must provide: names and phone numbers of your present and past job supervisors, salaries you earned in these positions, and similar information. On a private sector resume, this information is not expected. However, on a Federal Resume, you are usually asked and expected to provide this information and more.

COMPUTER-SCANNABLE RESUME, OR RESUMIX

The computer-scannable resume and Resumix are one and the same. Resumix is simply the name of the company that invented this form. This is an application document that several federal agencies have started to use.

Unlike the SF-171 or OF-612 (which are reviewed by actual people), the computer-scannable resume is fed into the database of a mainframe computer system. An artificial intelligence program then scans your material, looking for certain key words and phrases. As a result, in writing this kind of resume, you need to mirror the language contained in the vacancy announcement you are responding to because that is the key to this process.

You also need to produce a document that is physically capable of being scanned—or, in some cases, e-mailed. Forget the different fonts and stylistic creativity that you hope make your private-sector resume stand out in the pile. Here are some simple tips to follow:

- Do not underline for emphasis.
- Do not use bold or italics for emphasis.
- Do not use forward or backward slashes, such as "supervised each employee in drawing up his/her professional goals."
- Do not use fancy or unusual fonts. Simple typefaces are recommended, such as Courier, Arial, or Times New Roman. No part of any letter must touch any part of any other letter.
- Do not use very small or very large type sizes. The standard is 10-point or 12-point.
- As with every computer document, do not bend, fold, staple, tape, or mutilate your resume in any way.

The hiring agency that allows a Resumix may ask that you cover only specific points on it, so it may end up being rather short (compared to an SF-171). However, in those cases, the agency also will give you a *supplemental data sheet* with a list of questions, to be submitted as a separate document. The supplemental data sheet solicits the other information usually asked for on the SF-171, such as your lowest acceptable pay grade, willingness to accept temporary or part-time work, military experience, and so on. All this is in addition to the computer-scannable resume and the KSAs.

KSAS OR RANKING FACTORS

Almost every federal vacancy lists criteria that the hiring agency feels is essential for strong job performance. These criteria are called different names by different federal agencies. Some agencies call these "ranking factors," "selection criteria," or "rating factors." Some agencies actually call them "KSAs."

KSA stands for "knowledge, skill, ability," the general criteria an agency expects a successful candidate to possess in order to do the job. Some typical KSAs are "Ability to communicate orally and in writing," or "Knowledge of the federal budgeting system," or "Skill in negotiating contracts with vendors and suppliers." Usually there are four to six of these KSA factors for each vacancy announcement. Many KSAs repeat from one vacancy announcement to another, so if you're applying for eight different positions as an accounting technician, say, you'll probably find that all eight vacancy announcements are fairly similar and that the KSAs you wrote for the first one can be used again almost verbatim for the others.

You must respond in writing separately—apart from your entry document—to these KSAs in order to be selected for an interview. As a general rule of thumb, if you are applying for a position at the GS-5 level or below, a half-page response is usually sufficient. But if you are applying at the GS-7 level or above, you should submit a full-page written response to each factor, detailing examples of times when you used the type of knowledge, skill, or ability referred to in the vacancy announcement.

These KSAs are quite important in the final selection process. Don't ignore or neglect them because they usually make the difference between a decent application and a winning one.

WHICH FORM DO I CHOOSE?

Occasionally, a hiring agency will state in the job announcement the format that it prefers applicants to use. So, of course, in that instance, you will use the requested form. However, most agencies accept all the forms and say so in the announcement. From your point of view, it probably makes no difference. The questions that have been dropped from the SF-171 are relatively short anyway. In all cases, you should focus on describing your past duties and responsibilities, detailing the KSAs you developed, and quantifying or in some other way explicitly explaining what you did and what resulted.

Crafting Your Application to Match Career Area and Agency Standards

The federal government uses a two-stage screening process in selecting candidates to be interviewed and, ultimately, hired. The first stage involves the SF-171, the OF-612, a Federal Resume, or a computer-scannable resume that has been asked for in the vacancy announcement. In the first stage, these documents are screened by a federal personnel clerk to weed out those that are unacceptable or incomplete. Then they're screened by a panel of federal mid- to senior-level managers to see who is eligible to compete for the vacancy at the level that was announced. So, for example, your application as a GS-13 budget analyst might be complete in all its parts, but the panel may determine that you have enough experience for only a GS-11 level, which is not the advertised opening. At that point, your application will be out of the running.

If your application makes it through the panel, you face the second step in the screening process, in which the panel compares you directly to all the other applicants that have made it that far. The panel does this by using your KSAs to rank the "survivors." Thus, providing a wealth of detail on your application helps. You don't get a second chance to explain yourself; there is no back-up plan. Both the application and the KSAs must be as complete as possible from the very beginning.

To develop an effective and competitive SF-171, OF-612, Federal Resume, or computer-scannable resume for a federal position, you will need to keep the following points in mind:

- **Remember to describe your professional experience in detail.** You will have to provide more details than any private-sector job application ever requested. Some of the questions may seem obvious or repetitious. Complete them anyway.
- **Do more than redescribe your official job duties and job description.** Most competent employees do a lot more than their job descriptions because most official job descriptions don't capture the true complexity of the work that has to be done. Unfortunately, instead of writing about what they *really* do in their jobs, many people just repeat the official job description.

- **Give yourself credit.** You've earned it with your good work. But you've got to let people know. Federal screening panels are quite literal in the way they review and score your application. They give you points for what is relevant in your paperwork. And remember, they *don't* give you any points for what is not included. So don't feel bashful! You don't have to sound conceited, but you *do* have to point out your accomplishments.

- **Use your Federal Resume, SF-171, OF-612, KSAs, and scannable resumes to narrate your professional victories.** One good way to point out your accomplishments is to describe professional "victories." These could be times when you've made solid contributions; times when you've dealt effectively with problems, special projects, and troubleshooting assignments; or times when you've really demonstrated your value to the organizations for which you've worked. Properly described, these stories are like money in the bank. They make you and your abilities come alive to the screening panel, rather than being disguised by the verbiage of official job descriptions.

- **Highlight your professional skills by using an "action/result" presentation**. Show your skills actually being used. Most actions have a result, especially if your actions were effective. Don't shortchange yourself. If things you have done have generated bottom-line results for your employers, then say so. Did your innovative idea save money? Did your initiative and persistence make money? Say so—and say how much. Describe what happened. There's nothing more convincing to a skeptical screening panel than to see "Result" appear again and again throughout your application. This lets them know that *you* know where the bottom line is—and how to get there. *That's* what they are looking for in an employee.

- **Stop scaring yourself.** Writing an effective SF-171 or set of KSAs depends on your attitude more than on your writing skills. Filling out these forms is unpleasant, but don't let that discourage you. The task is certainly within your abilities. And remember, the application is not a test. There are no right or wrong answers. There are only other competitors like yourself who find the process just as difficult as you do. If you compete with these competitors effectively, you stand a good chance of winning.

And remember: *Someone's* going to be selected for these positions—it might as well be *you*.

"Before" and "After" Examples Taken from Federal Job Applications

What does a good 171 or KSA look like? The easiest way to learn how to write a good federal job application is to see the difference between some bad examples from several different fields contrasted with actual job-winning entries. Note that the "bad" examples won't really seem dreadful; they're just rather ordinary when seen next to the "good" entries.

DESCRIPTIONS OF MAJOR DUTIES

Bad:

> Coordinated complex civil cases. Developed detailed reviews and analyses. Researched and prepared comprehensive legal memoranda.

Now see how much detail has been added to the job-winning version:

Good:

> Coordinated complex civil cases with various departments or divisions within FDIC. Developed detailed reviews and analyses in preparation for counseling client representatives to improve their request for legal services.

> Researched and prepared comprehensive legal memoranda for clients, drawing on my extensive knowledge and experience litigating various issues under the FDI Act, FIRREA, the FDIC Improvement Act, commercial law, real estate law, and the Bankruptcy Code.

Take a look at another example:

Bad:

> Served as a contracting officer and contract administrator. Performed pre-award, award, and contract administration duties. Headed evaluation teams reviewing potential contractors. Prepared lease agreements.

The added details in the following show how the applicant's duties were much more responsible and varied:

Good:

> Served as contracting officer and contract administrator for multimillion-dollar supplies and services, construction, and architectural and engineering contracts. Possessed a contracting officer's warrant. Performed pre-award, award, and contract administration duties. Prepared *Commerce Business Daily* synopses and advertisements, developed and reviewed technical specifications, and issued solicitations and Requests for Proposals (RFPs). Headed evaluation teams reviewing potential contractors' financial data. Prepared lease agreements for properties where contractors performed construction work.

DESCRIPTIONS OF ADVANCED TRAINING

Bad:

> FBI/RTC Bank Failure School (December 7–10, 1993); Basic Examination School for Attorneys (January 1998).

Good:

> FBI/RTC Bank Failure School (December 7–10, 1993). This was a highly intensive course focusing on the aspects of fraud involving financial institutions, covering such topics as fraud detection and investigation, forensic accounting approach, prosecution of financial institution fraud cases, and the importance of CPAs to bank examiners and criminal investigations.

> Basic Examination School for Attorneys (January 1998). This was a week-long concentrated course focusing on fundamentals of bank supervision, basic report analysis, bank accrual accounting, loan classifications, and financial analysis.

DESCRIPTIONS OF KSAS OR RANKING FACTORS (FOR AN UPPER-LEVEL POSITION)

Bad:

> Knowledge of material life cycle management functions, programs and systems used to provide logistical support: Gained valuable understanding of military facilities planning while serving as Acting Chief of the Facilities Management Office. Responsible for issuing policy pertaining to the total acquisition life cycle baseline parameters. Strong working knowledge of PPBES. Broad experience writing, revising, and implementing policy.

Apparently the applicant didn't know that, at this job level, he or she should include a full page for each KSA, explaining how and when the knowledge, skills, or ability was demonstrated. The previous paragraph works as a bare-bones outline for the detailed job-winning entry that follows.

Good:

> Knowledge of material life cycle management functions, programs and systems used to provide logistical support.
>
> My current job includes a very substantial degree of life-cycle management responsibility. For example, I currently run the policy operation of Acquisition Life Cycle management. In this capacity, the information is related to guidance addressing Army's Acquisition Program Baselines (APBs) for Army Acquisition Category (ACAT) I, II, and some representative III programs. Examples of my strong working knowledge in this area include the following:
>
> Analyze the content of the APBs and ensure that APBs adequately address program requirements.
>
> continued

Result:

I recently issued APB policy that now requires APBs to address "total life cycle costs," which by definition includes operating and support (O&S) costs.

Keep Army and OSD leadership informed regarding how the Army executes cost, schedule, and performance parameters within respective APBs.

Result:

Maintain close ties and frequent contacts with officials at all levels in the Army and DOD, as well as the respective PEOs and PMs and Command Groups. Any known logistical support requirements would also be captured within the respective APBs.

I have gained substantial working knowledge and hands-on experience through interacting with officials in the comptroller and acquisition communities related to acquisition life cycle subject matter contained within APBs, SARs, and DAES reports, as well as through managing these processes.

Result:

My effort to include O&S costs within APBs is unique. To this point, the other military services have not yet followed suit but will likely do so soon because it is DOD policy to make program managers responsible for "total life cycle management." If and when this happens, these program managers would have total "cradle-to-grave" program responsibility, as well as operational control of the budget dollars to make sure that this level of responsibility is discharged fully and effectively.

The job-winning applicants might well have phrased their experience, background, and abilities as in the "bad" examples. If these had been private-sector resumes, that might have been enough. But the procedure is very different applying for a federal job.

Preparing for the Exam

Here are a few suggestions to help you use your study time effectively.

1. *Study alone.* You will concentrate better when you work by yourself. Keep a list of questions that you cannot answer and points that you are unsure of to talk over with a friend who is preparing for the same exam. Plan to exchange ideas at a joint review session just before the test.

2. *Eliminate distractions.* Disturbances caused by family and neighbor activities (telephone calls, chit-chat, TV programs, and so on) work to your disadvantage. Study in a quiet, private room.

3. *Don't try to learn too much in one study period.* If your mind starts to wander, take a short break and then return to your work.

4. *Review what you have learned.* When you have studied something thoroughly, be sure to review it the next day so that the information will be firmly fixed in your mind.

5. *Answer all the questions in this book.* Don't be satisfied merely with the correct answer to each question. Do additional research on the other choices that are given. You will broaden your background and be more adequately prepared for the actual exam. It's quite possible that a question on the exam that you are going to take may require you to be familiar with the other choices.

6. *Tailor your study to the subject matter. Skim or scan.* Don't study everything in the same manner. Obviously, certain areas are more important than others.

7. *Organize yourself.* Make sure that your notes are in good order. Valuable time is unnecessarily consumed when you can't find quickly what you are looking for.

8. *Keep physically fit.* You cannot retain information well when you are uncomfortable, when you have a headache, or when you are tense. Physical health promotes mental efficiency.

ANSWERING MULTIPLE-CHOICE QUESTIONS

General test questions always appear on machine-scored multiple-choice tests. Multiple-choice tests consist of a question booklet or booklets and a separate answer sheet. The question booklets begin with general instructions for taking the test. At the beginning of the question booklet you will learn the rules and regulations governing your exam, the number of questions, timing, signals, and so on. If there are specific directions for different types of questions in the exam, you will find these in the question booklet before each new type of question.

You may write in the question booklet—put a question mark next to the number of a question at which you took a guess, calculate the answers to math questions, cross out eliminated answer choices, underline key words, or even just plain doodle in the margins. The one thing you must not do with a question booklet is use it as an answer sheet.

The separate answer sheet that accompanies the test booklet is the only record of answers that is scored. You must mark every answer that you choose in the correct place on the answer sheet. Mark your answer choice by blackening its circle darkly and completely. If your answer is not registered by the scoring machine, you cannot get any credit for it. You must mark only one answer for each question. If there is more than one answer for any question, even if one of the answers is correct, the machine will give no credit for that question. You may change your mind and change your answer. However, when you change an answer, you must be careful to fully and cleanly erase the first answer. Also mark your new choice with extra care. You do not want the scoring machine to misread your choice. Never cross out an answer in favor of a new choice. You must erase.

Another very important aspect of working with the separate answer sheet is to mark every question in the right place. The scoring machine does not read question number and answer choice. The machine scans the page for a pattern of blackened spaces. If you have marked an answer in the wrong place, you will have it scored as wrong (unless, of course, the same letter was the correct answer for the space in which you made your mark). If you notice that you have slipped out of line, you must erase all answers from the point of the error and redo all those questions.

With the exception of clerical questions, most civil service tests are not heavily speeded. Even so, you do not have the luxury of time to waste erasing and reanswering large blocks of questions. Furthermore, an error of this type will fluster you and will lead to errors of judgment in choosing answers to other questions. Therefore, do not skip any questions. Do not jump around looking for easy questions to answer first. Do not omit a question even if you have no idea of the correct answer. If you are forced to guess so as to answer every question in order, then do so. If you guess, mark the question in the question booklet with a question mark. If you have time after you have completed all the questions, go back and give the marked questions more thought. If you answer every question in order, there should be no chance to slip. Even so, it is a good idea to check the question number against the answer space number as you mark each answer.

Multiple-choice questions consist of the question itself and four or five answer choices. The answer choices are lettered A, B, C, D, E. On the answer sheet next to each question number are answer spaces—circles, ovals, or boxes—lettered A, B, C, D, E. Each question has one *best* answer. You must read the question carefully, think, choose the best answer, and blacken the answer space that contains the letter of that answer. This method of answering is much easier than filling in a blank or circling a portion of a sentence or paragraph. Provided that you mark your answers neatly, there is no room for scoring error in marking a multiple-choice answer sheet. You can be sure of accuracy and objectivity.

In general, scoring of multiple-choice test questions is simple. You get one credit for each correct answer. You get no credit for a question that you do not answer at all. On most *General Test* subjects, you do not lose any credit for a wrong answer. A wrong answer is simply not a right answer. You get no credit, but the wrong answer itself does not work against you. On some *General Test* subjects, such as "Clerical Speed and Accuracy," there is a penalty for a wrong answer. The test instructions should tell you whenever there is a scoring penalty for wrong answers. If you are not certain, ask. On civil service tests, if there is a penalty for wrong answers, it is meant to be a penalty for inaccuracy. The kinds of questions with such penalties do not lend themselves to guessing. The questions that might tempt you to guess, those on which you might not know the right answer, do not generally have such a penalty. This means that a guess cannot hurt.

The best guess is the educated guess. Sometimes you may read a question and not be sure of the right answer. Try to eliminate those answers that are obviously wrong. If you have any idea at all of the answer, you may be able to rule out one or two of the choices. If you can narrow the field and guess from among fewer choices, you can raise your odds of guessing right. If you have no idea at all and must guess from among four, you have a 1 in 4 chance of guessing right. If you eliminate one choice, your odds are 1 in 3. If you can eliminate two of the four, then your odds become 1 in 2; that's 50–50. You could pick up a number of points by intelligent guessing. And always mark the guesses in the question booklet so that you can try again.

A blank space can do you no good, and a wrong answer can do you no harm, so it makes sense to answer every question. This means that you must keep track of time. Wear a watch. If you have worked slowly and methodically, and find that time is about to run out, pick a letter and mark all the remaining questions with the same response. By the law of averages, you should get some right and should pick up some credit. Of course, you should not randomly answer remaining questions when accuracy is paramount and there is a penalty for wrong answers. In such cases, work accurately and as quickly as possible right until you receive the signal that time is up. Then stop.

Aside from actually knowing the answer, of course, the single factor that most influences your choosing the right answer is careful reading. Misreading of directions causes the greatest damage. If the directions ask you to choose the word that means the *opposite* of the underlined word, and you choose the word that means the *same* as the underlined word, you will mark wrong answers for a whole series of questions and will do poorly on the exam. If the directions tell you to "Mark (D) if all the names being compared are *alike*," and you mark (D) when all the names are *different*, you will sabotage your score.

Careful reading must extend beyond reading of directions to reading of each individual question. Qualifying words such as *most, least, only, best, probably, definitely, not, all, every,* and *except* make a big difference in determining the correct answer to a specific question. You want to earn the highest possible score on your exam. A wrong answer caused by careless reading would be a shame.

FINAL SUGGESTIONS FOR TEST-TAKERS

1. Choose a comfortable, well-lighted study spot as far as possible from distractions of family life.
2. Make a study schedule, and stick to it. Regular, daily study is important.
3. Work your way through this book, giving special concentration to your areas of weakness. Never look at answers until you have completed answering a series of questions. Study answer explanations whenever they are supplied; they may give you extra insights, even into the questions that you answered correctly.
4. If the exam location is unfamiliar to you, make a dry run to be certain of route and timing.
5. On the evening before the exam, do something pleasant and go to bed early.
6. Allow ample time on test day so that you need not be unnerved by traffic tie-ups or unexpected delays.
7. Listen to directions; ask questions, if necessary; and read.
8. Follow the instructions you have just read concerning answering multiple-choice questions and marking the answer sheet.
9. Do not dwell too long on any question, even if it poses an interesting challenge. Even without heavy time pressure, your time is not unlimited. Make your best educated guess, mark the question, and return to give it more thought if time permits at the end.
10. Check and recheck. There is never a bonus for leaving early, so if you finish before the time is up, stay until the end of the exam. Check your answer sheet to be certain that you have answered every question and that you have marked every answer in the right place. Check to be certain that only one answer is marked for each question. Then look back into the question booklet for the questions that you marked as guesses only. This is your chance to give the difficult questions another try and to improve your chances by changing a wild guess into a calculated guess.

ONE

Clerical Ability

CONTENTS

Alphabetizing and Filing Answer Sheet

TEST 1

1. Ⓐ Ⓑ Ⓒ Ⓓ   4. Ⓐ Ⓑ Ⓒ Ⓓ   7. Ⓐ Ⓑ Ⓒ Ⓓ   10. Ⓐ Ⓑ Ⓒ Ⓓ
2. Ⓐ Ⓑ Ⓒ Ⓓ   5. Ⓐ Ⓑ Ⓒ Ⓓ   8. Ⓐ Ⓑ Ⓒ Ⓓ   11. Ⓐ Ⓑ Ⓒ Ⓓ
3. Ⓐ Ⓑ Ⓒ Ⓓ   6. Ⓐ Ⓑ Ⓒ Ⓓ   9. Ⓐ Ⓑ Ⓒ Ⓓ   12. Ⓐ Ⓑ Ⓒ Ⓓ

TEST 2

1. Ⓐ Ⓑ Ⓒ Ⓓ   3. Ⓐ Ⓑ Ⓒ Ⓓ   5. Ⓐ Ⓑ Ⓒ Ⓓ   7. Ⓐ Ⓑ Ⓒ Ⓓ   9. Ⓐ Ⓑ Ⓒ Ⓓ
2. Ⓐ Ⓑ Ⓒ Ⓓ   4. Ⓐ Ⓑ Ⓒ Ⓓ   6. Ⓐ Ⓑ Ⓒ Ⓓ   8. Ⓐ Ⓑ Ⓒ Ⓓ   10. Ⓐ Ⓑ Ⓒ Ⓓ

TEST 3

1. Ⓐ Ⓑ Ⓒ Ⓓ   4. Ⓐ Ⓑ Ⓒ Ⓓ   7. Ⓐ Ⓑ Ⓒ Ⓓ   10. Ⓐ Ⓑ Ⓒ Ⓓ   13. Ⓐ Ⓑ Ⓒ Ⓓ
2. Ⓐ Ⓑ Ⓒ Ⓓ   5. Ⓐ Ⓑ Ⓒ Ⓓ   8. Ⓐ Ⓑ Ⓒ Ⓓ   11. Ⓐ Ⓑ Ⓒ Ⓓ   14. Ⓐ Ⓑ Ⓒ Ⓓ
3. Ⓐ Ⓑ Ⓒ Ⓓ   6. Ⓐ Ⓑ Ⓒ Ⓓ   9. Ⓐ Ⓑ Ⓒ Ⓓ   12. Ⓐ Ⓑ Ⓒ Ⓓ   15. Ⓐ Ⓑ Ⓒ Ⓓ

TEST 4

1. Ⓐ Ⓑ Ⓒ Ⓓ   4. Ⓐ Ⓑ Ⓒ Ⓓ   7. Ⓐ Ⓑ Ⓒ Ⓓ   10. Ⓐ Ⓑ Ⓒ Ⓓ   13. Ⓐ Ⓑ Ⓒ Ⓓ
2. Ⓐ Ⓑ Ⓒ Ⓓ   5. Ⓐ Ⓑ Ⓒ Ⓓ   8. Ⓐ Ⓑ Ⓒ Ⓓ   11. Ⓐ Ⓑ Ⓒ Ⓓ   14. Ⓐ Ⓑ Ⓒ Ⓓ
3. Ⓐ Ⓑ Ⓒ Ⓓ   6. Ⓐ Ⓑ Ⓒ Ⓓ   9. Ⓐ Ⓑ Ⓒ Ⓓ   12. Ⓐ Ⓑ Ⓒ Ⓓ   15. Ⓐ Ⓑ Ⓒ Ⓓ

Clerical Speed and Accuracy Answer Sheet

TEST 1

1. Ⓐ Ⓑ Ⓒ Ⓓ   5. Ⓐ Ⓑ Ⓒ Ⓓ   9. Ⓐ Ⓑ Ⓒ Ⓓ   13. Ⓐ Ⓑ Ⓒ Ⓓ
2. Ⓐ Ⓑ Ⓒ Ⓓ   6. Ⓐ Ⓑ Ⓒ Ⓓ   10. Ⓐ Ⓑ Ⓒ Ⓓ   14. Ⓐ Ⓑ Ⓒ Ⓓ
3. Ⓐ Ⓑ Ⓒ Ⓓ   7. Ⓐ Ⓑ Ⓒ Ⓓ   11. Ⓐ Ⓑ Ⓒ Ⓓ   15. Ⓐ Ⓑ Ⓒ Ⓓ
4. Ⓐ Ⓑ Ⓒ Ⓓ   8. Ⓐ Ⓑ Ⓒ Ⓓ   12. Ⓐ Ⓑ Ⓒ Ⓓ   16. Ⓐ Ⓑ Ⓒ Ⓓ

TEST 2

1. Ⓐ Ⓑ Ⓒ Ⓓ   4. Ⓐ Ⓑ Ⓒ Ⓓ   7. Ⓐ Ⓑ Ⓒ Ⓓ   10. Ⓐ Ⓑ Ⓒ Ⓓ
2. Ⓐ Ⓑ Ⓒ Ⓓ   5. Ⓐ Ⓑ Ⓒ Ⓓ   8. Ⓐ Ⓑ Ⓒ Ⓓ   11. Ⓐ Ⓑ Ⓒ Ⓓ
3. Ⓐ Ⓑ Ⓒ Ⓓ   6. Ⓐ Ⓑ Ⓒ Ⓓ   9. Ⓐ Ⓑ Ⓒ Ⓓ   12. Ⓐ Ⓑ Ⓒ Ⓓ

TEST 3

1. Ⓐ Ⓑ Ⓒ Ⓓ   3. Ⓐ Ⓑ Ⓒ Ⓓ   5. Ⓐ Ⓑ Ⓒ Ⓓ   7. Ⓐ Ⓑ Ⓒ Ⓓ   9. Ⓐ Ⓑ Ⓒ Ⓓ
2. Ⓐ Ⓑ Ⓒ Ⓓ   4. Ⓐ Ⓑ Ⓒ Ⓓ   6. Ⓐ Ⓑ Ⓒ Ⓓ   8. Ⓐ Ⓑ Ⓒ Ⓓ   10. Ⓐ Ⓑ Ⓒ Ⓓ

ALPHABETIZING AND FILING

Rules for Alphabetic Filing

NAMES OF INDIVIDUALS

RULE 1: The names of individuals are filed in strict alphabetical order, first according to last name, then according to first name or initial, and finally according to middle name or initial. For example, *George Allen* comes before *Edward Bell*, and *Leonard P. Reston* comes before *Lucille B. Reston*.

RULE 2: When last names and first initials are the same, the one with the initial comes before the one with the name written out. For example, *A. Green* comes before *Agnes Green*.

RULE 3: When first and last names are the same, the name without a middle initial comes before the one with a middle name or initial. For example, *John Doe* comes before both *John A. Doe* and *John Alan Doe*.

RULE 4: When first and last names are the same, the name with a middle initial comes before the one with a middle name beginning with the same initial. For example, *Jack R. Hertz* comes before *Jack Richard Hertz*.

RULE 5: A quick summary of rules 2, 3, and 4 reads: "Nothing comes before something, and less comes before more."

Example:

> King
> King, D.
> King, D. A.
> King, D. Anne
> King, Dorothy
> King, Dorothy A.
> King, Dorothy Anne

The same rule applies to the filing of businesses and organizations. Thus, *A.A.A. Exterminating* is filed before *Atlas Exterminating*.

RULE 6: Prefixes such as *De, O' Mac, Mc*, and *Van* are filed exactly as written and treated as part of the names they come before. Ignore apostrophes for purposes of filing. For example, *Robert O'Dea* is filed before *David Olsen*, and *Gladys McTeague* is filed before *Frances Meadows*.

RULE 7: Foreign names are filed as spelled. Prefixes are not considered separately. Likewise, foreign language articles (*le, La, Les, El*, and so on), whether they begin with a lowercase or capital letter, are considered part of the name with which they appear.

Example:

> Da Costa, Carl
> D'Agnota, Ugo
> Des Verney, Elizabeth
> De Takacs, Maria
> L'Aiglon
> Les Miserables

RULE 8: Hyphenated surnames are indexed as though the hyphen joined the two parts, making one. Thus, *Lyttonet, Amadeus* is filed before *Lytton-Strachey, John.*

RULE 9: Abbreviated names are treated as if they were spelled out. For example, *Chas.* is filed as *Charles*, and *Thos.* is filed as *Thomas.*

RULE 10: Titles and designations, such as *Dr., Mr., Prof., Jr.*, or *II*, are given last consideration in filing.

NAMES OF BUSINESS ORGANIZATIONS

RULE 11: The names of business organizations, institutions, and buildings are filed according to the order in which each word in the name appears, except where these names include the full names of individuals.

Example:

> General Electric Company
> General Foods
> General Mills
> General Telephone and Telegraph

RULE 12: Where the names of firms, corporations, institutions, and buildings include the full names of individuals, the firm names are filed under the rules for filing individual names.

Example:

> Rice, Bernard, and Co.
> Rice Delivery Service
> Rice, Edward, and Sons Ltd.
> Rice Electronics
> Rice, Francis P.

RULE 13: When *the, of, and*, or an apostrophe are parts of a business name, they are disregarded for purposes of filing.

RULE 14: Names that include numerals should be filed as if the numerals were spelled out. Thus, *10th Street Bootery* is filed as *Tenth Street Bootery.*

Example:

> 8th Avenue Bookshop = Eighth Avenue Bookshop
> 5th Street Church = Fifth Street Church
> 4th National Bank = Fourth National Bank
> 7th Avenue Restaurant = Seventh Avenue Restaurant

RULE 15: When the same names appear with different addresses, arrange them alphabetically according to town or city, considering state only where there is a duplication of town or city names.

Example:

American Tobacco Co.	Norfolk, VA
American Tobacco Co.	Osceola, FL
American Tobacco Co.	Quincy, IL
American Tobacco Co.	Quincy, MA

RULE 16: Abbreviations are alphabetized as though the words were spelled out in full.

Example:

Indus. Bros. of America = Industrial Brothers…
Indus. Bldrs. of America = Industrial Builders…

RULE 17: Hyphenated firm names are treated as *separate* words.

Example:

Oil-O-Matic Heating Co.
Oilimatic Heating Co.

RULE 18: Compound geographic names written as separate words are always treated as separate words.

Example:

West Chester
West Milton
Westchester
Western Chicago Railway
Westinghouse

RULE 19: Bureaus, boards, offices, and departments of government are filed under the name of the chief governing body. For example, *Bureau of the Budget* would be filed as if written *Budget, Bureau of the.*

Practice Test 1

Directions: Each question consists of a CAPITALIZED word that is to be filed correctly before one of the alphabetized words listed. Indicate the word before which the key word should be filed by marking the letter of that word on the answer sheet at the beginning of this chapter.

1. CATHOLIC:
   - (A) catacombs
   - (B) catalogs
   - (C) catechisms
   - (D) cattle

2. DRAMA:
   - (A) drawing
   - (B) Drayton
   - (C) Dreyfus
   - (D) drugs

3. INQUISITION:
   - (A) industry
   - (B) insurance
   - (C) international
   - (D) interne

4. LUGUBRIOUS:
   - (A) Lucretius
   - (B) lumber
   - (C) Luther
   - (D) Lutheran

5. OCEANIC:
   - (A) occult
   - (B) Ohio
   - (C) Oklahoma
   - (D) optics

6. ENGLAND:
   - (A) engineering
   - (B) English
   - (C) engraving
   - (D) entomology

7. IRRIGATION:
   - (A) Ireland
   - (B) Irish
   - (C) iron
   - (D) Irving

8. MARINE:
   - (A) Margolin
   - (B) marketing
   - (C) Mary
   - (D) Maryland

9. PALEONTOLOGY:
   - (A) Pacific
   - (B) painting
   - (C) Palestine
   - (D) paltry

10. ASIATIC:
    - (A) ascetic
    - (B) assyriology
    - (C) astronomy
    - (D) astrophysics

11. ENTOMOLOGY:
    - (A) endocrine
    - (B) Erasmus
    - (C) Eskimo
    - (D) etching

12. GREAT BRITAIN:
    - (A) Grant
    - (B) Greece
    - (C) Greek
    - (D) Greeley

Practice Test 2

Directions: In each of the following questions, there is a name enclosed in a box followed by four names in proper alphabetic order. The spaces between the names are lettered. Decide where the boxed name belongs in the alphabetic series, and mark the letter of the space on the answer sheet at the beginning of this chapter.

1. | Eatley, Mary |
   (A)–
       Eagin, John
   (B)–
       Eagley, Robert
   (C)–
       Ebert, Jack
   (D)–
       Eckert, Wallace

2. | Pinch, Nathaniel |
   (A)–
       Payne, Briscoe
   (B)–
       Pearlman, Abe
   (C)–
       Pincus, Harry
   (D)–
       Pollaci, Angelina

3. | Raphan, Max |
   (A)–
       Rankin, H.
   (B)–
       Rappan, Sol
   (C)–
       Rascoll, Jon
   (D)–
       Rich, Harold

4. | Schwartz, H. |
   (A)–
       Scavone, John
   (B)–
       Schwartz, Harry

   (C)–
       Seiden, Burt
   (D)–
       Sheilds, Vera

5. | Hakim, Wm. |
   (A)–
       Hakiel, R.
   (B)–
       Hakim, Louis
   (C)–
       Hakim, M.
   (D)–
       Halabi, Joe

6. | Horn, Sol |
   (A)–
       Hormel, Max
   (B)–
       Horn, Harold
   (C)–
       Horn, Irving
   (D)–
       Hornbeck, J. W.

7. | Krommes, Selma |
   (A)–
       Kromolitz, J.
   (B)–
       Kromowitz, L.
   (C)–
       Kromwitz, Abe
   (D)–
       Kron, Harold

8. | Melzer, Max |

   (A)–

      Meltz, Lena

   (B)–

      Meltzer, Abe

   (C)–

      Meltzer, Alex

   (D)–

      Melzner, L.

9. | Nesbitt, Carl |

   (A)–

      Nesbiet, Jerry

   (B)–

      Nesbitt, Al

   (C)–

      Nesbitt, Gloria

   (D)–

      Nesci, Jas.

10. | Perron, Homer |

   (A)–

      Perrin, Larry

   (B)–

      Perron, Lewis

   (C)–

      Perrone, James

   (D)–

      Perrotta, Chas.

Practice Test 3

Directions: Consider each group of names as a unit. Determine in what position the name printed in ***boldface*** *would be if the names in the group were correctly alphabetized. If the name in* ***boldface*** *should be first, mark (A); if second, mark (B); if third, mark (C); and if fourth, mark (D). You may find it helpful to pencil in a numbered order of names on your test sheet. If you do so, be sure to mark your answer on the answer sheet at the beginning of this chapter.*

1. Albert Brown
    James Borenstein
    Frieda Albrecht
    Samuel Brown

2. Hugh F. Martenson
    A. S. Martinson
    Albert Martinsen
    Albert S. Martinson

3. Arthur Roberts
    James Robin
    J. B. Robin
    Arnold Robinson

4. **Eugene Thompkins**
    Alice Thompson
    Arnold G. Thomas
    B. Thomas

5. Albert Green
    Wm. Greenfield
    A. B. Green
    Frank E. Green

6. Dr. Francis Karell
    John Joseph Karelsen, Jr.
    John J. Karelsen, Sr.
    Mrs. Jeanette Kelly

7. Norman Fitzgibbons
    Charles F. Franklin
    Jas. Fitzgerald
    Andrew Fitzsimmons

8. **Chas. R. Connolly**
    Frank Conlon
    Charles S. Connolly
    Abraham Cohen

9. **The 5th Ave. Bus Co.**
    The Baltimore and Ohio Railroad
    3rd Ave. Elevated Co.
    Pennsylvania Railroad

10. James Ryn
    Francis Ryan
    Wm. Roanan
    Frances S. Ryan

11. **Aaron M. Michelson**
    Samuel Michels
    Arthur L. Michaelson, Sr.
    John Michell

12. Robt. Count
    Robert B. Count
    Steven Le Comte
    Steven M. Comte

13. Prof. David Towner
    Miss Edna Towner
    Dr. Frank I. Tower
    Mrs. K. C. Towner

14. The Jane Miller Shop
    Joseph Millard Corp.
    John Muller & Co.
    Jean Mullins, Inc.

15. **Anthony Delaney**
    A. De Landri
    A. M. D'Elia
    Alfred De Monte

Practice Test 4

Directions: *Each question consists of four names. For each question, select the one of the four names that should be third if the four names were arranged in alphabetical order in accordance with the rules for alphabetical filing. For each question, indicate in the correspondingly numbered row on the answer sheet on page 24 at the beginning of this chapter the letter preceding the name that should be third in alphabetical order.*

1. (A) Herbert Restman
   (B) H. Restman
   (C) Harry Restmore
   (D) H. Restmore

2. (A) Elm Trading Co.
   (B) El Dorado Trucking Corp.
   (C) James Eldred Jewelry Store
   (D) Eldridge Printing, Inc.

3. (A) Fifth Avenue Book Shop
   (B) Mr. Wm. A. Fifner
   (C) 52nd Street Association
   (D) Robert B. Fiffner

4. (A) Timothy Macalan
   (B) Fred McAlden
   (C) Thomas MacAllister
   (D) Mrs. Frank McAllen

5. (A) Peter La Vance
   (B) George Van Meer
   (C) Wallace De Vance
   (D) Leonard Vance

6. (A) 71st Street Theater
   (B) The Seven Seas Corp.
   (C) 7th Ave. Service Co.
   (D) Walter R. Sevan and Co.

7. (A) Dr. Chas. D. Peterson
   (B) Miss Irene F. Petersen
   (C) Lawrence E. Peterson
   (D) Prof. N. A. Petersen

8. (A) Edward La Gabriel
   (B) Marie Doris Gabriel
   (C) Marjorie N. Gabriel
   (D) Mrs. Marian Gabriel

9. (A) Adam Dunn
   (B) E. Dunn
   (C) A. Duncan
   (D) Edward Robert Dunn

10. (A) Paul Moore
    (B) William Moore
    (C) Paul A. Moore
    (D) William Allen Moore

11. (A) William Carver
    (B) Howard Cambell
    (C) Arthur Chambers
    (D) Charles Banner

12. (A) George Peters
    (B) Eric Petersen
    (C) G. Peters
    (D) E. Petersen

13. (A) Edward Hallam
    (B) Jos. Frank Hamilton
    (C) Edward A. Hanam
    (D) Joseph F. Hamilton

14. (A) William O'Hara
    (B) Arthur Gordon
    (C) James DeGraff
    (D) Anne von Glatin

15. (A) Theodore Madison
    (B) Timothy McCrill
    (C) Thomas MacLane
    (D) Thomas A. Madison

Answer Key for Practice Tests

TEST 1

1.	D	4.	B	7.	D	10.	B
2.	A	5.	B	8.	B	11.	B
3.	B	6.	B	9.	C	12.	B

TEST 2

1.	C	3.	B	5.	D	7.	A	9.	C
2.	C	4.	B	6.	D	8.	D	10.	B

TEST 3

1. (D) Albrecht, Frieda
Borenstein, James
Brown, Albert
Brown, Samuel

2. (D) Martenson, Hugh F.
Martinsen, Albert
Martinson, A. S.
Martinson, Albert S.

3. (C) Roberts, Arthur
Robin, J. B.
Robin, James
Robinson, Arnold

4. (C) Thomas, Arnold G.
Thomas, B.
Thompkins, Eugene
Thompson, Alice

5. (A) Green, A. B.
Green, Albert
Green, Frank E.
Greenfield, Wm.

6. (C) Karrell, Francis, Dr.
Karelsen, John J., Sr.
Karelsen, John Joseph, Jr.
Kelly, Jeanette, Mrs.

7. (A) Fitzgerald, Jas.
Fitzgibbons, Norman
Fitzsimmons, Andrew
Franklin, Charles, F.

8. (C) Cohen, Abraham
Conlon, Frank
Connolly, Chas. R.
Connolly, Charles S.

9. (B) Baltimore and Ohio Railroad, The
5th (Fifth) Ave. Bus. Co., The
Pennsylvania Railroad
3rd (Third) Ave. Elevated Co,

10. (C) Roanan, Wm.
Ryan, Frances S.
Ryan, Francis
Ryn, James

11. **(D)** Michaelson, Arthur L., Sr.
Michell, John
Michels, Samuel
Michelson, Aaron M.

12. **(D)** Comte, Steven M.
Count, Robt.
Count, Robert B.
La Comte, Steven

13. **(D)** Tower, Edna, Miss
Tower, Frank I., Dr.
Towner, David, Prof.
Towner, K. C., Mrs.

14. **(A)** **Millard, Joseph, Corp.**
Miller, Jane Shop, The
Muller, John & Co.
Mullins, Jean, Inc.

15. **(B)** De Landri, A.
Delaney, Anthony
D'Elia, A. M.
De Monte, Alfred

TEST 4

1. **(D)** (B) Restman, H.
(A) Restman, Herbert
(D) Restmore, H.
(C) Restmore, Harry

2. **(D)** (B) El Dorado Trucking Corp.
(C) Eldred, James Jewelry Store
(D) Eldridge Printing, Inc.
(A) Elm Trading Co.

3. **(A)** (D) Fiffner, Robert B.
(B) Fiffner, Wm. A., Mr.
(A) Fifth Avenue Book Shop
(C) 52nd (Fifty-second) Street
Association

4. **(B)** (A) Macalan, Timothy
(C) MacAllister, Thomas
(B) McAlden, Fred
(D) McAllen, Frank, Mrs.

5. **(D)** (C) De Vance, Wallace
(A) La Vance, Peter
(D) Vance, Leonard
(B) Van Meer, George

6. **(C)** (D) Sevan, Walter R. and Co.
(B) Seven Seas Corp., The
(C) 7th (Seventh) Ave. Service Co.
(A) 71st (Seventy-first) Street Theater

7. **(A)** (B) Petersen, Irene F., Miss
(D) Petersen, N.A., Prof.
(A) Peterson, Chas. D., Dr.
(C) Peterson, Lawrence E.

8. **(C)** (D) Gabriel, Marian, Mrs.
(B) Gabriel, Marie Doris
(C) Gabriel, Majorie N.
(A) La Gabriel, Edward

9. **(B)** (C) Duncan, A.
(A) Dunn, Adam
(B) Dunn, E.
(D) Dunn, Edward Robert

10. **(B)** (A) Moore, Paul
(C) Moore, Paul A.
(B) Moore, William
(D) Moore, William Allen

11. **(A)** (D) Banner, Charles
(B) Cambell, Howard
(A) Carver, William
(C) Chambers, Arthur

12. **(D)** (C) Peters, G.
(A) Peters, George
(D) Petersen, E.
(B) Petersen, Eric

13. (D) (A) Hallam, Edward
          (C) Hallam, Edward A.
          (D) Hamilton, Joseph F.
          (B) Hamilton, Jos. Frank

14. (A) (C) DeGraff, James
          (B) Gordon, Arthur

          (A) O'Hara, William
          (D) von Glatin, Anne

15. (D) (C) MacLane, Thomas
          (A) Madison, Theodore
          (D) Madison, Thomas A.
          (B) McGill, Timothy

CLERICAL SPEED AND ACCURACY

Comparison tests are the chief measure of clerical speed and accuracy in use today. Lots of practice with various forms of comparison questions should improve your skills in this area.

Part of clerical accuracy involves accuracy in reading directions. Each of the practice exercises in this chapter is governed by a different set of instructions. Read the directions slowly and carefully. The time you spend getting the directions straight is not a waste of time.

Generally, comparison questions are heavily timed. You probably will find that there are more questions than you can answer in the time allowed. Because accuracy is of prime importance, do not rush beyond your ability to focus on words and numbers, and do NOT guess. Work steadily until the time is called, and do NOT randomly answer the remaining questions.

The best way to read names, numbers, and addresses being compared is to read exactly what you see and to sound out words by syllables. For example:

If you see "St," read "es-tee," not "street."

If you see "NH," read "en aitch," not "New Hampshire."

If you see "1035," read "one oh three five," not "one thousand thirty-five."

Read "sassafrass" as "sas-sa-fras."

Psychologists have discovered that the human mind always tries to complete a figure. If you read "Pky" as "Parkway," you probably also will read "Pkwy" as "Parkway" and will never notice the difference. Your mind will complete the word without allowing you to focus on the letters. However, if you read the abbreviation as an abbreviation, you will notice that the two abbreviations are different. If you read "Kansas City, MO" as "Kansas City, Missouri," you are unlikely to catch the difference with "Kansas City, MD." But if you read "Kansas City, em oh," you will readily pick up on "Kansas City, em dee."

In answering comparison questions, you may find it helpful to look for differences in one area at a time. If you narrow your focus to compare only short numbers, abbreviations, or just the words, you are more likely to notice differences and are less apt to see what you expect to see rather than what is actually printed on the page.

Your best bet is to start with length of line, number of digits, middle initials, or small words. When you spot *any difference* at all, the two items being compared are different. If while concentrating on one area you happen to catch a difference in another area, by all means consider the items to be different, and go on to the next comparison. A system may be useful, but don't spend any more time on the question; move on.

Also trust yourself. Once you have decided that two items being compared are exactly alike, stick with your decision. Never look back and recheck two items.

Tests of clerical speed and accuracy put such a premium on accuracy that the scoring formula is sometimes "Score equals Number Correct minus Number Wrong." You must not allow fear of making errors to slow you down so that you plod along and answer very few questions; speed also is important. However, it should be clear to you that you must work steadily right until time is called, and then stop promptly.

Practice Test 1

Directions: *Each question lists four names or numbers. The names or numbers may or may not be exactly the same. Compare the four names or numbers in each question, and mark your answer as follows:*

Mark (A) if all four names or numbers are *DIFFERENT*.

Mark (B) if *TWO* of the names or numbers are exactly the same.

Mark (C) if *THREE* of the names or numbers are exactly the same.

Mark (D) if all *FOUR* names or numbers are exactly the same.

C **1.** W.E. Johnston
W.E. Johnson
W.E. Johnson
W.B. Johnson

D **2.** Vergil L. Muller
Vergil L. Muller
Vergil L. Muller
Vergil L. Muller

C **3.** 5261383
5263183
5263183
5623183

A **4.** Atherton R. Warde
Asheton R. Warde
Atherton P. Warde
Athertin P. Warde

B **5.** 8125690
8126690
8125609
8125609

B **6.** E. Owens McVey
E. Owen McVey
E. Owen McVay
E. Owen McVey

B **7.** Emily Neal Rouse
Emily Neal Rowse
Emily Neal Roose
Emily Neal Rowse

C **8.** Francis Ramsdell
Francis Ransdell
Francis Ramsdell
Francis Ramsdell

D **9.** 2395890
2395890
2395890
2395890

B **10.** 1926341
1962341
1963241
1926341

C **11.** H. Merritt Audubon
H. Merriott Audobon
H. Merritt Audobon
H. Merritt Audubon

C **12.** 6219354
6219354
6219345
6219354

13. Cornelius Detwiler
Cornelius Detwiler
Cornelius Detwiler
Cornelius Detwiler

15. Drusilla S. Ridgeley
Drusilla S. Ridgeley
Drucilla S. Ridgeley
Drucilla S. Ridgely

14. 2312793
2312973
2312973
2312973

16. Andrei I. Tourantzev
Andrei I. Toumantzev
Andrei I. Toumantzov
Andrei I. Tourantzov

Practice Test 2

Directions: Each question gives the name and identification number of an employee. You are to choose the ONE answer that has exactly the same identification number and name as those given in the question.

1. 176823 Katherine Blau
   (A) 176823 Catherine Blau
   (B) 176283 Katherine Blau
   (C) 176823 Katherine Blau
   (D) 176823 Katherine Blaw

2. 673403 Boris T. Frame
   (A) 673403 Boris P. Frame
   (B) 673403 Boris T. Frame
   (C) 673403 Boris T. Fraim
   (D) 673430 Boris T. Frame

3. 498832 Hyman Ziebart
   (A) 498832 Hyman Zeibart
   (B) 498832 Hiram Ziebart
   (C) 498832 Hyman Ziebardt
   (D) 498832 Hyman Ziebart

4. 506745 Barbara O'Dey
   (A) 507645 Barbara O'Day
   (B) 506745 Barbara O'Day
   (C) 506475 Barbara O'Day
   (D) 506745 Barbara O'Dey

5. 344223 Morton Sklar
   (A) 344223 Morton Sklar
   (B) 344332 Norton Sklar
   (C) 344332 Morton Sklaar
   (D) 343322 Morton Sklar

6. 816040 Betsy B. Voight
   (A) 816404 Betsy B. Voight
   (B) 814060 Betsy B. Voight
   (C) 816040 Betsy B. Voight
   (D) 816040 Betsey B. Voight

7. 913576 Harold Howritz
   (A) 913576 Harold Horwitz
   (B) 913576 Harold Howritz
   (C) 913756 Harold Howritz
   (D) 913576 Harald Howritz

8. 621190 Jayne T. Downs
   (A) 621990 Janie T. Downs
   (B) 621190 Janie T. Downs
   (C) 622190 Janie T. Downs
   (D) 621190 Jayne T. Downs

9. 004620 George McBoyd
   (A) 006420 George McBoyd
   (B) 006420 George MacBoyd
   (C) 006420 George McBoid
   (D) 004620 George McBoyd

10. 723495 Alice Appleton
   (A) 723495 Alice Appleton
   (B) 723594 Alica Appleton
   (C) 723459 Alice Appleton
   (D) 732495 Alice Appleton

11. 856772 Aaron B. Haynes
   (A) 856722 Aaron B. Haynes
   (B) 856722 Aaron B. Haynes
   (C) 856722 Aaron B. Haynes
   (D) 856772 Aaron B. Haynes

12. 121434 Veronica Pope
   (A) 121343 Veronica Pope
   (B) 121434 Veronica Pope
   (C) 121434 Veronica Popa
   (D) 121343 Veronica Popa

Practice Test 3

Directions: Each of the following questions consists of three sets of names and name codes. In each question, the two names and name codes on the same line are supposed to be exactly the same.

Mark (A) if there are mistakes in all THREE sets.

Mark (B) if there are mistakes in TWO of the sets.

Mark (C) if there are mistakes in only ONE set.

Mark (D) if there are NO MISTAKES in any of the sets.

1. Macabe, John N. – V 53162   Macade, John N. – V 53162
   Ware, Susan B. – A 45068   Ware, Susan B. – A 45968
   Howard, Joan S. – J 24791   Howard, Joan S. – J 24791

2. Powell, Michael C. – 78537F   Powell, Michael C. – 78537 F
   Martinez, Pablo J. – 24435 P   Martinez, Pablo J. – 24435 P
   MacBane, Eliot M. – 98674 E   MacBane, Eliot M. – 98674 E

3. Fitz-Kramer Machines Inc. – 259090   Fitz-Kramer Machines Inc. – 259090
   Marvel Cleaning Service – 482657   Marvel Cleaning Service – 482657
   Donato, Carl G. – 637418   Danato, Carl G. – 687418

4. Martin Davison Trading Corp. – 43108 T   Martin Davidson Trading Corp. – 43108 T
   Cotwald Lighting Fixtures – 76065 L   Cotwald Lighting Fixtures – 70056 L
   R. Crawford Plumbers – 23157 C   R. Crawford Plumbers – 23157 G

5. Fraiman Engineering Corp. – M4773   Friaman Engineering Corp. – M4773
   Neuman, Walter B. – N7745   Neumen, Walter B. – N7745
   Pierce, Eric M. – W6304   Pierce, Eric M. – W6304

6. Constable, Eugene – B 64837   Comstable, Eugene – B 64837
   Derrick, Paul – H 27119   Derrik, Paul – H 27119
   Heller, Karen – S 49606   Heller, Karen – S 46906

7. Hernando Delivery Service Co. – D 7456   Hernando Delivery Service Co. – D 7456
   Barettz Electrical Supplies – N 5392   Barettz Electrical Supplies – N 5392
   Tanner, Abraham – M 4798   Tanner, Abraham – M 4798

8. Kalin Associates	– R 38641	Kaline Associates	– R 38641
Sealey, Robert E.	– P 63533	Sealey, Robert E.	– P 63553
Scalsi Office Furniture	– R 36742	Scalsi Office Furniture	– R 36742
9. Janowsky, Philip M.	– 742213	Janowsky, Philip M.	– 742213
Hansen, Thomas H.	– 934816	Hanson, Thomas H.	– 934816
L. Lester and Son Inc.	– 294568	L. Lester and Son Inc.	– 294568
10. Majthenyi, Alexander	– P 4802	Majthenyi, Alexander	– B 4802
Prisco Pools, Inc.	– W 3641	Frisco Pools, Inc.	– W 3641
DePaso, Nancy G.	– X 4464	DePaso, Nancy G.	– X 4464

Answer Key for Practice Tests

TEST 1

1. **B**	5. **B**	9. **D**	13. **D**
2. **D**	6. **B**	10. **B**	14. **C**
3. **B**	7. **B**	11. **B**	15. **B**
4. **A**	8. **C**	12. **C**	16. **A**

TEST 2

1. **C**	4. **D**	7. **B**	10. **A**
2. **B**	5. **A**	8. **D**	11. **D**
3. **D**	6. **C**	9. **D**	12. **B**

TEST 3

1. **B**	3. **C**	5. **B**	7. **D**	9. **C**
2. **D**	4. **A**	6. **A**	8. **B**	10. **B**

TYPING

While typing is not strictly a part of the General Test, it is included in this book because nearly every applicant for any U.S. job must take a typing test. Most often, the typing test is merely a qualifying test—that is, the candidate must pass the test in order to be hired, but the score by which the test is passed is not a consideration. The candidate must simply prove that he or she knows how to type to a minimum speed and accuracy standard. For jobs in which typing is a very important skill, the typing test may be competitively scored. For such jobs, the score on the typing test enters into the overall civil service test score and affects hiring decisions.

The typing test that you take will consist of a passage that you must copy exactly as it is presented to you. You will have a specified length of time in which to type, and your score will be based upon the number of words per minute that you type within that time and upon the number of errors you make. The length of the test varies from one jurisdiction to another. Most typing tests last five minutes. The minimum performance standards for applicants also vary. For some positions, a minimum speed of 30 words per minute is adequate; for others, 35 words per minute, 40 words per minute, or even greater speeds are required. Likewise, the number of errors permitted varies according to governmental jurisdiction and according to the position for which you are applying.

In the typing test, you are faced with a single task—that of copying material exactly as it is presented. You must demonstrate how rapidly you can do so and with what degree of accuracy.

The plain copy test consists of a practice exercise and a specific test passage. The practice exercise, usually about 10 lines in length, enables candidates to warm up and to make certain that their typewriters are functioning properly. The practice exercise is not scored. After the practice exercise, candidates are instructed to put fresh paper into their machines for the actual test. They are given time to read both the plain copy directions and the actual test passage to be typed. Then the exam begins.

The basic principles in charging typing errors are as follows. One charge is made for each:

- WORD or PUNCTUATION MARK incorrectly typed or in which there was an erasure. (An error in spacing that follows an incorrect word or punctuation mark is not further charged.)
- SERIES of consecutive words omitted, repeated, inserted, transposed, or erased. A charge is made for errors within such series, but the total charge cannot exceed the number of words.
- LINE or part of line typed over other material, typed with all capitals, or apparently typed with the fingers on the wrong keys.
- CHANGE from the MARGIN where most lines are begun by the candidate or from the PARAGRAPH INDENTION most frequently used by the candidate.

Typing Exercise

Directions: Type the copy exactly as it is given below. Spell, space, punctuate, capitalize, and begin and end each line and paragraph precisely as shown. Make no erasures, insertions, or other corrections. Errors are penalized whether they are erased or otherwise corrected. Keep on typing even though you detect an error in your copy. If you finish typing the passage before the time limit is up, simply double-space once and start typing from the beginning of the passage. If you fill up one side of the paper, turn it over and continue typing on the other side.

LINE
COUNT   TIME: 5 Minutes

1   In the field of public administration in the narrower and more technical sense, significant trends are observable. These are closely related to the efficiency movement
3   in modern business and the new social background of administrative activity. The new movement involves larger administrative areas, consolidation of authority at
5   all levels, central control over subordinate authorities in the region, a professional personnel, and the application of new technical devices to the rationalization of
7   the service. These movements are especially apparent in the states and in the special fields of health, highways, education, and finance. Consolidation is also
9   seen in the cities, both under the council mayor and under the council manager forms of government.

11   The federal government has established an important form of administrative control by means of grants-in-aid. At the same time, an important relationship has
13   been developed in the cooperative exchange of administrative services between the United States and the states, and to a more limited extent between the states and
15   localities. The continuing involvement of federal agencies in these matters is a significant indicator of this new policy. It augurs well for the future.

EACH TIME YOU REACH THIS POINT, DOUBLE-SPACE ONCE AND BEGIN AGAIN.

TYPING SPEED ATTAINED: _____   NUMBER OF ERRORS: _____

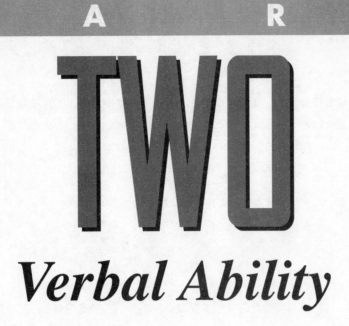

P A R T

TWO

Verbal Ability

CONTENTS

Correct Usage Test Answer Sheet

Test 1

1. Ⓐ Ⓑ Ⓒ Ⓓ   3. Ⓐ Ⓑ Ⓒ Ⓓ   5. Ⓐ Ⓑ Ⓒ Ⓓ   7. Ⓐ Ⓑ Ⓒ Ⓓ
2. Ⓐ Ⓑ Ⓒ Ⓓ   4. Ⓐ Ⓑ Ⓒ Ⓓ   6. Ⓐ Ⓑ Ⓒ Ⓓ   8. Ⓐ Ⓑ Ⓒ Ⓓ

Test 2

1. Ⓐ Ⓑ Ⓒ Ⓓ   3. Ⓐ Ⓑ Ⓒ Ⓓ   5. Ⓐ Ⓑ Ⓒ Ⓓ   7. Ⓐ Ⓑ Ⓒ Ⓓ   9. Ⓐ Ⓑ Ⓒ Ⓓ
2. Ⓐ Ⓑ Ⓒ Ⓓ   4. Ⓐ Ⓑ Ⓒ Ⓓ   6. Ⓐ Ⓑ Ⓒ Ⓓ   8. Ⓐ Ⓑ Ⓒ Ⓓ

Test 3

1. Ⓐ Ⓑ Ⓒ Ⓓ   3. Ⓐ Ⓑ Ⓒ Ⓓ   5. Ⓐ Ⓑ Ⓒ Ⓓ   7. Ⓐ Ⓑ Ⓒ Ⓓ   9. Ⓐ Ⓑ Ⓒ Ⓓ
2. Ⓐ Ⓑ Ⓒ Ⓓ   4. Ⓐ Ⓑ Ⓒ Ⓓ   6. Ⓐ Ⓑ Ⓒ Ⓓ   8. Ⓐ Ⓑ Ⓒ Ⓓ

Test 4

1. Ⓐ Ⓑ Ⓒ Ⓓ   3. Ⓐ Ⓑ Ⓒ Ⓓ   5. Ⓐ Ⓑ Ⓒ Ⓓ   7. Ⓐ Ⓑ Ⓒ Ⓓ
2. Ⓐ Ⓑ Ⓒ Ⓓ   4. Ⓐ Ⓑ Ⓒ Ⓓ   6. Ⓐ Ⓑ Ⓒ Ⓓ   8. Ⓐ Ⓑ Ⓒ Ⓓ

Test 5

1. Ⓐ Ⓑ Ⓒ Ⓓ   3. Ⓐ Ⓑ Ⓒ Ⓓ   5. Ⓐ Ⓑ Ⓒ Ⓓ   7. Ⓐ Ⓑ Ⓒ Ⓓ   9. Ⓐ Ⓑ Ⓒ Ⓓ
2. Ⓐ Ⓑ Ⓒ Ⓓ   4. Ⓐ Ⓑ Ⓒ Ⓓ   6. Ⓐ Ⓑ Ⓒ Ⓓ   8. Ⓐ Ⓑ Ⓒ Ⓓ   10. Ⓐ Ⓑ Ⓒ Ⓓ

Spelling Test Answer Sheet

Test 1

1. Ⓐ Ⓑ Ⓒ Ⓓ   3. Ⓐ Ⓑ Ⓒ Ⓓ   5. Ⓐ Ⓑ Ⓒ Ⓓ   7. Ⓐ Ⓑ Ⓒ Ⓓ   9. Ⓐ Ⓑ Ⓒ Ⓓ
2. Ⓐ Ⓑ Ⓒ Ⓓ   4. Ⓐ Ⓑ Ⓒ Ⓓ   6. Ⓐ Ⓑ Ⓒ Ⓓ   8. Ⓐ Ⓑ Ⓒ Ⓓ   10. Ⓐ Ⓑ Ⓒ Ⓓ

Test 2

1. Ⓐ Ⓑ Ⓒ Ⓓ	5. Ⓐ Ⓑ Ⓒ Ⓓ	9. Ⓐ Ⓑ Ⓒ Ⓓ	13. Ⓐ Ⓑ Ⓒ Ⓓ	17. Ⓐ Ⓑ Ⓒ Ⓓ
2. Ⓐ Ⓑ Ⓒ Ⓓ	6. Ⓐ Ⓑ Ⓒ Ⓓ	10. Ⓐ Ⓑ Ⓒ Ⓓ	14. Ⓐ Ⓑ Ⓒ Ⓓ	18. Ⓐ Ⓑ Ⓒ Ⓓ
3. Ⓐ Ⓑ Ⓒ Ⓓ	7. Ⓐ Ⓑ Ⓒ Ⓓ	11. Ⓐ Ⓑ Ⓒ Ⓓ	15. Ⓐ Ⓑ Ⓒ Ⓓ	19. Ⓐ Ⓑ Ⓒ Ⓓ
4. Ⓐ Ⓑ Ⓒ Ⓓ	8. Ⓐ Ⓑ Ⓒ Ⓓ	12. Ⓐ Ⓑ Ⓒ Ⓓ	16. Ⓐ Ⓑ Ⓒ Ⓓ	20. Ⓐ Ⓑ Ⓒ Ⓓ

Test 3

1. Ⓐ Ⓑ Ⓒ Ⓓ	5. Ⓐ Ⓑ Ⓒ Ⓓ	9. Ⓐ Ⓑ Ⓒ Ⓓ	13. Ⓐ Ⓑ Ⓒ Ⓓ	17. Ⓐ Ⓑ Ⓒ Ⓓ
2. Ⓐ Ⓑ Ⓒ Ⓓ	6. Ⓐ Ⓑ Ⓒ Ⓓ	10. Ⓐ Ⓑ Ⓒ Ⓓ	14. Ⓐ Ⓑ Ⓒ Ⓓ	18. Ⓐ Ⓑ Ⓒ Ⓓ
3. Ⓐ Ⓑ Ⓒ Ⓓ	7. Ⓐ Ⓑ Ⓒ Ⓓ	11. Ⓐ Ⓑ Ⓒ Ⓓ	15. Ⓐ Ⓑ Ⓒ Ⓓ	19. Ⓐ Ⓑ Ⓒ Ⓓ
4. Ⓐ Ⓑ Ⓒ Ⓓ	8. Ⓐ Ⓑ Ⓒ Ⓓ	12. Ⓐ Ⓑ Ⓒ Ⓓ	16. Ⓐ Ⓑ Ⓒ Ⓓ	20. Ⓐ Ⓑ Ⓒ Ⓓ

Test 4

1. Ⓐ Ⓑ Ⓒ Ⓓ	4. Ⓐ Ⓑ Ⓒ Ⓓ	7. Ⓐ Ⓑ Ⓒ Ⓓ	10. Ⓐ Ⓑ Ⓒ Ⓓ	13. Ⓐ Ⓑ Ⓒ Ⓓ
2. Ⓐ Ⓑ Ⓒ Ⓓ	5. Ⓐ Ⓑ Ⓒ Ⓓ	8. Ⓐ Ⓑ Ⓒ Ⓓ	11. Ⓐ Ⓑ Ⓒ Ⓓ	14. Ⓐ Ⓑ Ⓒ Ⓓ
3. Ⓐ Ⓑ Ⓒ Ⓓ	6. Ⓐ Ⓑ Ⓒ Ⓓ	9. Ⓐ Ⓑ Ⓒ Ⓓ	12. Ⓐ Ⓑ Ⓒ Ⓓ	15. Ⓐ Ⓑ Ⓒ Ⓓ

Synonyms Test Answer Sheet

Test 1

1. Ⓐ Ⓑ Ⓒ Ⓓ	6. Ⓐ Ⓑ Ⓒ Ⓓ	11. Ⓐ Ⓑ Ⓒ Ⓓ	16. Ⓐ Ⓑ Ⓒ Ⓓ	21. Ⓐ Ⓑ Ⓒ Ⓓ
2. Ⓐ Ⓑ Ⓒ Ⓓ	7. Ⓐ Ⓑ Ⓒ Ⓓ	12. Ⓐ Ⓑ Ⓒ Ⓓ	17. Ⓐ Ⓑ Ⓒ Ⓓ	22. Ⓐ Ⓑ Ⓒ Ⓓ
3. Ⓐ Ⓑ Ⓒ Ⓓ	8. Ⓐ Ⓑ Ⓒ Ⓓ	13. Ⓐ Ⓑ Ⓒ Ⓓ	18. Ⓐ Ⓑ Ⓒ Ⓓ	23. Ⓐ Ⓑ Ⓒ Ⓓ
4. Ⓐ Ⓑ Ⓒ Ⓓ	9. Ⓐ Ⓑ Ⓒ Ⓓ	14. Ⓐ Ⓑ Ⓒ Ⓓ	19. Ⓐ Ⓑ Ⓒ Ⓓ	24. Ⓐ Ⓑ Ⓒ Ⓓ
5. Ⓐ Ⓑ Ⓒ Ⓓ	10. Ⓐ Ⓑ Ⓒ Ⓓ	15. Ⓐ Ⓑ Ⓒ Ⓓ	20. Ⓐ Ⓑ Ⓒ Ⓓ	25. Ⓐ Ⓑ Ⓒ Ⓓ

Test 2

1. Ⓐ Ⓑ Ⓒ Ⓓ	6. Ⓐ Ⓑ Ⓒ Ⓓ	11. Ⓐ Ⓑ Ⓒ Ⓓ	16. Ⓐ Ⓑ Ⓒ Ⓓ	21. Ⓐ Ⓑ Ⓒ Ⓓ
2. Ⓐ Ⓑ Ⓒ Ⓓ	7. Ⓐ Ⓑ Ⓒ Ⓓ	12. Ⓐ Ⓑ Ⓒ Ⓓ	17. Ⓐ Ⓑ Ⓒ Ⓓ	22. Ⓐ Ⓑ Ⓒ Ⓓ
3. Ⓐ Ⓑ Ⓒ Ⓓ	8. Ⓐ Ⓑ Ⓒ Ⓓ	13. Ⓐ Ⓑ Ⓒ Ⓓ	18. Ⓐ Ⓑ Ⓒ Ⓓ	23. Ⓐ Ⓑ Ⓒ Ⓓ
4. Ⓐ Ⓑ Ⓒ Ⓓ	9. Ⓐ Ⓑ Ⓒ Ⓓ	14. Ⓐ Ⓑ Ⓒ Ⓓ	19. Ⓐ Ⓑ Ⓒ Ⓓ	24. Ⓐ Ⓑ Ⓒ Ⓓ
5. Ⓐ Ⓑ Ⓒ Ⓓ	10. Ⓐ Ⓑ Ⓒ Ⓓ	15. Ⓐ Ⓑ Ⓒ Ⓓ	20. Ⓐ Ⓑ Ⓒ Ⓓ	25. Ⓐ Ⓑ Ⓒ Ⓓ

Test 3

1. Ⓐ Ⓑ Ⓒ Ⓓ	6. Ⓐ Ⓑ Ⓒ Ⓓ	11. Ⓐ Ⓑ Ⓒ Ⓓ	16. Ⓐ Ⓑ Ⓒ Ⓓ	21. Ⓐ Ⓑ Ⓒ Ⓓ
2. Ⓐ Ⓑ Ⓒ Ⓓ	7. Ⓐ Ⓑ Ⓒ Ⓓ	12. Ⓐ Ⓑ Ⓒ Ⓓ	17. Ⓐ Ⓑ Ⓒ Ⓓ	22. Ⓐ Ⓑ Ⓒ Ⓓ
3. Ⓐ Ⓑ Ⓒ Ⓓ	8. Ⓐ Ⓑ Ⓒ Ⓓ	13. Ⓐ Ⓑ Ⓒ Ⓓ	18. Ⓐ Ⓑ Ⓒ Ⓓ	23. Ⓐ Ⓑ Ⓒ Ⓓ
4. Ⓐ Ⓑ Ⓒ Ⓓ	9. Ⓐ Ⓑ Ⓒ Ⓓ	14. Ⓐ Ⓑ Ⓒ Ⓓ	19. Ⓐ Ⓑ Ⓒ Ⓓ	24. Ⓐ Ⓑ Ⓒ Ⓓ
5. Ⓐ Ⓑ Ⓒ Ⓓ	10. Ⓐ Ⓑ Ⓒ Ⓓ	15. Ⓐ Ⓑ Ⓒ Ⓓ	20. Ⓐ Ⓑ Ⓒ Ⓓ	25. Ⓐ Ⓑ Ⓒ Ⓓ

Test 4

1. Ⓐ Ⓑ Ⓒ Ⓓ	6. Ⓐ Ⓑ Ⓒ Ⓓ	11. Ⓐ Ⓑ Ⓒ Ⓓ	16. Ⓐ Ⓑ Ⓒ Ⓓ	21. Ⓐ Ⓑ Ⓒ Ⓓ
2. Ⓐ Ⓑ Ⓒ Ⓓ	7. Ⓐ Ⓑ Ⓒ Ⓓ	12. Ⓐ Ⓑ Ⓒ Ⓓ	17. Ⓐ Ⓑ Ⓒ Ⓓ	22. Ⓐ Ⓑ Ⓒ Ⓓ
3. Ⓐ Ⓑ Ⓒ Ⓓ	8. Ⓐ Ⓑ Ⓒ Ⓓ	13. Ⓐ Ⓑ Ⓒ Ⓓ	18. Ⓐ Ⓑ Ⓒ Ⓓ	23. Ⓐ Ⓑ Ⓒ Ⓓ
4. Ⓐ Ⓑ Ⓒ Ⓓ	9. Ⓐ Ⓑ Ⓒ Ⓓ	14. Ⓐ Ⓑ Ⓒ Ⓓ	19. Ⓐ Ⓑ Ⓒ Ⓓ	24. Ⓐ Ⓑ Ⓒ Ⓓ
5. Ⓐ Ⓑ Ⓒ Ⓓ	10. Ⓐ Ⓑ Ⓒ Ⓓ	15. Ⓐ Ⓑ Ⓒ Ⓓ	20. Ⓐ Ⓑ Ⓒ Ⓓ	25. Ⓐ Ⓑ Ⓒ Ⓓ

Test 5

1. Ⓐ Ⓑ Ⓒ Ⓓ	6. Ⓐ Ⓑ Ⓒ Ⓓ	11. Ⓐ Ⓑ Ⓒ Ⓓ	16. Ⓐ Ⓑ Ⓒ Ⓓ	21. Ⓐ Ⓑ Ⓒ Ⓓ
2. Ⓐ Ⓑ Ⓒ Ⓓ	7. Ⓐ Ⓑ Ⓒ Ⓓ	12. Ⓐ Ⓑ Ⓒ Ⓓ	17. Ⓐ Ⓑ Ⓒ Ⓓ	22. Ⓐ Ⓑ Ⓒ Ⓓ
3. Ⓐ Ⓑ Ⓒ Ⓓ	8. Ⓐ Ⓑ Ⓒ Ⓓ	13. Ⓐ Ⓑ Ⓒ Ⓓ	18. Ⓐ Ⓑ Ⓒ Ⓓ	23. Ⓐ Ⓑ Ⓒ Ⓓ
4. Ⓐ Ⓑ Ⓒ Ⓓ	9. Ⓐ Ⓑ Ⓒ Ⓓ	14. Ⓐ Ⓑ Ⓒ Ⓓ	19. Ⓐ Ⓑ Ⓒ Ⓓ	24. Ⓐ Ⓑ Ⓒ Ⓓ
5. Ⓐ Ⓑ Ⓒ Ⓓ	10. Ⓐ Ⓑ Ⓒ Ⓓ	15. Ⓐ Ⓑ Ⓒ Ⓓ	20. Ⓐ Ⓑ Ⓒ Ⓓ	25. Ⓐ Ⓑ Ⓒ Ⓓ

Sentence Completion Test Answer Sheet

Test 1

1. Ⓐ Ⓑ Ⓒ Ⓓ	6. Ⓐ Ⓑ Ⓒ Ⓓ	11. Ⓐ Ⓑ Ⓒ Ⓓ	16. Ⓐ Ⓑ Ⓒ Ⓓ	21. Ⓐ Ⓑ Ⓒ Ⓓ
2. Ⓐ Ⓑ Ⓒ Ⓓ	7. Ⓐ Ⓑ Ⓒ Ⓓ	12. Ⓐ Ⓑ Ⓒ Ⓓ	17. Ⓐ Ⓑ Ⓒ Ⓓ	22. Ⓐ Ⓑ Ⓒ Ⓓ
3. Ⓐ Ⓑ Ⓒ Ⓓ	8. Ⓐ Ⓑ Ⓒ Ⓓ	13. Ⓐ Ⓑ Ⓒ Ⓓ	18. Ⓐ Ⓑ Ⓒ Ⓓ	23. Ⓐ Ⓑ Ⓒ Ⓓ
4. Ⓐ Ⓑ Ⓒ Ⓓ	9. Ⓐ Ⓑ Ⓒ Ⓓ	14. Ⓐ Ⓑ Ⓒ Ⓓ	19. Ⓐ Ⓑ Ⓒ Ⓓ	24. Ⓐ Ⓑ Ⓒ Ⓓ
5. Ⓐ Ⓑ Ⓒ Ⓓ	10. Ⓐ Ⓑ Ⓒ Ⓓ	15. Ⓐ Ⓑ Ⓒ Ⓓ	20. Ⓐ Ⓑ Ⓒ Ⓓ	25. Ⓐ Ⓑ Ⓒ Ⓓ

Test 2

1. Ⓐ Ⓑ Ⓒ Ⓓ	6. Ⓐ Ⓑ Ⓒ Ⓓ	11. Ⓐ Ⓑ Ⓒ Ⓓ	16. Ⓐ Ⓑ Ⓒ Ⓓ	21. Ⓐ Ⓑ Ⓒ Ⓓ
2. Ⓐ Ⓑ Ⓒ Ⓓ	7. Ⓐ Ⓑ Ⓒ Ⓓ	12. Ⓐ Ⓑ Ⓒ Ⓓ	17. Ⓐ Ⓑ Ⓒ Ⓓ	22. Ⓐ Ⓑ Ⓒ Ⓓ
3. Ⓐ Ⓑ Ⓒ Ⓓ	8. Ⓐ Ⓑ Ⓒ Ⓓ	13. Ⓐ Ⓑ Ⓒ Ⓓ	18. Ⓐ Ⓑ Ⓒ Ⓓ	23. Ⓐ Ⓑ Ⓒ Ⓓ
4. Ⓐ Ⓑ Ⓒ Ⓓ	9. Ⓐ Ⓑ Ⓒ Ⓓ	14. Ⓐ Ⓑ Ⓒ Ⓓ	19. Ⓐ Ⓑ Ⓒ Ⓓ	24. Ⓐ Ⓑ Ⓒ Ⓓ
5. Ⓐ Ⓑ Ⓒ Ⓓ	10. Ⓐ Ⓑ Ⓒ Ⓓ	15. Ⓐ Ⓑ Ⓒ Ⓓ	20. Ⓐ Ⓑ Ⓒ Ⓓ	25. Ⓐ Ⓑ Ⓒ Ⓓ

Test 3

1. Ⓐ Ⓑ Ⓒ Ⓓ	6. Ⓐ Ⓑ Ⓒ Ⓓ	11. Ⓐ Ⓑ Ⓒ Ⓓ	16. Ⓐ Ⓑ Ⓒ Ⓓ	21. Ⓐ Ⓑ Ⓒ Ⓓ
2. Ⓐ Ⓑ Ⓒ Ⓓ	7. Ⓐ Ⓑ Ⓒ Ⓓ	12. Ⓐ Ⓑ Ⓒ Ⓓ	17. Ⓐ Ⓑ Ⓒ Ⓓ	22. Ⓐ Ⓑ Ⓒ Ⓓ
3. Ⓐ Ⓑ Ⓒ Ⓓ	8. Ⓐ Ⓑ Ⓒ Ⓓ	13. Ⓐ Ⓑ Ⓒ Ⓓ	18. Ⓐ Ⓑ Ⓒ Ⓓ	23. Ⓐ Ⓑ Ⓒ Ⓓ
4. Ⓐ Ⓑ Ⓒ Ⓓ	9. Ⓐ Ⓑ Ⓒ Ⓓ	14. Ⓐ Ⓑ Ⓒ Ⓓ	19. Ⓐ Ⓑ Ⓒ Ⓓ	24. Ⓐ Ⓑ Ⓒ Ⓓ
5. Ⓐ Ⓑ Ⓒ Ⓓ	10. Ⓐ Ⓑ Ⓒ Ⓓ	15. Ⓐ Ⓑ Ⓒ Ⓓ	20. Ⓐ Ⓑ Ⓒ Ⓓ	25. Ⓐ Ⓑ Ⓒ Ⓓ

Test 4

1. Ⓐ Ⓑ Ⓒ Ⓓ	6. Ⓐ Ⓑ Ⓒ Ⓓ	11. Ⓐ Ⓑ Ⓒ Ⓓ	16. Ⓐ Ⓑ Ⓒ Ⓓ	21. Ⓐ Ⓑ Ⓒ Ⓓ
2. Ⓐ Ⓑ Ⓒ Ⓓ	7. Ⓐ Ⓑ Ⓒ Ⓓ	12. Ⓐ Ⓑ Ⓒ Ⓓ	17. Ⓐ Ⓑ Ⓒ Ⓓ	22. Ⓐ Ⓑ Ⓒ Ⓓ
3. Ⓐ Ⓑ Ⓒ Ⓓ	8. Ⓐ Ⓑ Ⓒ Ⓓ	13. Ⓐ Ⓑ Ⓒ Ⓓ	18. Ⓐ Ⓑ Ⓒ Ⓓ	23. Ⓐ Ⓑ Ⓒ Ⓓ
4. Ⓐ Ⓑ Ⓒ Ⓓ	9. Ⓐ Ⓑ Ⓒ Ⓓ	14. Ⓐ Ⓑ Ⓒ Ⓓ	19. Ⓐ Ⓑ Ⓒ Ⓓ	24. Ⓐ Ⓑ Ⓒ Ⓓ
5. Ⓐ Ⓑ Ⓒ Ⓓ	10. Ⓐ Ⓑ Ⓒ Ⓓ	15. Ⓐ Ⓑ Ⓒ Ⓓ	20. Ⓐ Ⓑ Ⓒ Ⓓ	25. Ⓐ Ⓑ Ⓒ Ⓓ

Test 5

1. Ⓐ Ⓑ Ⓒ Ⓓ	6. Ⓐ Ⓑ Ⓒ Ⓓ	11. Ⓐ Ⓑ Ⓒ Ⓓ	16. Ⓐ Ⓑ Ⓒ Ⓓ	21. Ⓐ Ⓑ Ⓒ Ⓓ
2. Ⓐ Ⓑ Ⓒ Ⓓ	7. Ⓐ Ⓑ Ⓒ Ⓓ	12. Ⓐ Ⓑ Ⓒ Ⓓ	17. Ⓐ Ⓑ Ⓒ Ⓓ	22. Ⓐ Ⓑ Ⓒ Ⓓ
3. Ⓐ Ⓑ Ⓒ Ⓓ	8. Ⓐ Ⓑ Ⓒ Ⓓ	13. Ⓐ Ⓑ Ⓒ Ⓓ	18. Ⓐ Ⓑ Ⓒ Ⓓ	23. Ⓐ Ⓑ Ⓒ Ⓓ
4. Ⓐ Ⓑ Ⓒ Ⓓ	9. Ⓐ Ⓑ Ⓒ Ⓓ	14. Ⓐ Ⓑ Ⓒ Ⓓ	19. Ⓐ Ⓑ Ⓒ Ⓓ	24. Ⓐ Ⓑ Ⓒ Ⓓ
5. Ⓐ Ⓑ Ⓒ Ⓓ	10. Ⓐ Ⓑ Ⓒ Ⓓ	15. Ⓐ Ⓑ Ⓒ Ⓓ	20. Ⓐ Ⓑ Ⓒ Ⓓ	25. Ⓐ Ⓑ Ⓒ Ⓓ

Reading Comprehension Test Answer Sheet

Test 1

1. Ⓐ Ⓑ Ⓒ Ⓓ	3. Ⓐ Ⓑ Ⓒ Ⓓ	5. Ⓐ Ⓑ Ⓒ Ⓓ	7. Ⓐ Ⓑ Ⓒ Ⓓ	9. Ⓐ Ⓑ Ⓒ Ⓓ
2. Ⓐ Ⓑ Ⓒ Ⓓ	4. Ⓐ Ⓑ Ⓒ Ⓓ	6. Ⓐ Ⓑ Ⓒ Ⓓ	8. Ⓐ Ⓑ Ⓒ Ⓓ	10. Ⓐ Ⓑ Ⓒ Ⓓ

Test 2

1. Ⓐ Ⓑ Ⓒ Ⓓ   3. Ⓐ Ⓑ Ⓒ Ⓓ   5. Ⓐ Ⓑ Ⓒ Ⓓ   7. Ⓐ Ⓑ Ⓒ Ⓓ   9. Ⓐ Ⓑ Ⓒ Ⓓ

2. Ⓐ Ⓑ Ⓒ Ⓓ   4. Ⓐ Ⓑ Ⓒ Ⓓ   6. Ⓐ Ⓑ Ⓒ Ⓓ   8. Ⓐ Ⓑ Ⓒ Ⓓ   10. Ⓐ Ⓑ Ⓒ Ⓓ

Test 3

1. Ⓐ Ⓑ Ⓒ Ⓓ   3. Ⓐ Ⓑ Ⓒ Ⓓ   5. Ⓐ Ⓑ Ⓒ Ⓓ   7. Ⓐ Ⓑ Ⓒ Ⓓ   9. Ⓐ Ⓑ Ⓒ Ⓓ

2. Ⓐ Ⓑ Ⓒ Ⓓ   4. Ⓐ Ⓑ Ⓒ Ⓓ   6. Ⓐ Ⓑ Ⓒ Ⓓ   8. Ⓐ Ⓑ Ⓒ Ⓓ   10. Ⓐ Ⓑ Ⓒ Ⓓ

Test 4

1. Ⓐ Ⓑ Ⓒ Ⓓ Ⓔ   3. Ⓐ Ⓑ Ⓒ Ⓓ Ⓔ   5. Ⓐ Ⓑ Ⓒ Ⓓ Ⓔ

2. Ⓐ Ⓑ Ⓒ Ⓓ Ⓔ   4. Ⓐ Ⓑ Ⓒ Ⓓ Ⓔ   6. Ⓐ Ⓑ Ⓒ Ⓓ Ⓔ

Effective Expression Test Answer Sheet

1. Ⓐ Ⓑ Ⓒ Ⓓ	21. Ⓐ Ⓑ Ⓒ Ⓓ	41. Ⓐ Ⓑ Ⓒ Ⓓ	61. Ⓐ Ⓑ Ⓒ Ⓓ	81. Ⓐ Ⓑ Ⓒ Ⓓ
2. Ⓐ Ⓑ Ⓒ Ⓓ	22. Ⓐ Ⓑ Ⓒ Ⓓ	42. Ⓐ Ⓑ Ⓒ Ⓓ	62. Ⓐ Ⓑ Ⓒ Ⓓ	82. Ⓐ Ⓑ Ⓒ Ⓓ
3. Ⓐ Ⓑ Ⓒ Ⓓ	23. Ⓐ Ⓑ Ⓒ Ⓓ	43. Ⓐ Ⓑ Ⓒ Ⓓ	63. Ⓐ Ⓑ Ⓒ Ⓓ	83. Ⓐ Ⓑ Ⓒ Ⓓ
4. Ⓐ Ⓑ Ⓒ Ⓓ	24. Ⓐ Ⓑ Ⓒ Ⓓ	44. Ⓐ Ⓑ Ⓒ Ⓓ	64. Ⓐ Ⓑ Ⓒ Ⓓ	84. Ⓐ Ⓑ Ⓒ Ⓓ
5. Ⓐ Ⓑ Ⓒ Ⓓ	25. Ⓐ Ⓑ Ⓒ Ⓓ	45. Ⓐ Ⓑ Ⓒ Ⓓ	65. Ⓐ Ⓑ Ⓒ Ⓓ	85. Ⓐ Ⓑ Ⓒ Ⓓ
6. Ⓐ Ⓑ Ⓒ Ⓓ	26. Ⓐ Ⓑ Ⓒ Ⓓ	46. Ⓐ Ⓑ Ⓒ Ⓓ	66. Ⓐ Ⓑ Ⓒ Ⓓ	86. Ⓐ Ⓑ Ⓒ Ⓓ
7. Ⓐ Ⓑ Ⓒ Ⓓ	27. Ⓐ Ⓑ Ⓒ Ⓓ	47. Ⓐ Ⓑ Ⓒ Ⓓ	67. Ⓐ Ⓑ Ⓒ Ⓓ	87. Ⓐ Ⓑ Ⓒ Ⓓ
8. Ⓐ Ⓑ Ⓒ Ⓓ	28. Ⓐ Ⓑ Ⓒ Ⓓ	48. Ⓐ Ⓑ Ⓒ Ⓓ	68. Ⓐ Ⓑ Ⓒ Ⓓ	88. Ⓐ Ⓑ Ⓒ Ⓓ
9. Ⓐ Ⓑ Ⓒ Ⓓ	29. Ⓐ Ⓑ Ⓒ Ⓓ	49. Ⓐ Ⓑ Ⓒ Ⓓ	69. Ⓐ Ⓑ Ⓒ Ⓓ	89. Ⓐ Ⓑ Ⓒ Ⓓ
10. Ⓐ Ⓑ Ⓒ Ⓓ	30. Ⓐ Ⓑ Ⓒ Ⓓ	50. Ⓐ Ⓑ Ⓒ Ⓓ	70. Ⓐ Ⓑ Ⓒ Ⓓ	90. Ⓐ Ⓑ Ⓒ Ⓓ
11. Ⓐ Ⓑ Ⓒ Ⓓ	31. Ⓐ Ⓑ Ⓒ Ⓓ	51. Ⓐ Ⓑ Ⓒ Ⓓ	71. Ⓐ Ⓑ Ⓒ Ⓓ	91. Ⓐ Ⓑ Ⓒ Ⓓ
12. Ⓐ Ⓑ Ⓒ Ⓓ	32. Ⓐ Ⓑ Ⓒ Ⓓ	52. Ⓐ Ⓑ Ⓒ Ⓓ	72. Ⓐ Ⓑ Ⓒ Ⓓ	92. Ⓐ Ⓑ Ⓒ Ⓓ
13. Ⓐ Ⓑ Ⓒ Ⓓ	33. Ⓐ Ⓑ Ⓒ Ⓓ	53. Ⓐ Ⓑ Ⓒ Ⓓ	73. Ⓐ Ⓑ Ⓒ Ⓓ	93. Ⓐ Ⓑ Ⓒ Ⓓ
14. Ⓐ Ⓑ Ⓒ Ⓓ	34. Ⓐ Ⓑ Ⓒ Ⓓ	54. Ⓐ Ⓑ Ⓒ Ⓓ	74. Ⓐ Ⓑ Ⓒ Ⓓ	94. Ⓐ Ⓑ Ⓒ Ⓓ
15. Ⓐ Ⓑ Ⓒ Ⓓ	35. Ⓐ Ⓑ Ⓒ Ⓓ	55. Ⓐ Ⓑ Ⓒ Ⓓ	75. Ⓐ Ⓑ Ⓒ Ⓓ	95. Ⓐ Ⓑ Ⓒ Ⓓ
16. Ⓐ Ⓑ Ⓒ Ⓓ	36. Ⓐ Ⓑ Ⓒ Ⓓ	56. Ⓐ Ⓑ Ⓒ Ⓓ	76. Ⓐ Ⓑ Ⓒ Ⓓ	96. Ⓐ Ⓑ Ⓒ Ⓓ
17. Ⓐ Ⓑ Ⓒ Ⓓ	37. Ⓐ Ⓑ Ⓒ Ⓓ	57. Ⓐ Ⓑ Ⓒ Ⓓ	77. Ⓐ Ⓑ Ⓒ Ⓓ	97. Ⓐ Ⓑ Ⓒ Ⓓ
18. Ⓐ Ⓑ Ⓒ Ⓓ	38. Ⓐ Ⓑ Ⓒ Ⓓ	58. Ⓐ Ⓑ Ⓒ Ⓓ	78. Ⓐ Ⓑ Ⓒ Ⓓ	98. Ⓐ Ⓑ Ⓒ Ⓓ
19. Ⓐ Ⓑ Ⓒ Ⓓ	39. Ⓐ Ⓑ Ⓒ Ⓓ	59. Ⓐ Ⓑ Ⓒ Ⓓ	79. Ⓐ Ⓑ Ⓒ Ⓓ	99. Ⓐ Ⓑ Ⓒ Ⓓ
20. Ⓐ Ⓑ Ⓒ Ⓓ	40. Ⓐ Ⓑ Ⓒ Ⓓ	60. Ⓐ Ⓑ Ⓒ Ⓓ	80. Ⓐ Ⓑ Ⓒ Ⓓ	100. Ⓐ Ⓑ Ⓒ Ⓓ

Verbal Analogy Test Answer Sheet

Test 1

1. Ⓐ Ⓑ Ⓒ Ⓓ	3. Ⓐ Ⓑ Ⓒ Ⓓ	5. Ⓐ Ⓑ Ⓒ Ⓓ	7. Ⓐ Ⓑ Ⓒ Ⓓ	9. Ⓐ Ⓑ Ⓒ Ⓓ
2. Ⓐ Ⓑ Ⓒ Ⓓ	4. Ⓐ Ⓑ Ⓒ Ⓓ	6. Ⓐ Ⓑ Ⓒ Ⓓ	8. Ⓐ Ⓑ Ⓒ Ⓓ	10. Ⓐ Ⓑ Ⓒ Ⓓ

Test 2

1. Ⓐ Ⓑ Ⓒ Ⓓ	3. Ⓐ Ⓑ Ⓒ Ⓓ	5. Ⓐ Ⓑ Ⓒ Ⓓ	7. Ⓐ Ⓑ Ⓒ Ⓓ	9. Ⓐ Ⓑ Ⓒ Ⓓ
2. Ⓐ Ⓑ Ⓒ Ⓓ	4. Ⓐ Ⓑ Ⓒ Ⓓ	6. Ⓐ Ⓑ Ⓒ Ⓓ	8. Ⓐ Ⓑ Ⓒ Ⓓ	10. Ⓐ Ⓑ Ⓒ Ⓓ

Test 3

1. Ⓐ Ⓑ Ⓒ Ⓓ	3. Ⓐ Ⓑ Ⓒ Ⓓ	5. Ⓐ Ⓑ Ⓒ Ⓓ	7. Ⓐ Ⓑ Ⓒ Ⓓ	9. Ⓐ Ⓑ Ⓒ Ⓓ
2. Ⓐ Ⓑ Ⓒ Ⓓ	4. Ⓐ Ⓑ Ⓒ Ⓓ	6. Ⓐ Ⓑ Ⓒ Ⓓ	8. Ⓐ Ⓑ Ⓒ Ⓓ	10. Ⓐ Ⓑ Ⓒ Ⓓ

Test 4

1. Ⓐ Ⓑ Ⓒ Ⓓ	3. Ⓐ Ⓑ Ⓒ Ⓓ	5. Ⓐ Ⓑ Ⓒ Ⓓ	7. Ⓐ Ⓑ Ⓒ Ⓓ	9. Ⓐ Ⓑ Ⓒ Ⓓ
2. Ⓐ Ⓑ Ⓒ Ⓓ	4. Ⓐ Ⓑ Ⓒ Ⓓ	6. Ⓐ Ⓑ Ⓒ Ⓓ	8. Ⓐ Ⓑ Ⓒ Ⓓ	10. Ⓐ Ⓑ Ⓒ Ⓓ

Test 5

1. Ⓐ Ⓑ Ⓒ Ⓓ	3. Ⓐ Ⓑ Ⓒ Ⓓ	5. Ⓐ Ⓑ Ⓒ Ⓓ	7. Ⓐ Ⓑ Ⓒ Ⓓ	9. Ⓐ Ⓑ Ⓒ Ⓓ
2. Ⓐ Ⓑ Ⓒ Ⓓ	4. Ⓐ Ⓑ Ⓒ Ⓓ	6. Ⓐ Ⓑ Ⓒ Ⓓ	8. Ⓐ Ⓑ Ⓒ Ⓓ	10. Ⓐ Ⓑ Ⓒ Ⓓ

ENGLISH GRAMMAR AND USAGE

Rules You Must Know

The following list of rules is far from comprehensive. In fact, it has been purposely kept brief so that you can learn every rule and every hint. These are rules that you will find invaluable for all your writing.

CAPITALIZATION

1. Capitalize the first word of a sentence.

2. Capitalize all proper names.

    Example: China, First National Bank, Reggie Jackson

3. Capitalize days of the week, months of the year, and holidays.

    Example: The check was mailed on *Thursday,* the day before *Christmas*.

    Note: Do NOT capitalize the seasons.

    Example: In Florida, *winter* is mild.

4. Capitalize the first and all other important words in a title.

    Example: The Art of Salesmanship

5. Capitalize nouns that are not regularly capitalized when they are used as part of proper names.

    Example: Yesterday I visited *Uncle Charles,* my favorite *uncle*.

    Example: *Locust Street* is an exceptionally narrow *street*.

6. Capitalize the points of the compass only when referring to a specific place or area.

    Example: Many retired persons spend the winter in the *South*.

    Note: Do NOT capitalize the points of the compass when referring to a direction.

    Example: Many birds fly *south* in the winter.

7. Capitalize languages and specific place names used as modifiers. Do *not* capitalize any other school subjects.

    Example: Next year I will study *French,* biology, *English* literature, mathematics, *European* history, and ancient philosophy.

8. Capitalize the first word of a direct quotation.

Example: It was Alexander Pope who wrote, "*A little learning is a dangerous thing.*"

Note: Do NOT capitalize the first word within quotation marks if it does not begin a complete sentence, when a directly quoted sentence is broken.

Example: "I tore my stocking," she told us, "*because* the drawer was left open."

PUNCTUATION
The Apostrophe

1. Use an apostrophe to indicate possession. Place the apostrophe according to this rule: "The apostrophe, when used to indicate possession, means *belonging to everything to the left of the apostrophe.*"

   Examples: lady's = belonging to the lady
                ladies' = belonging to the ladies
       children's = belonging to the children

   Note: To test for correct placement of the apostrophe, read "of the."

   Example: childrens' = of the childrens (obviously incorrect)

   The placement rule applies at all times, even with regard to compound nouns separated by hyphens and with regard to entities made up of two or more names.

   Example: father-in-law's = belonging to a father-in-law

   Example: Lansdale, Jackson, and Roosevelt's law firm = the law firm belonging to Lansdale, Jackson, and Roosevelt

   Example: Brown and Sons' delivery truck = the delivery truck of Brown and Sons

2. Use an apostrophe in a contraction in place of the omitted letter or letters.

   Examples: haven't = have not
             we're = we are
             let's = let us
          o'clock = of the clock
      class of '85 = class of 1985

   Note: Do NOT begin a paragraph with a contraction that begins with an apostrophe.

3. Use an apostrophe to form plurals of numbers, letters, and phrases referred to as words.

   Example: The toddler pronounced her *t's* as *b's.*

   Example: Solution of the puzzle involves crossing out all the *3's* and *9's.*

   Example: His speech was studded with *you know's.*

The Colon

1. Use a colon after the salutation in a business letter.

    Example: Dear Board Member:

2. Use a colon to separate hours from minutes.

    Example: The eclipse occurred at 10:36 A.M.

3. Use of the colon is optional in the following cases:
    (a) to introduce a list, especially after an expression such as *as follows*
    (b) to introduce a long quotation
    (c) to introduce a question

    Example: My question is this: Are you willing to punch a time clock?

The Comma

1. Use a comma after the salutation of a personal letter.

    Example: Dear Mary,

2. Use a comma after the complimentary close of a letter.

    Example: Cordially yours,

3. Use a comma or pair of commas to set off a noun of address.

    Example: When you finish your homework, Jeff, please take out the garbage.

4. Use a pair of commas to set off an appositive, a phrase that follows a noun or pronoun and means the same as that noun or pronoun.

    Example: Mr. Burke, our lawyer, gave us some good advice.

5. Use a pair of commas to set off parenthetical expressions, words that interrupt the flow of the sentence, such as *however, though, for instance, by the way*.

    Example: We could not, however, get him to agree.

    Example: This book, I believe, is the best of its kind.

    Note: Test for placement of commas in a parenthetical expression by reading aloud. If you would pause before and after such an expression, then it should be set off by commas.

6. Use a comma between two or more adjectives that modify a noun equally.

    Example: The young, nervous, first-grade teacher stood at the front of his class of 25 six-year-olds.

    Note: If you can add the word *and* between the adjectives without changing the sense of the sentence, then use commas.

7. Use a comma to separate words, phrases, or clauses in a series. The use of a comma before *and* is optional. If the series ends in *etc.,* use a comma before *etc.* Do not use a comma after *etc.* in a series, even if the sentence continues.

    Example: Coats, umbrellas, and boots should be placed in the closet at the end of the hall.

    Example: Pencils, scissors, paper clips, etc. belong in your top desk drawer.

8. Use a comma to separate a short direct quotation from the speaker.

    Example: She said, "I must leave work on time today."

    Example: "Tomorrow I begin my summer job," he told us.

9. Use a comma after an introductory phrase of five or more words.

    Example: Because the prisoner had a history of attempted jailbreaks, he was put under heavy guard.

10. Use a comma after a short introductory phrase whenever the comma would aid clarity.

    Example: As a child she was a tomboy. (comma unnecessary)

    Example: To Dan, Phil was friend as well as a brother. (comma clarifies)

    Example: In 1978, 300 people lost their lives in one air disaster. (comma clarifies)

    Note: A comma is not generally used before a subordinate clause that ends a sentence, though in long, unwieldy sentences like this one, use of such comma is optional.

11. Use a comma before a coordinating conjunction unless the two clauses are very short.

    Example: The boy wanted to borrow a book from the library, but the librarian would not allow him to take it until he had paid his fines.

    Example: Roy washed the dishes and Helen dried.

12. Use a pair of commas to set off a nonrestrictive adjective phrase or clause. A nonrestrictive phrase or clause is one that can be omitted without essentially changing the meaning of the sentence.

    Example: Our new sailboat, which has bright orange sails, is very seaworthy.

    A restrictive phrase or clause is vital to the meaning of a sentence and cannot be omitted. Do NOT set it off with commas.

    Example: A sailboat without sails is useless.

13. Use a comma if the sentence might be subject to different interpretations without it.

    Example: The banks which closed yesterday are in serious financial difficulty.
                  (Some banks closed yesterday, and those banks are in trouble.)
                  The banks, which closed yesterday, are in serious financial difficulty.
                  (All banks closed yesterday, and all are in trouble.)

    Example: My brother Bill is getting married.
                  (The implication is that I have more than one brother.)
                  My brother, Bill, is getting married.
                  (Here *Bill* is an appositive. Presumably he is the only brother.)

14. Use a comma if a pause would make the sentence clearer and easier to read.

   Example: Inside the people were dancing. (confusing)
               Inside, the people were dancing. (clearer)

   Example: After all crime must be punished. (confusing)
               After all, crime must be punished. (clearer)

The pause rule is not infallible, but it is your best resort when all other rules governing use of the comma fail you.

The Dash

1. Use a dash—or parentheses—for emphasis or to set off an explanatory group of words.

   Example: The tools of her trade—probe, mirror, cotton swabs—were neatly arranged on the dentist's tray.

   Note: Unless the set-off expression ends a sentence, dashes, like parentheses, must be used in pairs.

2. Use a dash to break up a thought.

   Example: There are five—remember, I said five—good reasons to refuse their demands.

3. Use a dash to mark a sudden break in thought that leaves a sentence unfinished.

   Example: He opened the door a crack and saw—

The Exclamation Mark

1. Use an exclamation mark only to express strong feeling or emotion, or to imply urgency.

   Example: Congratulations! You broke the record.

   Example: Rush! Perishable contents.

The Hyphen

1. Use a hyphen to divide a word at the end of a line. Always divide words between syllables.

2. Use a hyphen in numbers from *twenty-one to ninety-nine.*

3. Use a hyphen to join two words serving together as a single adjective before a noun.

   Example: We left the highway and proceeded on a well-paved road.

   Example: That baby-faced man is considerably older than he appears to be.

4. Use a hyphen with the prefixes *ex-, self-,* and *all-,* and the suffix *-elect.*

   Examples: ex-Senator, self-appointed, all-state, Governor-elect

5. Use a hyphen to avoid ambiguity.

   Example: After the custodian recovered the use of his right arm, he re-covered the office chairs.

6. Use a hyphen to avoid an awkward union of letters.

   Example: semi-independent, shell-like

The Period

1. Use a period at the end of a sentence that makes a statement, gives a command, or makes a "polite request" in the form of a question that does not require an answer.

   Example: I am preparing for my exam.

   Example: Proofread everything you type.

   Example: Would you please hold the script so that I may see if I have memorized my lines.

2. Use a period after an abbreviation and after the initial in a person's name.

   Example: Gen. Robert E. Lee led the Confederate forces.

   Note: Do NOT use a period after postal service state name abbreviations such as AZ (for Arizona) or MI (for Michigan).

The Question Mark

1. Use a question mark after a request for information.

   Example: At what time does the last bus leave?

   Note: A question must end with a question mark even if the question does not encompass the entire sentence.

   Example: "Daddy, are we there yet?" the child asked.

Quotation Marks

1. Use quotation marks to enclose all directly quoted material. Words not quoted must remain outside the quotation marks.

   Example: "If it is hot on Sunday," she said, "we will go to the beach."

   Note: Do NOT enclose an indirect quote in quotation marks.

   Example: She said that we might go to the beach on Sunday.

2. Use quotation marks around words used in an unusual way.

   Example: A surfer who "hangs ten" is performing a tricky maneuver on a surfboard, not staging a mass execution.

3. Use quotation marks to enclose the title of a short story, essay, short poem, song, or article.

    Example: Robert Louis Stevenson wrote a plaintive poem called "Bed in Summer."

    Note: Titles of books and plays are NOT enclosed in quotation marks. They are printed in italics. In handwritten or typed manuscript, underscore titles of books and plays.

    Example: The song "Tradition" is from *Fiddler on the Roof*.

Placement of Quotation Marks

1. A period ALWAYS goes inside the quotation marks, whether the quotation marks are used to denote quoted material, to set off titles, or to isolate words used in a special sense.

    Example: The principal said, "Cars parked in the fire lane will be ticketed."

    Example: The first chapter of *The Andromeda Strain* is entitled "The Country of Lost Borders."

    Example: Pornography is sold under the euphemism "adult books."

2. A comma ALWAYS goes inside the quotation marks.

    Example: "We really must go home," said the dinner guests.

    Example: If your skills become "rusty," you must study before you take the exam.

    Example: Three stories in Kurt Vonnegut's *Welcome to the Monkey House* are "Harrison Bergeron," "Next Door," and "Epicac."

3. A question mark goes inside the quotation marks if it is part of the quotation. If the whole sentence containing the quotation is a question, the question mark goes outside the quotation marks.

    Example: He asked, "Was the airplane on time?"

    Example: What did you really mean when you said "I do"?

4. An exclamation mark goes inside the quotation marks if the quoted words are an exclamation; it goes outside if the entire sentence, including the quoted words, is an exclamation.

    Example: The sentry shouted, "Drop your gun!"

    Example: Save us from our "friends"!

5. A colon and a semicolon ALWAYS go outside the quotation marks.

    Example: He said, "War is destructive"; she added, "Peace is constructive."

6. When a multiple-paragraph passage is quoted, each paragraph of the quotation must begin with quotation marks, but ending quotation marks are used only at the end of the last quoted paragraph.

The Semicolon

1. Use a semicolon to separate a series of phrases or clauses, each of which contains commas.

    Example: The old gentleman's heirs were Margaret Whitlock, his half-sister; James Bagley, the butler; William Frame, companion to his late cousin, Robert Bone; and his favorite charity, the Salvation Army.

2. Use a semicolon to avoid confusion with numbers.

    Example: Add the following: $1.25; $7.50; and $12.89.

3. You may use a semicolon to join two short, related independent clauses.

    Example: Anne is working at the front desk on Monday; Ernie will take over on Tuesday.

    Note: Two main clauses must be separated by a conjunction *or* by a semicolon, *or* they must be written as two sentences. A semicolon never precedes a coordinating conjunction. The same two clauses maybe written in any one of three ways:

    Example: Autumn had come, and the trees were almost bare.
    Autumn had come; the trees were almost bare.
    Autumn had come. The trees were almost bare.

4. You may use a semicolon to separate two independent clauses that are joined by an adverb such as *however, therefore, otherwise,* or *nevertheless.* The adverb must be followed by a comma.

    Example: You may use a semicolon to separate this clause from the next; however, you will not be incorrect if you choose to write two separate sentences.

    Note: If you are uncertain about how to use the semicolon to connect independent clauses, write two sentences instead.

The Essentials of English Grammar

PARTS OF SPEECH

A **noun** is the name of a person, place, thing, or idea: teacher   city   desk   democracy

Pronouns substitute for nouns: he   they   ours   those

An **adjective** describes a noun: warm   quick   tall   blue

A **verb** expresses action or state of being: yell   interpret   feel   are

An **adverb** modifies a verb, an adjective, or another adverb: fast   slowly   friendly   well

Conjunctions join words, sentences, and phrases: and   but   or

A **preposition** shows position in time or space: in   during   after   behind

Nouns

There are different kinds of nouns:

Common nouns are general: house   girl   street   city

Proper nouns are specific: White House   Jane   Main Street   New York

Collective nouns name groups: team   crowd   organization   Congress

Nouns have *cases*:

Nominative—The subject, noun of address, or predicate noun

Objective—The direct object, indirect object, or object of the preposition

Possessive—The form that shows possession

Pronouns

Antecedent of the pronoun—The noun to which a pronoun refers. A pronoun must agree with its antecedent in gender, person, and number. There are several kinds of pronouns. (Pronouns also have cases.)

Demonstrative pronouns: this, that, these, those

Indefinite pronouns: all, any, anybody

Interrogative pronouns: who, which, what

Personal pronouns:			Nominative Case	Objective Case	Possessive Case
	Singular	1st person	I	me	mine
		2nd person	you	you	yours
		3rd person	he, she, it	him, her, it	his, hers, its
	Plural	1st person	we	us	ours
		2nd person	you	you	your
		3rd person	they	them	theirs

Adjectives

Adjectives answer the following questions: Which one? What kind? and How many?

There are three uses of adjectives:

A **noun modifier** is usually placed directly before the noun it describes: He is a *tall* man.

A **predicate adjective** follows an inactive verb and modifies the subject: He is *happy*. I feel *terrible*.

An **article** or **noun marker** are other names for these adjectives: the, a, an

Adverbs

Adverbs answer the following questions: Why? How? Where? When? and To what degree? Adverbs should NOT be used to modify nouns.

SELECTED RULES OF GRAMMAR

1. The subject of a verb is in the nominative case even if the verb is understood and not expressed.

   Example: They are as old as *we*. (as we are)

2. The word *who* is in the nominative case. *Whom* is in the objective case.

   Example: The trapeze artist who ran away with the clown broke the lion tamer's heart. (*Who* is the subject of the verb *ran*.)

   Example: The trapeze artist whom he loved ran away with the circus clown. (*Whom* is the object of the verb *loved*.)

3. The word *whoever* is in the nominative case. *Whomever* is in the objective case.

   Example: Whoever comes to the door is welcome to join the party. (*Whoever* is the subject of the verb *comes*.)

   Example: Invite whomever you wish to accompany you. (*Whomever* is the object of the verb *invite*.)

4. Nouns or pronouns connected by a form of the verb *to be* should always be in the nominative case.

   Example: It is *I*. (Not *me*)

5. The object of a preposition or of a transitive verb should use a pronoun in the objective case.

   Example: It would be impossible for *me* to do that job alone. (*Me* is the object of the preposition *for*.)

   Example: The attendant gave *me* the keys to the locker. (*Me* is the indirect object of the verb *gave*.)

   Note: When the first person pronoun is used in conjunction with one or more proper names, you may confirm the choice of *I* or *me* by eliminating the proper names and reading the sentence with the pronoun alone.

   Example: John, George, Marylou, and (me or I) went to the movies last night. (By eliminating the names, you can readily choose that *I went to the movies* is correct.)

   Example: It would be very difficult for Mae and (I or me) to attend the wedding. (Without *Mae*, it is clear that it is *difficult for me* to attend.)

6. *Each, either, neither, anyone, anybody, somebody, someone, every, everyone, one, no one,* and *nobody* are singular pronouns. Each of these words takes a singular verb and a singular pronoun.

   Examples: *Neither likes* the pets of the other.
                 Everyone must wait *his* turn.
                 Each of the patients *carries* insurance.
                 Neither of the women *has* completed *her* assignment.

7. When the correlative conjunctions *either/or* and *neither/nor* are used, the number of the verb agrees with the number of the last subject.

   Example: Neither John nor *Greg eats* meat.

   Example: Either the cat or the *mice take* charge in the barn.

8. A subject consisting of two or more nouns joined by a coordinating conjunction takes a plural verb.

    Example: Paul *and* Sue *were* the last to arrive.

9. The number of the verb is not affected by the addition to the subject of words introduced by *with, together with, no less than, as well as,* etc.

    Example: The *captain,* together with the rest of the team, *was delighted* by the victory celebration.

10. A verb agrees in number with its subject. A verb should not be made to agree with a noun that is part of a phrase following the subject.

    Example: *Mount Snow,* one of my favorite ski areas, *is* in Vermont.

    Example: The *mountains* of Colorado, like those of Switzerland, *offer* excellent skiing.

11. A verb should agree in number with the subject, not with the predicate noun or pronoun.

    Example: Poor study *habits are* the leading cause of unsatisfactory achievement in school.

    Example: The leading *cause* of unsatisfactory achievement in school *is* poor study habits.

12. A pronoun agrees with its antecedent in person, number, gender, and case.

    Example: Since you were absent on Tuesday, you will have to ask Mary or Beth for her notes on the lecture. (Use *her,* not their, because two singular antecedents joined by *or* take a singular pronoun.)

13. *Hardly, scarcely, barely, only,* and *but* (when it means *only*) are negative words. Do NOT use another negative in conjunction with any of these words.

    Example: He *didn't have but* one hat. (WRONG)

    He had *but* one hat. OR He had *only* one hat.

    Example: I *can't hardly* read the small print. (WRONG)

    I *can hardly* read the small print. OR I *can't* read the small print.

14. *As* is a conjunction introducing a subordinate clause, while *like* is a preposition. The object of a preposition is a noun or phrase.

    Example: Winston tastes good, as a cigarette should. (*Cigarette* is the subject of the clause; *should* is its verb.)

    Example: He behaves *like* a fool.

    Example: The gambler accepts only hard currency *like* gold coins.

15. When modifying the words *kind* and *sort,* the words *this* and *that* always remain in the singular.

    Example: *This kind* of apple makes the best pie.

    Example: *That sort* of behavior will result in severe punishment.

16. In sentences beginning with *there is* and *there are,* the verb should agree in number with the noun that follows it.

   Example: There isn't an unbroken bone in her body. (The singular subject *bone* takes the singular verb *is*.)

   Example: There are many choices to be made. (The plural subject *choices* takes the plural verb *are*.)

17. A noun or pronoun modifying a gerund should be in the possessive case.

   Example: Is there any criticism of Arthur's going? (*Going* is a gerund. It must be modified by Arthur's, not by Arthur.)

18. Do NOT use the possessive case when referring to an inanimate object.

   Example: He had difficulty with the *store's* management. (WRONG)
   He had difficulty with the management of the store.

19. When expressing a condition contrary to fact or a wish, use the subjunctive form *were.*

   Example: I wish I *were* a movie star.

20. Statements equally true in the past and in the present are usually expressed in the present tense. The contents of a book are also expressed in the present tense.

   Example: He said that Venus is a planet. (Even though he made the statement in the past, the fact remains that Venus *is* a planet.)

   Example: In the book *Peter Pan,* Wendy says, "I can fly." (Every time one reads the book, Wendy *says* it again.)

ANTECEDENTS AND MODIFIERS

1. When used as a relative pronoun, *it* refers to the nearest noun. In your writing, you must be certain that the grammatical antecedent is indeed the intended antecedent.

   Example: Since the mouth of the cave was masked by underbrush, *it* provided an excellent hiding place. (Do you really mean that the underbrush is an excellent hiding place, or do you mean the cave?)

2. *Which* is another pronoun with which reference errors are often made. In fact, whenever using pronouns, you must ask yourself whether the reference of the pronoun is clear.

   Example: The first chapter awakens your interest in cloning, which continues to the end of the book. (What continues, cloning or your interest?)

   Example: Jim told Bill that he was about to be fired. (Who is about to be fired? This sentence can be interpreted to mean that Jim was informing Bill about Bill's impending termination or about his, Jim's, own troubles.)

In your writing, you may find that the most effective way to clear up an ambiguity is to recast the sentence.

Example: The first chapter awakens your interest in cloning. The following chapters build upon this interest and maintain it throughout the book.

Example: Jim told Bill, "I am about to be fired." OR Jim told Bill, "You are about to be fired."

3. Adjectives modify only nouns and pronouns. Adverbs modify verbs, adjectives, and other adverbs.

Example: One can swim in a lake as *easy* as in a pool. (WRONG)
One can swim in a lake as *easily* as in a pool. (The adverb *easily* must modify the verb *can swim.*)

Example: I was *real* happy. (WRONG)
I was *really* happy. (The adverb *really* must be used to modify the adjective *happy*.)

Sometimes context determines the use of adjective or adverb.

Example: The old man looked *angry*. (*Angry* is an adjective describing the old man: angry old man.)

The old man looked *angrily* out the window. (*Angrily* is an adverb describing the man's manner of looking out the window.)

4. Phrases should be placed near the words they modify.

Example: The author says that she intends to influence your life *in the first chapter*. (WRONG)
The author *in the first chapter* says….OR *In the first chapter,* the author says….

Example: He played the part *in Oklahoma* of Jud. (WRONG)
He played the part of Jud *in Oklahoma.*

5. Adverbs should be placed near the words they modify.

Example: The man was *only* willing to sell one horse. (WRONG)
The man was willing to sell *only* one horse.

6. Clauses should be placed near the words they modify.

Example: He will reap a good harvest *who sows early*. (WRONG)
He who sows early will reap a good harvest.

7. A modifier must modify something.

Example: Having excellent control, a no-hitter was pitched. (WRONG)
(*Having excellent control* does not modify anything.)
Having excellent control, the pitcher pitched a no-hitter. (*Having excellent control* modifies the pitcher.)

Example: The day passed quickly, climbing the rugged rocks. (WRONG)
The day passed quickly as we climbed the rugged rocks.

Example: While away on vacation, the pipes burst. (WRONG) (The pipes were not away on vacation.)
While we were away on vacation, the pipes burst.

Example: To run efficiently, the serviceman should oil the lawnmower. (WRONG)

                       The serviceman should oil the lawnmower to make it run efficiently.

Note: The best test for the placement of modifiers is to read the sentence literally. If you read a sentence literally and it is literally ridiculous, it is WRONG. The meaning of a sentence must be clear to any reader. The words of the sentence *must make sense*.

SENTENCE STRUCTURE

1. Every sentence must contain a verb. No matter how long they are, a group of words without a verb is a sentence fragment, not a sentence. A verb may consist of one, two, three, or four words.

   Examples: The girl *studies* hard.

                     The girl *will study* hard.

                     The girl *has been studying* hard.

                     The girl *should have been studying* hard.

   The words that make up a single verb may be separated.

   Examples: It *is* not *snowing*.

                     It *will* almost certainly *snow* tomorrow.

2. Every sentence must have a subject. The subject may be a noun, a pronoun, or a word or group of words functioning as a noun.

   Examples: *Fish* swim. (noun)

                     Boats are sailed. (noun)

                     She is young. (pronoun)

                     Running is good exercise. (gerund)

                     To argue is pointless. (infinitive)

                     That he was tired was evident. (noun clause)

   In commands, the subject is usually not expressed but is understood to be *you*.

   Example: Mind your own business.

3. A phrase cannot stand by itself as a sentence. A phrase is any group of related words that has no subject or predicate and that is used as a single part of speech. Phrases may be built around prepositions, particles, gerunds, or infinitives.

   Example: The boy *with curly hair* is my brother. (prepositional phrase used as an adjective modifying *boy*)

   Example: My favorite cousin lives *on a farm*. (prepositional phrase used as an adverb modifying *lives*)

   Example: *Beyond the double white line* is out of bounds. (prepositional phrase used as a noun, the subject of the sentence)

   Example: A thunderstorm *preceding a cold front* is often welcome. (participial phrase used as an adjective modifying *thunderstorm*)

Example: We eagerly awaited the pay envelopes *brought by the messenger.* (participial phrase used as an adjective modifying *envelopes*)

Example: *Running a day camp* is an exhausting job. (gerund phrase used as a noun, subject of the sentence)

Example: The director is paid well for *running the day camp.* (gerund phrase used as a noun, the object of the preposition *for*)

Example: *To breathe unpolluted air* should be every person's birthright. (infinitive phrase used as a noun, the subject of the sentence)

Example: The child began *to unwrap his gift.* (infinitive phrase used as a noun, the object of the verb *began*)

Example: The boy ran away from home *to become a marine.* (infinitive phrase used as an adverb modifying *ran away*)

4. A *main, independent,* or *principal* clause can stand alone as a complete sentence. A main clause has a subject and a verb. It may stand by itself or be introduced by a coordinating conjunction.

Example: The sky darkened ominously and rain began to fall. (two independent clauses joined by a coordinating conjunction)

A *subordinate* or *dependent* clause must never stand alone. It is not a complete sentence, only a sentence fragment, despite the fact that is has a subject and a verb. A subordinate clause usually is introduced by a subordinating conjunction. Subordinate clauses may act as adverbs, adjectives, or nouns. Subordinate adverbial clauses are generally introduced by the subordinating conjunctions *when, while, because, as soon as, if, after, although, as before, since, than, though, until,* and *unless.*

Example: *While we were waiting for the local train,* the express roared past.

Example: The woman applied for a new job *because she wanted to earn more money.*

Example: *Although a subordinate clause contains both subject and verb,* it cannot stand alone *because it is introduced by a subordinating word.*

Subordinate adjective clauses may be introduced by the pronouns *who, which,* and *that.*

Example: The play *which he liked best* was a mystery.

Example: I have a neighbor *who served in the Peace Corps.*

Subordinate noun clauses may be introduced by *who, what,* or *that.*

Example: The stationmaster says *that the train will be late.*

Example: I asked the waiter *what the stew contained.*

Example: I wish I knew *who backed into my car.*

5. Just as a subordinate clause cannot stand alone but must be incorporated into a sentence that features an independent clause, so two independent clauses cannot share one sentence without some form of connective. If they do, they form a run-on sentence. Two principal clauses may be joined by a coordinating conjunction, by a comma followed by a coordinating conjunction, or by a semicolon. They may form two distinct sentences. Two main clauses may NEVER be joined by a comma without a coordinating conjunction. This error is called a comma splice.

    Example:
    • A college education has never been more important than it is today it has never cost more. (WRONG—run-on sentence)

    • A college education has never been more important than it is today, it has never cost more. (WRONG—comma splice)

    • A college education has never been more important than it is today and it has never cost more. (WRONG—The two independent clauses are not equally short, so a comma is required before the coordinating conjunction.)

    • A college education has never been more important than it is today, and it has never cost more. (correct form)

    • A college education has never been more important than it is today; and it has never cost more. (WRONG—A semicolon is never used before a coordinating conjunction.)

    • A college education has never been more important than it is today; it has never cost more. (correct form)

    • A college education has never been more important than it is today. It has never cost more. (correct form)

    • A college education has never been more important than it is today. And it has never cost more. (correct form)

    • While a college education has never been more important than it is today, it has never cost more. (correct form—An introductory subordinate clause is separated from the main clause by a comma.)

6. Direct quotations are bound by all the rules of sentence formation. Beware of comma splices in divided quotations.

    Example: "Your total is wrong," he said, "add the column again." (WRONG)
    "Your total is wrong," he said. "Add the column again." (The two independent clauses form two separate sentences.)

    Example: "Are you lost?" she asked, "may I help you?" (WRONG)
    "Are you lost?" she asked. "May I help you?" (two main clauses; two separate sentences)

7. Comparisons must be logical and complete. Train yourself to concentrate on each sentence so that you can recognize errors.

    Example: Wilmington is larger than any city in Delaware. (WRONG)
    Wilmington is larger than any *other* city in Delaware.

    Example: He is as short, if not shorter, than his uncle. (WRONG)
    He is as short *as,* if not shorter than, his uncle.

Example: I hope to find a summer job other than a lifeguard. (WRONG)
I hope to find a summer job other than *that of* lifeguard.

Example: Law is a better profession than an accountant. (WRONG)
Law is a better profession than accounting. (Parallel)

8. Avoid the "is when" and "is where" construction.

Example: A limerick is when a short poem has a catchy rhyme. (WRONG)
A limerick is a short poem with a catchy rhyme.

Example: To exile is where a person must live in another place. (WRONG)
To exile a person is to force him to live in another place.

9. Errors in parallelism are often quite subtle, but you should learn to recognize and avoid them.

Example: Skiing and to skate are both winter sports. (WRONG)
Skiing and *skating* are both winter sports.

Example: She spends all her time eating, asleep, and on her studies. (WRONG)
She spends all her time *eating, sleeping,* and *studying*.

Example: The work is neither difficult nor do I find it interesting. (WRONG)
The work is neither difficult nor interesting.

Example: His heavy drinking and the fact that he gambles makes him a poor role model. (WRONG)
His heavy *drinking* and *gambling make* him a poor role model.

10. Avoid needless shifts in point of view. A shift in point of view is a change within the sentence from one tense or mood to another, from one subject or voice to another, or from one person or number to another. Shifts in point of view destroy parallelism within the sentence.

Example: After he *rescued* the kitten, he *rushes* down the ladder to find its owner. (shift from past tense to present tense) CHANGE TO: After he rescued the kitten, he rushed down the ladder to find its owner.

Example: First *stand* at attention, and then you *should salute* the flag. (shift from imperative to indicative mood) CHANGE TO: First *stand* at attention, and then *salute* the flag.

Example: Mary especially likes math, but history is also enjoyed by her. (The subject shifts from *Mary* to *history*; the mood shifts from active to passive.) CHANGE TO: Mary especially likes math, but she also enjoys history.

Example: George rowed around the island, and soon the mainland came into sight. (The subject changes from *George* to *the mainland*.) CHANGE TO: George rowed around the island and soon came in sight of the mainland.

Example: The captain welcomed *us* aboard, and the crew enjoyed showing *one* around the boat. (The object shifts from first to third person. *Us* may be the subject of *showing*.) CHANGE TO: The captain welcomed us aboard, and the crew enjoyed showing us around the boat.

Example: *One* should listen to the weather forecast so that *they* may anticipate a hurricane. (The subject shifts from singular to plural.) CHANGE TO: *One* should listen to the weather forecast so that *he* may anticipate a hurricane.

Correct Usage Test 1

Directions: In each of the following questions, there are four sentences. One of them is grammatically incorrect. Mark the answer sheet (on page 46) with the letter of the incorrect sentence.

1. (A) Everyone at camp must have his or her medical certificate on file before participating in competitive sports.
   (B) A crate of oranges were sent from Florida for all the children in cabin 6.
   (C) John and Danny's room looks as if they were prepared for inspection.
   (D) Three miles is too far for a young child to walk.

2. (A) The game over, the spectators rushed out on the field and tore down the goal posts.
   (B) The situation was aggravated by disputes over the captaincy of the team.
   (C) Yesterday they lay their uniforms aside with the usual end-of-the-season regret.
   (D) It is sometimes thought that politics is not for the high-minded.

3. (A) Sandburg's autobiography, as well as his poems, are familiar to many readers.
   (B) A series of authentic records of American Indian tribes is being published.
   (C) The Smokies is the home of the descendants of this brave tribe.
   (D) Five dollars is really not too much to pay for a book of this type.

4. (A) Being tired, I stretched out on a grassy knoll.
   (B) While we were rowing on the lake, a sudden squall almost capsized the boat.
   (C) Entering the room, a strange mark on the floor attracted my attention.
   (D) Mounting the curb, the empty car crossed the sidewalk and came to rest against a building.

5. (A) The text makes the process of developing and sustaining a successful home zoo appear to be a pleasant and profitable one.
   (B) The warmth and humor, the clear characterization of the Walmsey family, which includes three children, two dogs, and two cats, is such fun to read that this reviewer found herself reading it all over again.
   (C) You will be glad, I am sure, to give the book to whoever among your young friends has displayed an interest in animals.
   (D) The consensus among critics of children's literature is that the book is well worth the purchase price.

6. (A) Not one in a thousand readers take the matter seriously.
   (B) He was able to partially accomplish his purpose.
   (C) You are not as tall as he.
   (D) The people began to realize how much she had done.

7. (A) In the case of members who are absent, a special letter will be sent.
   (B) The visitors were all ready to see it.
   (C) I like Burns's poem, "To a Mountain Daisy."
   (D) John told William that he was sure he seen it.

8. (A) B. Nelson & Co. has a sale on sport shirts today.
   (B) Venetian blinds—called that although they probably did not originate in Venice—are no longer used as extensively as they were at one time.
   (C) He determined to be guided by the opinion of whoever spoke first.
   (D) There was often disagreement as to whom was the better Shakespearean actor, Evans or Gielgud.

Correct Usage Test 2

Directions: *In each of the following questions, there are four sentences. One of them is grammatically incorrect. Mark the answer sheet (on page 46) with the letter of the incorrect sentence.*

1. (A) Everyone can have a wonderful time in New York if they will just not try to see the entire city in one week.
   (B) Being a stranger in town myself, I know how you feel.
   (C) New York is a city of man-made wonders, as awe-inspiring as those found in nature.
   (D) He felt deep despair (as who has not?) at the evidence of man's inhumanity to man.

2. (A) A clerk should be careful as well as punctual, even though he or she are otherwise efficient.
   (B) Regardless of whether it may be true, some students are not very studious.
   (C) Not every writer can say that his opinion is always the best.
   (D) We often think of people who assume airs as being affected.

3. (A) This is the woman whom I saw.
   (B) She could solve even this problem.
   (C) She divided the money among the three of us.
   (D) Either she or I are guilty.

4. (A) Consider that the person which is always idle can never be happy.
   (B) Because a man understands a woman does not mean they are necessarily compatible.
   (C) He said that accuracy and speed are both essential.
   (D) Can it be said that the better of the two books is less expensive?

5. (A) Neither the critics nor the author were right about the reaction of the public.
   (B) The senator depended upon whoever was willing to assist him.

   (C) I don't recall any time when Edgar has broken his word.
   (D) Every one of the campers but John and me is going on the hike.

6. (A) Everyone entered promptly but her.
   (B) Each of the messengers were busily occupied.
   (C) At which exit did you leave him?
   (D) The work was not done well.

7. (A) Never before have I seen anyone who has the skill John has when he repairs engines.
   (B) If anyone can be wholly just in his decisions, it is he.
   (C) Because of his friendliness, the new neighbor was immediately accepted by the community.
   (D) Imagine our embarrassment when us girls saw Miss Maltinge sitting with her beau in the front row.

8. (A) I wondered why it was that the Mayor objected to the Governor's reference to the new tax law.
   (B) I have never read *Les Miserables,* but I plan to do so this summer.
   (C) After much talking and haranguing, the workers received an increase in wages.
   (D) The author and myself were the only cheerful ones at the macabre gathering.

9. (A) The doctor had carelessly left all the instruments on the operating table.
   (B) Was it them whom the professor regarded with such contempt?
   (C) Despite all the power he has, I should still hate to be in his shoes.
   (D) I feel badly because I gave such a poor performance in the play tonight.

Correct Usage Test 3

Directions: *In each of the following questions, there are four sentences. One of them is grammatically incorrect. Mark the answer sheet (on page 46) with the letter of the incorrect sentence.*

1. (A) The general regarded whomever the colonel honored with disdain.
    (B) Everyone who reads this book will think themselves knights errant on missions of heroism.
    (C) The reason why the new leader was so unsuccessful was that he had fewer responsibilities.
    (D) All the new mechanical devices we have today have made our daily living a great deal simpler, it is said.

2. (A) The town consists of three distinct sections, of which the western one is by far the larger.
    (B) Of London and Paris, the former is the wealthier.
    (C) Chicago is larger than any other city in Illinois.
    (D) America is the greatest nation, and of all other nations England is the greatest.

3. (A) I can but do my best.
    (B) I cannot help comparing him with his predecessor.
    (C) I wish that I was in Florida now.
    (D) I like this kind of grapes better than any other.

4. (A) Neither Tom nor John was present for the rehearsal.
    (B) The happiness or misery of men's lives depends on their early training.
    (C) Honor as well as profit are to be gained by these studies.
    (D) The egg business is only incidental to the regular business of the general store.

5. (A) It was superior in every way to the book previously used.
    (B) His testimony today is different from that of yesterday.
    (C) If you would have studied the problem carefully, you would have found the solution more quickly.
    (D) The flowers smelled so sweet that the whole house was perfumed.

6. (A) When either or both habits become fixed, the student improves.
    (B) Neither his words nor his action was justifiable.
    (C) A calm almost always comes before a storm.
    (D) The gallery with all its pictures were destroyed.

7. (A) Who did they say won?
    (B) The man whom I thought was my friend deceived me.
    (C) Send whoever will do the work.
    (D) The question of who should be leader arose.

8. (A) A box of choice figs was sent to him for Christmas.
    (B) Neither Charles nor his brother finished his assignment.
    (C) There goes the last piece of cake and the last spoonful of ice cream.
    (D) Diamonds are more desired than any other precious stones.

9. (A) As long as you are ready, you may as well start promptly.
    (B) My younger brother insists that he is as tall as me.
    (C) We walked as long as there was any light to guide us.
    (D) Realizing I had forgotten my gloves, I returned to the theater.

Correct Usage Test 4

Directions: *In each of the following questions, there are four sentences. One of them is grammatically incorrect. Mark the answer sheet (on page 46) with the letter of the incorrect sentence.*

1. (A) His knowledge of methods and proce-
        dures enable him to assist the director
        in many ways.
    (B) A new set of rules and regulations has
        been made.
    (C) Reports that the strike has been settled
        were circulated yesterday.
    (D) The cracks in the teapot my aunts gave
        for Christmas make it useless.

2. (A) The Credit Bureau rates you as high as her.
    (B) He is no better than you or me.
    (C) You will be notified as soon as I.
    (D) We were ready sooner than they.

3. (A) Neither the stenographer nor the typist
        has returned from lunch.
    (B) Either the operators or the machines
        are at fault.
    (C) One or the other of those clerks are
        responsible for these errors.
    (D) Either the clerk or the receptionist is
        available by this time of day.

4. (A) The Board of Directors has prepared a
        manual for their own use.
    (B) The company has announced its new
        policy of advertising.
    (C) The jury was out about 30 minutes
        when they returned a verdict.
    (D) The flock of geese creates a health
        hazard for visitors with allergies.

5. (A) Who does he think he is?
    (B) Whom does he consider in making a
        decision?
    (C) Whom did they say is to be appointed?
    (D) Whom do they contact in such
        emergencies?

6. (A) Who shall I say called?
    (B) The water has frozen the pipes.
    (C) Everyone has left except them.
    (D) Every one of the salesmen must
        supply their own car.

7. (A) Two-thirds of the building is finished.
    (B) Where are Mr. Keene and Mr.
        Herbert?
    (C) Neither the salesladies nor the floor
        walker want to work overtime.
    (D) The committee was agreed.

8. (A) Amends have been made for the
        damage to one of our cars.
    (B) Neither the customer nor the clerk
        were aware of the fire in the store.
    (C) A box of spare pencils is on the desk.
    (D) There is the total number of
        missing pens.

9. (A) The company insist on everyone's
        being prompt.
    (B) Each one of our salesmen takes an
        aptitude test.
    (C) It is the location that appeals to me.
    (D) Most of the men have left the
        building.

10. (A) The students in the dormitories
        were forbidden, unless they had
        special passes, from staying out
        after 11:30 P.M.
    (B) The Student Court rendered a decision
        satisfactory to both the defendant and
        the accuser.
    (C) Margarine is being substituted for
        butter to a considerable extent.
    (D) In this school there are at least
        15 minor accidents a year which are
        due to this traffic violation.

Correct Usage Test 5

Directions: In each of the following questions, there are four sentences. One of them is grammatically incorrect. Mark the answer sheet (on page 46) with the letter of the incorrect sentence.

1. (A) Sailing along New England's craggy coastline, you will relive a bygone era of far-roving whalers and graceful clipper ships.
   (B) The march of history is reenacted in folk festivals, outdoor pageants, and fiestas—local in theme, but national in import.
   (C) Visiting the scenes of the past, our interest in American history is renewed and enlivened.
   (D) What remained was a few unrecognizable fragments.

2. (A) I knew it to be him by the style of his clothes.
   (B) No one saw him doing it.
   (C) Her going away is a loss to the community.
   (D) Illness prevented him graduating in June.

3. (A) No one but her could have recognized him.
   (B) She knew the stranger to be him whom she had given up as lost.
   (C) He looked like he had been in some strange land where age advanced at a double pace.
   (D) It is impossible to include that item; the agenda has already been mimeographed.

4. (A) You have probably heard of the new innovation in the regular morning broadcast.
   (B) During the broadcast you are expected to stand, to salute, and to sing the fourth stanza of "America."
   (C) None of the rocks which form the solid crust of our planet is more than two billion years old.
   (D) "I have finished my assignment," said the pupil. "May I go home now?"

5. (A) The coming of peace effected a change in her way of life.
   (B) Spain is as weak, if not weaker, than she was in 1900.

   (C) In regard to that, I am not certain what my attitude will be.
   (D) That unfortunate family faces the problem of adjusting itself to a new way of life.

6. (A) Participation in active sports produces both release from tension as well as physical well-being.
   (B) The problem of taxes is still with them.
   (C) Every boy and every girl in the auditorium was thrilled when the curtain went up.
   ✓(D) At length our club decided to send two representatives to the meeting, you and me.

7. (A) Remains of an ancient civilization were found near Mexico City.
   (B) It is interesting to compare the interior of one of the pyramids in Mexico with the interior of one of the pyramids in Egypt.
   (C) In two days' journey you will be reminded of political upheavals comparable to the volcanic eruptions still visible and audible in parts of Mexico.
   ✓(D) There is little danger of the laws being broken, so drastic is the penalty.

8. (A) Instead of looking disdainfully at London grime, think of it as a mantle of tradition.
   (B) Nobody but the pilot and the co-pilot was permitted to handle the mysterious package.
   (C) Not only is industry anxious to hire all available engineers, but they are being offered commissions by the armed forces.
   (D) For immediate service go directly to the store manager.

Correct Usage—Answer Key for Practice Tests

Test 1

1. **B**	3. **A**	5. **B**	7. **D**
2. **C**	4. **C**	6. **A**	8. **D**

Test 2

1. **A**	3. **D**	5. **A**	7. **D**	9. **B**
2. **A**	4. **A**	6. **B**	8. **D**	

Test 3

1. **B**	3. **C**	5. **C**	7. **B**	9. **B**
2. **A**	4. **C**	6. **D**	8. **C**	

Test 4

1. **A**	3. **C**	5. **C**	7. **C**	9. **A**
2. **B**	4. **A**	6. **D**	8. **B**	10. **A**

Test 5

1. **C**	3. **C**	5. **B**	7. **D**
2. **D**	4. **A**	6. **A**	8. **C**

SPELLING

Spelling questions appear on all tests. Examinations for general positions include anywhere from 5 to 25 spelling questions among the many different subjects tested. Examinations for typists and stenographers may place a much heavier emphasis upon spelling ability. For such positions, some jurisdictions may administer a 90- or 100-question spelling test. Because spelling might be an important part of your civil service exam, we suggest that you give a great deal of attention to the rules that follow. These 24 rules will see you through almost any spelling question you may face. Study these rules and the most common exceptions that we have highlighted. Memorize as many as you can.

Spelling Rules

RULE 1:   *i* before *e*

Except after *c*

Or when sounding like *ay*

As in *neighbor* or *weigh*.

Exception: neither, leisured, foreigner, seized, weird, heights

RULE 2:   If a word ends in *y* preceded by a vowel, keep the *y* when adding a suffix.
Examples: day, days; attorney, attorneys.

RULE 3:   If a word ends in *y* preceded by a consonant, change the *y* to *i* before adding a suffix
Examples: try, tries, tried; lady, ladies.

Exceptions: To avoid double *i*, retain the *y* before *-ing* and *-ish*. For example, *fly, flying*; *baby, babyish.*

RULE 4:   Silent *e* at the end of a word is usually dropped before a suffix beginning with a vowel.
Examples: dine + ing   = dining
locate + ion   = location
use + able   = usable
offense + ive   = offensive

Exception: Words ending in *ce* and *ge* retain *e* before *-able* and *-ous* in order to retain the soft sounds of *c* and *g*. For example, *peace + able = peaceable*; *courage + ous = courageous.*

RULE 5:   Silent *e* is usually kept before a suffix beginning with a consonant.
Examples: care + less   = careless
late + ly   = lately
one + ness   = oneness
game + ster = gamester

RULE 6:   Some exceptions must simply be memorized. Some exceptions to the last two rules are: *truly, duly, awful, argument, wholly, ninth, mileage, dyeing, acreage, canoeing.*

RULE 7: A one-syllable word that ends in a <u>single</u> consonant preceded by a <u>single</u> vowel doubles the final consonant before a suffix beginning with a vowel or <u>y</u>.

Examples: hit, hitting; drop, dropped; big, biggest; mud, muddy

But: help, *helping* because *help* ends in two consonants; *need, needing* because the final consonant is preceded by two vowels

RULE 8: A word with more than one syllable that accents the <u>last</u> syllable and ends in a <u>single</u> consonant preceded by a <u>single</u> vowel doubles the final consonant when adding a suffix beginning with a vowel.

Examples: begin, beginner; admit, admitted

But: enter, *entered* because the accent is <u>not</u> on the last syllable

RULE 9: A word ending in <u>er</u> or <u>ur</u> doubles the <u>r</u> in the past tense if the word is accented on the <u>last</u> syllable.

Examples: occur, occurred; prefer, preferred; transfer, transferred

RULE 10: A word ending in <u>er</u> does not double the <u>r</u> in the past tense if the accent does not fall on the last syllable.

Examples: answer, answered; offer, offered; differ, differed

RULE 11: When <u>-full</u> is added to the end of a noun to form an adjective, the final <u>l</u> is dropped.

Examples: cheerful, cupful, hopeful

RULE 12: All words beginning with <u>over</u> are one word.

Examples: overcast, overcharge, overhear

RULE 13: All words with the prefix <u>self</u> are hyphenated.

Examples: self-control, self-defense, self-evident

RULE 14: The letter <u>q</u> is always followed by <u>u.</u>

Examples: quiz, bouquet, acquire

RULE 15: Numbers from twenty-one to ninety-nine are hyphenated.

RULE 16: <u>Per cent</u> is <u>never</u> hyphenated. It may be written as one word (*percent*) or as two words (*per cent*).

RULE 17: <u>Welcome</u> is one word with one <u>l</u>.

RULE 18: <u>All right</u> is always two words. There is no such word as *alright*.

RULE 19: <u>Already</u> means "prior to some specified time." <u>All ready</u> means "completely ready."

Example: By the time I was <u>all ready</u> to go to the play, the bus had <u>already</u> left.

RULE 20: <u>Altogether</u> means "entirely."

<u>All together</u> means "in sum or collectively."

Example: There are <u>altogether</u> too many people to seat in this room when we are <u>all together</u>.

RULE 21: <u>Their</u> is the possessive of *they.*

<u>They're</u> is the contraction for <u>they are.</u>

<u>There</u> is "that place."

Example: They're going to put their books over there.

RULE 22: *Your* is the possessive of *you*.

You're is the contraction for *you are*.

Example: You're certainly planning to leave your muddy boots outside.

RULE 23: *Whose* is the possessive of *who*.

Who's is the contraction for *who is*.

Example: Do you know who's ringing the doorbell or whose car is in the street?

RULE 24: *Its* is the possessive of *it*.

It's is the contraction for *it is*.

Example: It's I who put its stamp on the letter.

Spelling Tests

If you have left yourself ample time to study for your exam, then you can go beyond memorizing rules and answering practice exercises, and you can develop a personal program for improving your own spelling. Think of your own private "devils," the words that you must look up every time you write a note or letter, and the words that gave you trouble all through school. Everyone has such words. Make a list of these words, correctly spelled. Add to the list words that you often look up, words of which you are just not sure. Keep adding to this list right up to exam day. Each day that you have a bit of study time, type through the list three times. By typing your troublesome words correctly, your hands and fingers will get used to the "feel" of the correct spelling, and your eye will become accustomed to seeing the words correctly spelled. Frequent repetition will embed the correct spelling in your mind.

One way to enlarge your personal spelling list is to add to it those words that give you trouble in the exercises that follow. These exercises illustrate the three most common types of spelling questions found on civil service clerical exams.

One common variety of spelling question looks like this:

Directions: *In each group of four words, one word is misspelled. Find the misspelled word, and mark its letter on your answer sheet.*

1. (A) business
   (B) manufacturer   Ⓐ Ⓑ Ⓒ ●
   (C) possibly
   (D) recieved

(D) is marked because the word is misspelled; the correct spelling is <u>received</u> (spelling rule 1).

2. (A) alphabetic
   (B) erasure   Ⓐ Ⓑ ● Ⓓ
   (C) industrey
   (D) requirement

(C) is the word spelled incorrectly; the correct spelling is <u>industry</u>.

A second common spelling question looks like this:

Directions: *In each group of three words, one word may be misspelled. If you find one word that is incorrectly spelled, mark its letter on your answer sheet. If all the words are spelled correctly, mark **(D)**.*

3. (A) anticipate
   (B) similiar   Ⓐ ● Ⓒ Ⓓ
   (C) benefit

   (B) is the misspelled word; the correct spelling is <u>similar</u>.

4. (A) foreign
   (B) acreage   Ⓐ Ⓑ Ⓒ ●
   (C) occurred

   All three words are spelled correctly, so the answer is **(D).** If you thought one of these words was spelled incorrectly, refer back to spelling rules 1, 6, and 9.

Or, you might run into spelling questions with somewhat more complicated instructions, like this:

> **Directions:** *Each question consists of three words, any or all of which may be spelled incorrectly. On your answer sheet:*

> Mark **(A)** *if ONLY ONE WORD* is misspelled.

> Mark **(B)** if *TWO WORDS* are misspelled.

> Mark **(C)** if *ALL THREE* words are misspelled.

> Mark **(D)** if *NO* words are misspelled.

5. (A) offered
   (B) hopefull   Ⓐ ● Ⓒ Ⓓ
   (C) usable

   (B) is the correct answer because the first two words are misspelled; the correct spellings are <u>offered</u> (rule 10) and <u>hopeful</u> (rule 11). (The correct spelling of <u>usable</u> is shown in rule 4.).

6. (A) welcome
   (B) acquire   ● Ⓑ Ⓒ Ⓓ
   (C) per-cent

   (A) is the correct answer because only the word <u>per-cent</u> is misspelled; it should be spelled <u>percent</u> or <u>per cent</u> (see rule 16). (See rules 17 and 14 to see why the first and third words, respectively, are spelled correctly.)

The spelling exercises that follow will give you lots of practice spotting words spelled incorrectly. The exercises are short so that you may do one or two a day as part of a balanced study program. Take time to look at each word, even if you believe that you have found the incorrect word in one of the first words in the series; you may miss an obviously misspelled word by not looking. The three most common types of spelling tests are included. All the misspelled words are spelled correctly at the end of the series of exercises. Where applicable, the rule that applies to the misspelled word is given beside that word.

Spelling Test 1

Directions: *In each group of four words, one word is misspelled. Find the misspelled word, and mark its letter on your answer sheet (on page 46).*

1. (A) afford
   (B) closeing
   (C) latter
   (D) headache

2. (A) gravel
   (B) artifishal
   (C) lodge
   (D) lilies

3. (A) document
   (B) handsome
   (C) frighten
   (D) incorect

4. (A) atached
   (B) flakes
   (C) distributed
   (D) continue

5. (A) conducter
   (B) choice
   (C) particular
   (D) streamline

6. (A) thunder
   (B) speaking
   (C) recreation
   (D) rockey

7. (A) provided
   (B) runner
   (C) sugested
   (D) principle

8. (A) throughout
   (B) silense
   (C) political
   (D) operation

9. (A) truth
   (B) organized
   (C) potatoe
   (D) production

10. (A) worried
    (B) spinach
    (C) guilt
    (D) suceeded

Spelling Test 2

Directions: *In each group of four words, one word is misspelled. Find the misspelled word, and mark its letter on your answer sheet (on page 47).*

1. (A) hyphen
   (B) index
   (C) office
   (D) diferent

2. (A) corporation
   (B) spindel
   (C) foreign
   (D) material

3. (A) adress
   (B) exactly
   (C) research
   (D) vertical

4. (A) occupation
   (B) accross
   (C) authority
   (D) invoice

5. (A) guardian
    (B) certified
    (C) voucher
    (D) mispelled

6. (A) trustee
    (B) multipal
    (C) promissory
    (D) valuable

7. (A) traveller
    (B) pamphlet
    (C) agencys
    (D) permit

8. (A) automatic
    (B) proportion
    (C) announcement
    (D) municiple

9. (A) recruitment
    (B) mentioned
    (C) optional
    (D) commision

10. (A) responsibility
    (B) disabled
    (C) vetran
    (D) misleading

11. (A) competetive
    (B) review
    (C) erroneous
    (D) license

12. (A) familiarity
    (B) accredited
    (C) payment
    (D) distributer

13. (A) localities
    (B) servise
    (C) central
    (D) occupation

14. (A) offerred
    (B) jobbing
    (C) threaten
    (D) throughway

15. (A) vending
    (B) tomorrow
    (C) strangly
    (D) barometer

16. (A) anounce
    (B) local
    (C) grasshopper
    (D) farmer

17. (A) historical
    (B) dustey
    (C) kindly
    (D) humbug

18. (A) current
    (B) comunity
    (C) cement
    (D) calves

19. (A) changeing
    (B) explained
    (C) diameter
    (D) consent

20. (A) sword
    (B) reckord
    (C) signed
    (D) taste

Spelling Test 3

Directions: In each question, one of the words may be spelled incorrectly, or all three may be spelled correctly. If one of the words is spelled incorrectly, mark the letter of this word on your answer sheet. If all three words are spelled correctly, blacken (D). The answer sheet is on page 47.

1. (A) gratful
   (B) census
   (C) analysis

2. (A) installment
   (B) retreive
   (C) concede

3. (A) dismissal
   (B) conscientious
   (C) indelible

4. (A) percieve
   (B) anticipate
   (C) acquire

5. (A) facility
   (B) reimburse
   (C) assortment

6. (A) plentifull
   (B) advantageous
   (C) similar

7. (A) guarantee
   (B) repel
   (C) ommission

8. (A) maintenance
   (B) liable
   (C) announcement

9. (A) exaggerate
   (B) sieze
   (C) condenm

10. (A) pospone
    (B) altogether
    (C) grievance

11. (A) argument
    (B) reciept
    (C) complain

12. (A) sufficient
    (B) declaim
    (C) visible

13. (A) expirience
    (B) dissatisfy
    (C) alternate

14. (A) occurred
    (B) noticable
    (C) appendix

15. (A) anxious
    (B) guarantee
    (C) calender

16. (A) fundamental
    (B) dissapear
    (C) accidentally

17. (A) guidance
    (B) across
    (C) correer

18. (A) pamphlet
    (B) always
    (C) commit

19. (A) excessive
    (B) permited
    (C) appointment

20. (A) personnel
    (B) resource
    (C) colledge

Spelling Test 4

Directions: *Each question consists of three words, any or all of which may be spelled incorrectly. On your answer sheet (on page 47):*

Mark **(A)** if ONLY ONE word is misspelled.

Mark **(B)** if TWO WORDS are misspelled.

Mark **(C)** if ALL THREE words are misspelled.

Mark **(D)** if NO WORDS are misspelled.

1. professor	satisfactorally	weight
2. sabbatical	accomplishment	occasionally
3. associate	bookeeping	carefuly
4. dictater	beforhand	deceit
5. accidently	supervisor	efficiently
6. bureau	manifest	scheduling
7. auxilary	machinary	distorsion
8. synthesis	harrassment	exemplify
9. receiveable	bankrupcy	chronological
10. facsimile	requisition	liability
11. proxey	pollish	courtesy
12. negotiable	acknowledgment	notarary
13. confidential	typograpfical	memmoranda
14. pertainent	codify	ellimination
15. corrective	performance	clogging

Answer Key to Practice Tests

Spelling Test 1

1. **(B)** closing (rule 4)
2. **(B)** artificial
3. **(D)** incorrect
4. **(A)** attached
5. **(A)** conductor

6. **(D)** rocky
7. **(C)** suggested
8. **(B)** silence
9. **(C)** potato
10. **(D)** succeeded

Spelling Test 2

1. **(D)** different
2. **(B)** spindle
3. **(A)** address
4. **(B)** across
5. **(D)** misspelled
6. **(B)** multiple
7. **(C)** agencies (rule 3)

8. **(D)** municipal
9. **(D)** commission
10. **(C)** veteran
11. **(A)** competitive
12. **(D)** distributor
13. **(B)** service
14. **(A)** offered (rule 10)

15. **(C)** strangely (rule 5)
16. **(A)** announce
17. **(B)** dusty

18. **(B)** community
19. **(A)** changing (rule 4)
20. **(B)** record

Spelling Test 3

1. **(A)** grateful (rule 5)
2. **(B)** retrieve(rule l)
3. **(D)**
4. **(A)** perceive (rule 1)
5. **(D)**
6. **(A)** plentiful (rule 11)
7. **(C)** omission
8. **(D)**
9. **(C)** condemn
10. **(A)** postpone

11. **(B)** receipt (rule l)
12. **(D)**
13. **(A)** experience
14. **(B)** noticeable (rule 4 — exception)
15. **(C)** calendar
16. **(B)** disappear
17. **(C)** career
18. **(D)**
19. **(B)** permitted (rule 8)
20. **(C)** college

Spelling Test 4

1. **(A)**—satisfactorily
2. **(D)**
3. **(B)**—bookkeeping; carefully (careful + ly)
4. **(B)**—dictator; beforehand
5. **(A)**—accidentally
6. **(D)**
7. **(C)**—auxiliary; machinery; distortion

8. **(A)**—harassment
9. **(B)**—receivable (rule 4); bankruptcy
10. **(D)**
11. **(B)**—proxy; polish
12. **(A)**—notary
13. **(B)**—typographical; memoranda
14. **(B)**—pertinent; elimination
15. **(A)**—performance

SYNONYMS

Two words are **synonyms** if they mean the same thing. In a synonym question, you must pick the word or phrase closest in meaning to the given word. This is the simplest kind of vocabulary question.

How to Answer Synonym Questions

1. Read each question carefully.
2. If you know that some of the answer choices are wrong, eliminate them.
3. From the answer choices that seem possible, select the one that *most nearly* means the same as the given word, even if it is a word that you don't normally use. The correct answer may not be a perfect synonym, but of the choices offered, it is the *closest* in meaning to the given word.
4. Make up a sentence using the given word. Then test your answer by putting it in the place of the given word in your sentence. The meaning of the sentence should be unchanged.
5. First answer the questions you know. You can come back to the others later.

Sample Questions

Before doing the practice tests, study the following examples.

1. We had to *terminate* the meeting because a fire broke out in the hall. *Terminate* most nearly means:
   (A) continue   (C) end
   (B) postpone   (D) extinguish

Some actual tests will give you the word in a sentence. You must then make sure that your answer (1) makes sense in the given sentence, and (2) does not change the meaning of the sentence.

The correct answer is (C) *end*. Even if you don't know what *terminate* means, you can eliminate choice (A) *continue* because it doesn't make much sense to say, "We had to continue the meeting because a fire broke out in the hall." Choice (B) *postpone* means "to put off until another time." It makes sense in the given sentence, but it also changes the meaning of the sentence. Choice (D) *extinguish* is similar in meaning to *terminate,* but not as close as *end.* One can *extinguish* (put an end to) a fire, but not a meeting.

2. pertinent
   (A) relevant   (C) true
   (B) prudent   (D) respectful

The correct answer is (A) *relevant. Pertinent* means "having some bearing on or relevance to." In the sentence "Her testimony was pertinent to the investigation," you could put *relevant* in the place of pertinent without changing the meaning. Choice (B) *prudent* means "careful" or "wise." Although it sounds somewhat like *pertinent,* its meaning is different. Choice (C) may seem possible because something that is *pertinent* should also be *true.* However, not everything that is true is pertinent. Choice (D) *respectful* is misleading. Its opposite, *disrespectful,* is a synonym for the word *impertinent.* You might logically guess, then, that *respectful* is a synonym for *pertinent.* The best way to avoid a trap like this is to remember how you've heard or seen the word used. You never see *pertinent* used to mean *respectful.*

3. facsimile
   (A) summary
   (B) exact copy
   (C) list
   (D) artist's sketch

This is a straightforward vocabulary question. The given word is rather difficult, but the choices are not tricky. The correct answer is (B) *exact copy*. A *facsimile* is a copy that looks exactly like the original, such as a photocopy. The word contains the root *simile*, meaning "like." Choice (C) *list* has no connection with *facsimile*. Both a *summary* (A) and an *artist's sketch* (D) are in a sense copies of something else, but not exact copies.

4. severe
   (A) cut off
   (B) surprising
   (C) serious
   (D) unusual

The correct answer is (C) *serious*. Severe means "harsh," "extreme," or "serious." You cannot use *serious* in every place where you can use *severe,* or vice versa, but it is the best of the choices offered. For instance, in the sentence "A severe case of the flu kept him in bed for three weeks," you could use *serious* in place of *severe* without changing the meaning. A synonym for choice (A) *cut off* is *sever*, which looks like *severe* but means something different. You can eliminate (A). Choices (B) and (D) seem more likely. Something that is severe—a snowstorm, for example—may also be *surprising* or *unusual*; it doesn't have to be, though. Severe snowstorms are not unusual in cold, wet climates. Severe hardship is not unusual in poverty-stricken areas.

Practice Test 1

Directions: *Select the word or phrase closest in meaning to the given word. Mark its letter on the sample answer sheet on page 47.*

1. retain
   (A) pay out   (B) play
   (C) keep   (D) inquire

2. endorse
   (A) sign up for   (B) announce support for
   (C) lobby for   (D) renounce

3. intractable
   (A) confused   (B) misleading
   (C) instinctive   (D) unruly

4. correspondence
   (A) letters   (B) files
   (C) testimony   (D) response

5. obliterate
   (A) praise   (B) doubt
   (C) erase   (D) reprove

6. legitimate
   (A) democratic   (B) legal
   (C) genealogical (D) underworld

7. deduct
   (A) conceal   (B) withstand
   (C) subtract   (D) terminate

8. mutilate
   (A) paint   (B) damage
   (C) alter   (D) rebel

9. egress
   (A) extreme   (B) extra supply
   (C) exit   (D) high price

10. horizontal
   (A) marginal   (B) in a circle
   (C) left and right (D) up and down

11. controversy
    (A) publicity (B) debate
    (C) revolution (D) revocation

12. preempt
    (A) steal (B) empty
    (C) preview (D) appropriate

13. category
    (A) class (B) adherence
    (C) simplicity (D) cataract

14. apathy
    (A) sorrow (B) indifference
    (C) aptness (D) sickness

15. tentative
    (A) persistent (B) permanent
    (C) thoughtful (D) provisional

16. per capita
    (A) for an entire population
    (B) by income
    (C) for each person
    (D) for every adult

17. deficient
    (A) sufficient (B) outstanding
    (C) inadequate (D) bizarre

18. inspect
    (A) disregard (B) look at
    (C) annoy (D) criticize

19. optional
    (A) not required (B) infrequent
    (C) choosy (D) for sale

20. implied
    (A) acknowledged (B) stated
    (C) predicted (D) hinted

21. presumably
    (A) positively (B) helplessly
    (C) recklessly (D) supposedly

22. textile
    (A) linen (B) cloth
    (C) page (D) garment

23. fiscal
    (A) critical (B) basic
    (C) personal (D) financial

24. stringent
    (A) demanding (B) loud
    (C) flexible (D) clear

25. proceed
    (A) go forward (B) parade
    (C) refrain (D) resume

Practice Test 2

Directions: Select the word or phrase closest in meaning to the given word. Mark its letter on the sample answer sheet on page 47.

1. brochure
    (A) ornament (B) flowery statement
    (C) breakage (D) pamphlet

2. permeable
    (A) penetrable (B) durable
    (C) unending (D) allowable

3. limit
    (A) budget (B) sky
    (C) point (D) boundary

4. scrupulous
    (A) conscientious (B) unprincipled
    (C) intricate (D) neurotic

5. stalemate
   (A) pillar   (B) deadlock
   (C) maneuver   (D) work slowdown

6. competent
   (A) inept   (B) informed
   (C) capable   (D) caring

7. somatic
   (A) painful   (B) drowsy
   (C) indefinite   (D) physical

8. obstacle
   (A) imprisonment   (B) hindrance
   (C) retaining wall (D) leap

9. redundant
   (A) concise   (B) reappearing
   (C) superfluous   (D) lying down

10. supplant
    (A) prune   (B) conquer
    (C) uproot   (D) replace

11. haphazard
    (A) devious   (B) without order
    (C) aberrant   (D) risky

12. commensurate
    (A) identical   (B) of the same age
    (C) proportionate (D) measurable

13. accelerate
    (A) drive fast   (B) reroute
    (C) decline rapidly (D) speed up

14. purchased
    (A) charged   (B) bought
    (C) ordered   (D) supplied

15. zenith
    (A) depths   (B) astronomical system
    (C) peak   (D) solar system

16. succor
    (A) assistance   (B) Mayday
    (C) vitality   (D) distress

17. restrict
    (A) limit   (B) replace
    (C) watch   (D) record

18. strident
    (A) booming   (B) austere
    (C) swaggering   (D) shrill

19. dispatch
    (A) omit mention of
    (B) send out on an errand
    (C) hurry up
    (D) do without

20. inventory
    (A) catalog of possessions
    (B) statement of purposes
    (C) patent office
    (D) back order

21. assiduous
    (A) untrained   (B) unrestricted
    (C) diligent   (D) negligent

22. portable
    (A) drinkable   (B) convenient
    (C) having wheels (D) able to be carried

23. annual
    (A) yearly   (B) seasonal
    (C) occasional   (D) infrequent

24. endeavored
    (A) managed   (B) expected
    (C) attempted   (D) promised

25. acumen
    (A) caution   (B) strictness
    (C) inability   (D) keenness

Practice Test 3

Directions: Select the word or phrase closest in meaning to the given word. Mark its letter on the sample answer sheet on page 48.

1. excess
   (A) surplus   (B) exit
   (C) inflation   (D) luxury

2. verbose
   (A) vague   (B) brief
   (C) wordy   (D) verbal

3. collusion
   (A) decision   (B) connivance
   (C) insinuation (D) conflict

4. subversive
   (A) secret   (B) foreign
   (C) evasive   (D) destructive

5. vacillating
   (A) changeable (B) equalizing
   (C) decisive   (D) progressing

6. coincide
   (A) agree   (B) disregard
   (C) collect   (D) conflict

7. petty
   (A) lengthy   (B) communal
   (C) small   (D) miscellaneous

8. concede
   (A) confess   (B) ebb
   (C) enact   (D) give in

9. intrepid
   (A) willing   (B) fanciful
   (C) cowardly   (D) fearless

10. prolonged
    (A) refined   (B) drawn out
    (C) tiresome   (D) ardent

11. transcribe
    (A) write a copy (B) invent
    (C) interpret   (D) dictate

12. negotiate
    (A) suffer   (B) think
    (C) speak   (D) bargain

13. credible
    (A) believable (B) correct
    (C) intelligent (D) gullible

14. objective
    (A) strict   (B) courteous
    (C) fair   (D) pleasant

15. examine
    (A) file   (B) collect
    (C) distribute (D) inspect

16. quantity
    (A) flow   (B) type
    (C) amount   (D) difficulty

17. expedite
    (A) obstruct   (B) advise
    (C) accelerate (D) demolish

18. coordinator
    (A) enumerator (B) organizer
    (C) spokesman (D) advertiser

19. reprisal
    (A) retaliation (B) warning
    (C) advantage   (D) denial

20. relevant
    (A) controversial (B) recent
    (C) applicable   (D) impressive

21. sterile
    (A) antique   (B) germ-free
    (C) unclean   (D) perishable

22. mortgagor
    (A) lender   (B) receiver
    (C) giver   (D) judge

23. assist
    (A) malign   (B) incur
    (C) advise   (D) aid

24. maximum
    (A) greatest   (B) limited
    (C) oldest   (D) smallest

25. construe
    (A) violate   (B) contradict
    (C) question   (D) interpret

Practice Test 4

Directions: *Select the word or phrase closest in meaning to the given word. Mark its letter on the sample answer sheet on page 48.*

1. customary
    (A) methodical   (B) usual
    (C) curious   (D) procedural

2. minute
    (A) quick   (B) protracted
    (C) tiny   (D) shrunken

3. preclude
    (A) arise from   (B) account for
    (C) prevent   (D) define

4. abundant
    (A) plentiful   (B) accessible
    (C) concentrated (D) scattered

5. invoice
    (A) speech   (B) bill
    (C) offense   (D) liability

6. recreation
    (A) sport   (B) recess
    (C) diversion   (D) escapade

7. futile
    (A) medieval   (B) unfortunate
    (C) wasteful   (D) useless

8. expenditure
    (A) exhaustion   (B) budgeting
    (C) conservation (D) spending

9. stamina
    (A) part of a flower
    (B) incentive
    (C) staying power
    (D) reservation

10. advantageous
    (A) profitable   (B) winning
    (C) enterprising (D) shrewd

11. merchant
    (A) producer   (B) executive
    (C) advertiser   (D) storekeeper

12. observable
    (A) noticeable   (B) understandable
    (C) keen   (D) blatant

13. parole
    (A) sentence   (B) conditional release
    (C) good behavior (D) granting of privileges

14. reveal
    (A) describe fully (B) make known
    (C) guess at   (D) question seriously

15. fraud
    (A) guilt   (B) criminality
    (C) cheating   (D) disguise

16. asserted
    (A) decided   (B) agreed
    (C) contradicted   (D) declared

17. durable
    (A) thick   (B) waterproof
    (C) lasting   (D) costly

18. vindictive
    (A) revengeful   (B) boastful
    (C) aggressive   (D) impolite

19. bourgeois
    (A) middle-class   (B) affluent
    (C) decadent   (D) prevalent

20. absurd
    (A) careless   (B) foolish
    (C) impulsive   (D) regrettable

21. hospitable
    (A) careful   (B) incurable
    (C) relaxed   (D) welcoming

22. graft
    (A) undercover activity
    (B) political influence
    (C) illegal payment for political favor
    (D) giving jobs to relatives

23. emendations
    (A) illustrations
    (B) new problems
    (C) unexplained actions
    (D) corrections

24. punctuality
    (A) partiality   (B) being on time
    (C) precision   (D) being delayed

25. fatigue
    (A) illness   (B) worry
    (C) weariness   (D) indolence

Practice Test 5

Directions: Select the word or phrase closest in meaning to the given word. Mark its letter on the sample answer sheet on page 48.

1. affluence
    (A) persuasion   (B) power
    (C) inspiration   (D) wealth

2. related
    (A) subordinated   (B) connected
    (C) detached   (D) finished

3. designate
    (A) name   (B) illustrate
    (C) accuse   (D) change

4. chagrin
    (A) enjoyment   (B) disappointment
    (C) smirk   (D) disgust

5. anomalous
    (A) out of place   (B) vague
    (C) similar   (D) unknown

6. altitude
    (A) outlook   (B) height
    (C) distance   (D) magnitude

7. precise
    (A) short   (B) picky
    (C) exact   (D) trivial

8. ignominy
    (A) fame   (B) disgrace
    (C) bad luck   (D) despair

9. normal
   (A) comfortable   (B) right
   (C) usual   (D) necessary

10. increase
    (A) decline   (B) plenty
    (C) quantity (D) growth

11. collate
    (A) destroy   (B) separate
    (C) assemble (D) copy

12. authorize
    (A) permit   (B) write
    (C) train   (D) constrain

13. platitude
    (A) data   (B) length
    (C) theory (D) trite remark

14. entrenched
    (A) firmly established
    (B) at war
    (C) eternal
    (D) earthy

15. constant
    (A) absent   (B) unchanging
    (C) perpetrated (D) tiring

16. misnomer
    (A) wrong address (B) mistaken identity
    (C) crime   (D) wrong name

17. monitor
    (A) preserve   (B) warn
    (C) keep ahead of (D) keep track of

18. sufficient
    (A) interesting (B) enough
    (C) excessive   (D) accepting

19. prior
    (A) previous   (B) official
    (C) conflicting (D) important

20. anticipated
    (A) required (B) revised
    (C) expected (D) extraordinary

21. substitute
    (A) excuse   (B) replacement
    (C) arrangement (D) pretense

22. rapidity
    (A) idleness (B) delay
    (C) speed   (D) efficiency

23. verify
    (A) control (B) line up
    (C) confirm (D) decide

24. attain
    (A) mar   (B) exhaust
    (C) reach (D) attack

25. requisition
    (A) payment   (B) written order
    (C) formality (D) cancellation

Answer Key for Practice Tests

TEST 1

1. C	6. B	11. B	16. C	21. D
2. B	7. C	12. D	17. C	22. B
3. D	8. B	13. A	18. B	23. D
4. A	9. C	14. B	19. A	24. A
5. C	10. C	15. D	20. D	25. A

TEST 2

1. D	6. C	11. B	16. A	21. C
2. A	7. D	12. C	17. A	22. D
3. D	8. B	13. D	18. D	23. A
4. A	9. C	14. B	19. B	24. C
5. B	10. D	15. C	20. A	25. D

TEST 3

1. A	6. A	11. A	16. C	21. B
2. C	7. C	12. D	17. C	22. A
3. B	8. D	13. A	18. B	23. D
4. D	9. D	14. C	19. A	24. A
5. A	10. B	15. D	20. C	25. D

TEST 4

1. B	6. C	11. D	16. D	21. D
2. C	7. D	12. A	17. C	22. C
3. C	8. D	13. B	18. A	23. D
4. A	9. C	14. B	19. A	24. B
5. B	10. A	15. C	20. B	25. C

TEST 5

1. D	6. B	11. C	16. D	21. B
2. B	7. C	12. A	17. D	22. C
3. A	8. B	13. D	18. B	23. C
4. B	9. C	14. A	19. A	24. C
5. A	10. D	15. B	20. C	25. B

SENTENCE COMPLETIONS

In a sentence completion question, you are given a sentence or longer passage in which something has been left blank. A number of words or phrases are suggested to fill that blank. You must select the word or phrase that will *best* complete the meaning of the passage as a whole.

Sentence completion questions are more complex than synonym questions. They test not only your knowledge of basic vocabulary, but also your ability to understand what you read. While studying individual words may be helpful, the best way to prepare for this type of question is to read a lot. A dictionary will tell you what a word means; reading will teach you how it is actually used.

How to Answer Sentence Completion Questions

1. Read each question carefully, looking at all the answer choices.
2. Eliminate any answer choices that seem obviously wrong.
3. Of the remaining choices, select the one that *best* completes the meaning of the sentence or passage given. Although more than one answer may make sense, the best choice will be the one that is most exact, appropriate, or likely, considering the information given in the sentence or passage.
4. To check yourself, read the sentence or passage through again, putting your answer in the blank.
5. First answer the questions you know. If you have trouble with a question, leave it and come back to it later.

Sample Questions

Before doing the practice tests, study the following examples.

1. Trespassing on private property is _____ by law.
    (A) proscribed   (C) prescribed
    (B) warranted   (D) eliminated

The most likely—and, therefore, correct—answer is (A) *proscribed*, which means "forbidden" or "outlawed." *Warranted* (B) may remind you of a *warrant* for arrest, which might be a result of trespassing. *Warranted*, however, means "justified," which would make the given sentence obviously untrue. Choice (C) *prescribed* looks similar to the correct answer but means "recommended." Like *warranted*, it makes nonsense out of the given sentence. Choice (D) *eliminated* is also less likely than (A). The law may be intended to eliminate trespassing, but it can never be completely successful in doing so.

2. Despite the harsh tone of her comments, she did not mean to _____ any criticism of you personally.
    (A) infer   (C) comply
    (B) aim   (D) imply

The correct answer is (D) *imply*, which means "suggest indirectly." Choice (A) *infer* is a word often confused with *imply*. It means "conclude from reasoning or implication." A speaker implies; a listener infers. Choice (C) *comply*, meaning "obey," makes no sense in this context. Choice (B) *aim* is more likely, but it doesn't work in the sentence as given. You might say, "she did not mean to *aim* any criticism *at* you," but you would not normally say, "she did not mean to *aim* any criticism *of* you."

3. The department's _____ does not allow for unlimited copying by all the instructors in the program. Each instructor can be reimbursed for copying expenses only up to $10.
    (A) paperwork   (C) organization
    (B) staff   (D) budget

Because the concern here is with money, the correct answer is (D) *budget*. It is a *budget* that puts limits on spending. Choices (A) *paperwork* and (B) *staff* are not appropriate to the meaning of the passage. Choice (C) *organization* is barely possible, but only because it is so vague. *Budget* both makes sense and is much more exact.

4. If the company offered a settlement commensurate with the damages sustained, the couple would _____ their right to a hearing.
    (A) cancel   (C) waive
    (B) ensue   (D) assert

The correct answer is (C) *waive*, which means "forgo" or "give up." One *waives* something to which one is entitled, such as a right. Choice (A) *cancel* is similar in meaning but is not used in this way. One can cancel a hearing but not a right. Choice (B) *ensue* may mislead you by its similarity to *sue*. The sentence does imply that the couple is suing or planning to sue the company for damages of some sort. However, *ensue* simply means "follow as a result," and so makes no sense in this context. Choice (D) *assert* here means the opposite of *waive*. One can assert a right, but the meaning of the first part of the sentence makes this choice unlikely.

Practice Test 1

Directions: *Each of the following sentences or passages contains a blank. Select the word or phrase that will best complete the meaning of the sentence or passage as a whole. Mark its letter on the sample answer sheet on page 48.*

1. He was the chief _____ of his uncle's will. After taxes, he was left with an inheritance worth close to $20,000.
    (A) exemption   (C) beneficiary
    (B) pensioner   (D) contestant

2. In view of the extenuating circumstances and the defendant's youth, the judge recommended _____.
    (A) conviction   (C) a mistrial
    (B) a defense   (D) leniency

3. The basic concept of civil service is that where a public job exists, all those who possess the _____ shall have an opportunity to compete for it.
    (A) potential   (C) qualifications
    (B) contacts   (D) credits

4. They would prefer to hire someone fluent in Spanish because the neighborhood in which the clinic is located is _____ Hispanic.
    (A) imponderably (C) consistently
    (B) sparsely   (D) predominantly

5. The lover of democracy has an _____ toward totalitarianism.
   (A) antipathy   (C) empathy
   (B) attitude   (D) idolatry

6. The candidate's _____ was carefully planned; she traveled to six cities and spoke at nine rallies.
   (A) pogrom   (C) adjournment
   (B) itinerary   (D) apparition

7. _____ recommendations are generally more constructive than vague complaints or blanket praise.
   (A) Justified   (C) Sweeping
   (B) Nebulous   (D) Specific

8. In the face of an uncooperative Congress, the Chief Executive may find himself _____ to accomplish the political program to which he is committed.
   (A) impotent   (C) neutral
   (B) equipped   (D) contingent

9. The authorities declared an _____ on incoming freight because of the trucking strike.
   (A) impression   (C) embargo
   (B) immolation   (D) opprobrium

10. The information we have available on that question is _____: The form, scope, and reliability of the documents vary tremendously.
    (A) essential   (C) minimal
    (B) homogeneous (D) heterogeneous

11. The _____ on the letter indicated that it had been mailed in Minnesota three weeks previously.
    (A) address   (C) postmark
    (B) stamp   (D) envelope

12. The television ads _____ an unprecedented public response. Sales skyrocketed, and within a few months the brand name had become a household word.
    (A) boosted   (C) elicited
    (B) promised   (D) favored

13. The chairman submitted a _____ for the new equipment, but it won't be delivered for two weeks.
    (A) requisition (C) proposal
    (B) reason   (D) plea

14. With all his courtroom experience, the attorney was able to pry very little information out of the _____ witness.
    (A) cooperative (C) reactionary
    (B) recalcitrant (D) testifying

15. Although for years substantial resources had been devoted to alleviating the problem, a satisfactory solution remained _____.
    (A) costly   (C) elusive
    (B) probable   (D) esoteric

16. The local police department will not accept for _____ a report of a person missing from his residence if such residence is located outside of the city.
    (A) foreclosure (C) investigation
    (B) convenience (D) control

17. The consumer group is optimistic about the _____ of the new regulations on the industry's safety standards.
    (A) incision   (C) affectation
    (B) effect   (D) input

18. The mayor sent a letter _____ our invitation and commending us on our work; she regrets that she will be unable to attend the opening ceremonies due to a prior commitment.
    (A) rebuffing   (C) returning
    (B) reconsidering (D) acknowledging

19. His wealth of practical experience and his psychological acuity more than _____ his lack of formal academic training.
    (A) concede to (C) compensate for
    (B) comprise   (D) educate for

20. Suffering from _____, she was forced to spend almost all her time indoors.
    (A) claustrophobia (C) anemia
    (B) agoraphobia   (D) ambivalence

21. The treaty cannot go into effect until it has been _____ by the Senate.
(A) considered   (C) ratified
(B) debated   (D) shelved

22. You will have to speak to the head of the agency; I am not _____ to give out that information.
(A) willing   (C) programmed
(B) authorized   (D) happy

23. When new individuals have proved their capability and reliability, they ought to achieve journeyman status in the company _____.

(A) intrinsically (C) automatically
(B) permanently   (D) decisively

24. The objective may be _____, but the plan as presented is far from practicable.
(A) compensatory (C) precarious
(B) laudable   (D) subversive

25. You must _____ a copy of your latest federal income tax return before your loan application can be considered.
(A) surrender   (C) supplement
(B) replicate   (D) submit

Practice Test 2

Directions: Each of the following sentences or passages contains a blank. Select the word or phrase that will best complete the meaning of the sentence or passage as a whole. Mark its letter on the sample answer sheet on page 49.

1. It is easy to see the difference between the two photographs when they are placed in _____.
(A) disarray   (C) composition
(B) juxtaposition (D) collaboration

2. The criticism that supervisors are discriminatory in their treatment of subordinates is to some extent _____, for the subjective nature of many supervisory decisions makes it probable that many employees who have not progressed will attribute their lack of success to supervisory favoritism.
(A) knowledgeable (C) detrimental
(B) unavoidable   (D) deniable

3. Traditionally, the more _____ sectors of the population in the northern states tend to belong to the Republican Party.
(A) democratic   (C) conciliatory
(B) radical   (D) conservative

4. Short of a further major _____ of business conditions, it is difficult to see how inventory liquidation could continue at current rates much beyond mid-year.
(A) infiltration (C) deterioration
(B) obliteration (D) machination

5. Students with grade averages of 3.5 or better in the course work were _____ from the final exam.
(A) expelled   (C) selected
(B) barred   (D) exempt

6. The Freedom of Information Act gives private citizens _____ government files.
(A) access to   (C) redress of
(B) excess of   (D) release from

7. Among the most serious emergencies for which first aid should be taught is _____ from asphyxiation, such as may result from drowning, electric shock, or exhaust-gas poisoning.
(A) salvation   (C) humiliation
(B) resuscitation (D) overstimulation

8. Because I wanted to use a synonym, I looked the word up in the _____.
   (A) thesaurus (C) encyclopedia
   (B) directory (D) dictionary

9. Her position in the agency authorized her to award contracts and to _____ obligations for payment of salaries.
   (A) rescind (C) procure
   (B) incur (D) recur

10. It is wise to get a written _____ of the costs of labor and materials before commissioning someone to do the work.
    (A) account (C) estimate
    (B) promise (D) invoice

11. His remarks were so _____ that we could not decide which of the possible meanings was correct.
    (A) ambiguous (C) impalpable
    (B) facetious (D) congruent

12. With such controversial subjects, there is always the risk that any standards set up will yield or be _____ in one way or another.
    (A) dismantled (C) enforced
    (B) intercepted (D) circumvented

13. Publication of the article was timed to _____ with the professor's 50th birthday.
    (A) coincide (C) amalgamate
    (B) harmonize (D) terminate

14. A policy on noncooperation can be a certain method of _____ the friends with whom you work.
    (A) abominating (C) aborting
    (B) alienating (D) evacuating

15. The effects of the drug can be _____ by drinking large quantities of water.
    (A) reprimanded (C) neutralized
    (B) implemented (D) admitted

16. When the desk was placed facing the window, he found himself _____ from his work by the activity in the street.

    (A) distraught (C) distracted
    (B) destroyed (D) decimated

17. Because she is not _____ to using this kind of copier, you had better instruct her on how to add paper.
    (A) amenable (C) adaptable
    (B) accustomed (D) impartial

18. Compulsory education was instituted for the purpose of preventing _____ of young children and of guaranteeing them a minimum of education.
    (A) malnutrition (C) homelessness
    (B) usurpation (D) exploitation

19. A man who commits a wrong may be required to _____ his property as a penalty.
    (A) confiscate (C) forfeit
    (B) destroy (D) assess

20. When human relationships are involved in a job, it is difficult to set precise _____ for judging how well the job is being done. Merely physical or monetary standards are inadequate.
    (A) options (C) behavior
    (B) criteria (D) reports

21. The assigned task _____ the ability to analyze the available data and to draw conclusions about their implications.
    (A) inculcates (C) precludes
    (B) obtrudes (D) entails

22. In his suit against the government, the veteran claimed that he had been sent into an area _____ by the carcinogenic defoliant without being informed of the risk or being provided with adequate protective gear.
    (A) affected (C) irradiated
    (B) sterilized (D) contaminated

23. An accident report should be written as soon as possible after the necessary _____ has been obtained.
    (A) bystander (C) information
    (B) formulation (D) permission

24. To give in to the terrorists' demands would be a betrayal of our responsibilities; such _____ would only encourage others to adopt similar methods for gaining their ends.
(A) defeats   (C) appeals
(B) appeasement   (D) subterfuge

25. To protect the respondents' privacy, names and Social Security numbers are _____ the questionnaires before the results are tabulated.
(A) referred to   (C) retained in
(B) deleted from   (D) appended to

Practice Test 3

Directions: Each of the following sentences or passages contains a blank. Select the word or phrase that will best complete the meaning of the sentence or passage as a whole. Mark its letter on the sample answer sheet on page 49.

1. A legal _____ arose when the legislature passed a new law prohibiting such sales.
(A) miscellany   (C) aid
(B) morass   (D) impediment

2. The cause of the child's death was _____ from the fire's thick smoke.
(A) myopia   (C) strangulation
(B) asphyxiation   (D) hemorrhage

3. It has come to the attention of the court that a newspaper recently published a series of photographs _____ taken during a court session.
(A) surreptitiously (C) patently
(B) judiciously   (D) patiently

4. The woman sued the magazine, claiming that the article _____ her character.
(A) demoted   (C) denigrated
(B) deplored   (D) implicated

5. A charlatan is likely to give you _____ advice.
(A) desirable   (C) profitable
(B) unreliable   (D) lethal

6. He is studying the language _____ in preparation for the assignment; he spends several hours a day practicing with the tapes.
(A) sporadically   (C) profoundly
(B) superficially   (D) intensively

7. During the campaign, the politician presented tax reforms as a _____ for the high cost of living.
(A) rectitude   (C) sanction
(B) panacea   (D) reimbursement

8. The arresting officer is expected to testify that he saw the _____ thief fleeing from the scene of the crime.
(A) convicted   (C) alleged
(B) delinquent   (D) offensive

9. In certain tropical areas, malaria is an _____ disease.
(A) endocrine   (C) inevitable
(B) endemic   (D) intestinal

10. While fewer documents are being kept, the usefulness of those _____ is now insured by an improved cataloguing system.
(A) printed   (C) read
(B) discarded   (D) retained

11. In a country where public offices are created solely for the benefit of the people, no one person has any more _____ right to official station than another.
(A) intrinsic   (C) technical
(B) sincere   (D) confidential

12. The _____, assumed for the sake of the discussion, was that business would get better for the next five years.
    (A) labyrinth   (C) outlay
    (B) hypothesis   (D) itinerary

13. The man _____ the speaker at the meeting by shouting false accusations.
    (A) corrected   (C) disconcerted
    (B) interfered   (D) acknowledged

14. The only fair way to choose who will have to work over the holiday is to pick someone _____ by drawing lots.
    (A) covertly   (C) randomly
    (B) conspicuously   (D) carefully

15. Although he has a reputation for aloofness, his manner on that occasion was so _____ that everyone felt perfectly at ease.
    (A) reluctant   (C) malign
    (B) gracious   (D) plausible

16. Do not undertake a daily program of _____ exercise such as jogging without first having a physical checkup.
    (A) light   (C) hazardous
    (B) spurious   (D) strenuous

17. She was _____ for her outspoken and well-founded criticisms of her fellow representatives.
    (A) rewarded   (C) reprimanded
    (B) notorious   (D) alienated

18. The commissioner tolerates no _____ in the application of these procedures; the regulations of the agency must in all cases be followed to the letter.
    (A) laxity   (C) censure
    (B) rupture   (D) enthusiasm

19. Research in that field has become so _____ that researchers on different aspects of the same problem may be unfamiliar with each other's work.

    (A) secure   (C) partial
    (B) specialized   (D) departmental

20. A shift to greater use of renewable or inexhaustible resources in the production of power would slow the depletion of _____ fuel materials.
    (A) regional   (C) chemical
    (B) irradiated   (D) irreplaceable

21. The day will come when _____ will look back upon us and our time with a sense of superiority.
    (A) teachers   (C) scientists
    (B) posterity   (D) ancestors

22. A change in environment is very likely to _____ a change in one's work habits.
    (A) affect   (C) effect
    (B) inflict   (D) prosper

23. She revolutionized the way things were done, but many of the _____ for which she broke ground were left to be fully realized by others.
    (A) innovations   (C) foundations
    (B) initiations   (D) provocations

24. The overseer certified that the temporary _____ was the result of an injury incurred on the job. The employee was transferred to another position until he was able to resume his usual duties.
    (A) disease   (C) leave
    (B) disability   (D) condition

25. The _____ of such crimes between the hours of midnight and 6 A.M. has been reduced 30 percent since April.
    (A) threat   (C) incidence
    (B) circumstance   (D) graph

Practice Test 4

Directions: *Each of the following sentences or passages contains a blank. Select the word or phrase that will best complete the meaning of the sentence or passage as a whole. Mark its letter on the sample answer sheet on page 49.*

1. To arrest a person is to _____ his liberty by legal authority so that he may be held to answer for a crime.
   (A) confer on him   (C) deprive him of
   (B) set bail for   (D) dispel from him

2. Their ceaseless _____ was out of place on that solemn occasion.
   (A) viscosity   (C) acuity
   (B) banter   (D) infinity

3. In order to save time, the supervisor directed that some forms be consolidated and others _____ entirely.
   (A) eliminated   (C) combined
   (B) incorporated   (D) disconnected

4. For the sake of public confidence, public officials should avoid even the _____ of a conflict of interest.
   (A) appearance   (C) actuality
   (B) resistance   (D) apparition

5. One function of professional _____ is to exclude from comprehension those hearers not initiated into the special knowledge that constitutes the profession.
   (A) translation   (C) elocution
   (B) jargon   (D) conduct

6. A string of lies had landed her in such a hopeless _____ that she didn't know how to extricate herself.
   (A) status   (C) enigma
   (B) pinnacle   (D) predicament

7. They _____ all acts of terrorism by the revolutionaries.
   (A) abdicate   (C) abominate
   (B) debase   (D) defray

8. Because he made _____ for the merchandise he had stolen, the judge reduced his sentence.
   (A) desuetude   (C) restitution
   (B) destitution (D) contrition

9. Although she was otherwise efficient and responsible, _____ was not one of her virtues. She was rarely in the office by 9 A.M.
   (A) conscientiousness   (C) politeness
   (B) tardiness   (D) punctuality

10. In developing photographic film, a highly concentrated _____ containing a caustic alkali such as sodium hydroxide is essential.
    (A) solution   (C) concoction
    (B) coalition (D) cremation

11. A professional journalist will attempt to _____ the facts learned in an interview by an independent investigation.
    (A) retell   (C) query
    (B) endorse   (D) verify

12. Her transcript indicates that she has satisfactorily completed the _____ number of courses for an associate degree.
    (A) requited   (C) requisite
    (B) rescinded (D) relative

13. The police received a(n) _____ call giving them valuable information that led to an arrest. The caller refused to give his name out of fear of reprisals.
    (A) anonymous   (C) private
    (B) asinine   (D) candid

14. In an attempt to _____ a strike, the parties agreed to negotiate through the night.
    (A) trigger   (C) arbitrate
    (B) avert   (D) herald

15. While lenses and frames form the focus of operations, the company also makes a host of other _____ products, such as artificial eyes and instruments used to correct vision defects, as well as eyeglass cases.
    (A) panoramic   (C) ocular
    (B) corporate   (D) optimistic

16. More residents turned out for the town meeting than the board had anticipated. There were not enough seats to _____ them all.
    (A) count   (C) ascertain
    (B) hear   (D) accommodate

17. The _____ of the factory into three new departments has improved its productivity.
    (A) collaboration   (C) partition
    (B) deliberation   (D) rehabilitation

18. Because of their previous exposure to this strain of influenza, they are fortunately _____ to the current outbreak.
    (A) immune   (C) oblivious
    (B) adamant   (D) not liable

19. A majority of the membership constitutes a _____ to do business in the Senate.
    (A) forum   (C) podium
    (B) quorum   (D) minority

20. The _____ of the award stopped by the financial aid office to pick up his check.

    (A) recipient   (C) donor
    (B) subject   (D) sponsor

21. Her expertise is vital to our operation. We could not _____ her services.
    (A) redouble   (C) define
    (B) dispense with   (D) invest in

22. The ability to grow or reproduce and to change or mutate has long been regarded as a special _____ of living agents.
    (A) evolution   (C) vitality
    (B) detriment   (D) characteristic

23. The study produced a _____ amount of data—so much, in fact, that it will take several weeks to prepare the report.
    (A) considerate   (C) considerable
    (B) minuscule   (D) constant

24. Because the evidence is incomplete, we will have to come to a decision based on what seem to be reasonable _____.
    (A) actions   (C) proofs
    (B) operations   (D) assumptions

25. At the outset, opposition to the planned highway seemed futile, but the neighborhood association _____ its campaign until the city agreed to reconsider the route.
    (A) proclaimed   (C) insisted on
    (B) persisted in   (D) refrained from

Practice Test 5

Directions: Each of the following sentences or passages contains a blank. Select the word or phrase that will best complete the meaning of the sentence or passage as a whole. Mark its letter on the sample answer sheet on page 49.

1. The field of _____ medicine concerns not treatment, but the avoidance of disease. Studies of diet, exercise, drinking habits, and other factors are contributing to a better understanding of what constitutes good health.
   (A) curative   (C) veterinary
   (B) surgical   (D) preventive

2. Unfortunately, these favorable influences can be expected to _____ or even disappear within the next few years.
   (A) defray   (C) abate
   (B) recur   (D) vanish

3. No one knows more about the special program than she does; she has been its director since its _____.
   (A) operation   (C) culmination
   (B) inception   (D) fulfillment

4. Repetition of words and ideas can confuse as well as emphasize a point, and may make your speech _____.
   (A) redundant   (C) illiterate
   (B) concise   (D) effective

5. The secretary was unfailingly _____ to the clients, no matter how demanding and unreasonable they were.
   (A) irksome   (C) superficial
   (B) courteous   (D) related

6. Supported by aid from the federal government, university research activity enjoyed a period of unprecedented _____.
   (A) expansion   (C) reprieve
   (B) collapse   (D) extenuation

7. An arithmetic average or mean is arrived at by adding up the value of all the items and then dividing the _____ by the number of items.
   (A) remainder   (C) value
   (B) quotient   (D) total

8. Though brilliantly presented, the report was _____ because the information on which it was based was erroneous.
   (A) informative   (C) worthless
   (B) verbose   (D) marred

9. Her _____ manner embarrassed the others at the party.
   (A) affable   (C) gracious
   (B) gauche   (D) amiable

10. Because every society produces cultural elements—customs, artifacts, and so forth—unique to itself, translation of terms from its language to that of another society must sometimes be _____.
    (A) wrong   (C) rectified
    (B) unnatural   (D) imprecise

11. The committee was so uninformed about the legitimate sources of the students' unrest that its recommendations were _____ value.
    (A) of moderate   (C) depreciating in
    (B) devoid of   (D) of incontestable

12. Out of modesty, he often _____ his own contribution; without his efforts, however, the program would still be in the planning stage.
    (A) affirms   (C) belittles
    (B) represses   (D) rescinds

13. The pioneers did not settle in this area because the land was _____.
    (A) decimated   (C) barren
    (B) robust   (D) lucid

14. As citizens, we would be _____ if we did not make these facts public.
    (A) nominative   (C) private
    (B) elective   (D) derelict

15. Given a clear knowledge of what is expected of him, the subordinate requires, in addition, the definite assurance that he will have the _____ of his superiors as long as his actions are consistent with established policies and are taken within the limits of his responsibility.
    (A) independence (C) authority
    (B) satisfaction (D) support

16. As the workload increased, she _____ responsibility for many routine tasks to an assistant.
    (A) preserved   (C) handled
    (B) delegated   (D) abased

17. The principal object of the _____ law is to define crime and prescribe punishments.
    (A) penal   (C) state
    (B) parole   (D) federal

18. The use of a roadblock is simply an adaptation to police practices of the military _____ of encirclement.
    (A) aggression   (C) concept
    (B) consequence (D) flanking

19. Monetary policy was _____ primarily through the flexible use of both open-market operations and adjustments in the discount rate.
(A) implemented (C) unified
(B) associated (D) deliberated

20. The Constitution provides that no person shall twice be put in _____ for the same offense.
(A) prison (C) the army
(B) jeopardy (D) court

21. A _____ in the diplomatic service, she had not yet encountered such a question of protocol.
(A) success (C) veteran
(B) volunteer (D) novice

22. News reports alleged that high officials had been aware of the _____, and even illegal, covert activities of the group.

(A) open (C) explicit
(B) unethical (D) administrative

23. The _____ report was submitted, subject to such revisions as would be made before the final draft.
(A) preliminary (C) ultimate
(B) ubiquitous (D) obsolete

24. Because of the fire hazard, regulations forbid the use of highly _____ materials in certain items, such as children's pajamas.
(A) synthetic (C) inflammatory
(B) flammable (D) flame-retardant

25. The new secretary has a more businesslike manner than her _____ in the job.
(A) precedent (C) successor
(B) ancestor (D) predecessor

Answer Key for Practice Tests

TEST 1

1. **C**	6. **B**	11. **C**	16. **C**	21. **C**
2. **D**	7. **D**	12. **C**	17. **B**	22. **B**
3. **C**	8. **A**	13. **A**	18. **D**	23. **C**
4. **D**	9. **C**	14. **B**	19. **C**	24. **B**
5. **A**	10. **D**	15. **C**	20. **B**	25. **D**

TEST 2

1. **B**	6. **A**	11. **A**	16. **C**	21. **D**
2. **B**	7. **B**	12. **D**	17. **B**	22. **D**
3. **D**	8. **A**	13. **A**	18. **D**	23. **C**
4. **C**	9. **B**	14. **B**	19. **C**	24. **B**
5. **D**	10. **C**	15. **C**	20. **B**	25. **B**

TEST 3

1. **D**	6. **D**	11. **A**	16. **D**	21. **B**
2. **B**	7. **B**	12. **B**	17. **B**	22. **C**
3. **A**	8. **C**	13. **C**	18. **A**	23. **A**
4. **C**	9. **B**	14. **C**	19. **B**	24. **B**
5. **B**	10. **D**	15. **B**	20. **D**	25. **C**

TEST 4

1. **C**	6. **D**	11. **D**	16. **D**	21. **B**
2. **B**	7. **C**	12. **C**	17. **C**	22. **D**
3. **A**	8. **C**	13. **A**	18. **A**	23. **C**
4. **A**	9. **D**	14. **B**	19. **B**	24. **D**
5. **B**	10. **A**	15. **C**	20. **A**	25. **B**

TEST 5

1. **D**	6. **A**	11. **B**	16. **B**	21. **D**
2. **C**	7. **D**	12. **C**	17. **A**	22. **B**
3. **B**	8. **C**	13. **C**	18. **C**	23. **A**
4. **A**	9. **B**	14. **D**	19. **A**	24. **B**
5. **B**	10. **D**	15. **D**	20. **B**	25. **D**

READING COMPREHENSION

It would appear to the average person taking a civil service examination that reading comprehension is adequately tested in the exam itself. Without being able to read and understand both the complex sets of directions and some of the tricky questions posed on some tests, failure is imminent. Nonetheless, most civil service exams test the test-taker's ability to read a passage, understand the point being made, and answer questions based on what is said in the passage being read.

This section is designed to help you overcome any fears you may have about taking this part of the civil service test. If you follow the simple suggestions listed here and do the exercises that follow, you will know what to look for when reading the passages and what to expect to find in the questions. You will then be one step ahead of the game.

1. Skim the passage to get a general idea of the subject matter and of the point that is being made.
2. Reread the passage, paying attention to details and point of view. Be alert for the author's hints as to what he or she thinks is important. Phrases such as "Note that …," "Of importance is …," and "Do not overlook …" give clues to what the writer is stressing.
3. If the author has quoted material from another source, be sure that you understand the purpose of the quote. Does the author agree or disagree?
4. Carefully read the question or incomplete statement. Determine exactly what is being asked. Watch for negatives or all-inclusive words, such as *always*, *never*, *all*, *only*, *every*, *absolutely*, *completely*, *none*, *entirely*, and *no*. These words can affect your answer.
5. Read all the answer choices. Do not rush to choose the first answer that might be correct. Eliminate those choices that are obviously incorrect. Reread the remaining choices, and refer to the passage, if necessary, to determine the *best* answer.
6. Avoid inserting your judgments into your answers. Even if you disagree with the author or spot a factual error in the passage, you must answer on the basis of what is stated or implied in the passage.
7. Do not allow yourself to spend too much time on any one question. If looking back at the passage does not help you to find or figure out the answer, choose from among the answers remaining after you eliminate the obviously wrong answers, and go on to the next question or the next reading passage.

Practice Test 1

Directions: Answer each question on the basis of the information stated or implied in the accompanying reading passage. The answer sheet is on page 49.

1. Unfortunately, specialization in industry creates workers who lack versatility. When a laborer is trained to perform only one task, he or she is almost entirely dependent for employment upon the demand for that particular skill. If anything happens to interrupt that demand, he or she is unemployed.

   This paragraph indicates that
   (A) the unemployment problem is a direct result of specialization in industry.
   (B) the demand for labor of a particular type is constantly changing.
   (C) the average laborer is not capable of learning more than one task at a time.
   (D) some cases of unemployment are due to laborers' lack of versatility.

2. Good management is needed now more than ever. The essential characteristic of management is organization. An organization must be capable of handling responsibility and authority. It also must be able to maintain the balance and perspective necessary to make the weighty decisions thrust upon it today.

   This paragraph is a plea for
   (A) better business.
   (B) adequately controlled responsibility.
   (C) well-regulated authority.
   (D) better management through organization.

3. The increasing size of business organizations has resulted in less personal contact between superior and subordinate. Consequently, business executives today depend more upon records and reports to secure information and exercise control over the operations of various departments.

   According to this paragraph, the increasing size of business organizations

   (A) has caused a complete cleavage between employer and employee.
   (B) has resulted in less personal contact between superior and subordinate.
   (C) has tended toward class distinctions in large organizations.
   (D) has resulted in a more direct means of controlling the operations of various departments.

4. In large organizations, some standardized, simple, inexpensive method of giving employees information about company policies and rules, as well as specific instructions regarding their duties, is practically essential. This is the purpose of all office manuals of whatever type.

   This section notes that office manuals
   (A) are all about the same.
   (B) should be simple enough for the average employee to understand.
   (C) are necessary to large organizations.
   (D) act as constant reminders to the employee of her duties.

5. Direct lighting is the least satisfactory lighting arrangement. The desk or ceiling light with a reflector that diffuses all the rays downward is sure to cause glare on the working surface.

   This paragraph indicates that direct lighting is least satisfactory as a method of lighting chiefly because
   (A) the light is diffused, causing eye strain.
   (B) the shade on the individual lamp is not constructed along scientific lines.
   (C) the working surface is usually obscured by the glare.
   (D) the ordinary reflector causes the rays to fall perpendicularly.

6. The principal advantage of wood over steel office equipment lies, surprisingly, in the greater safety afforded papers in a fire. While the wooden exterior of a file cabinet may burn somewhat, the papers will not be charred as quickly as they would in a steel cabinet. This is because wood burns slowly and does not transmit heat, while steel, although it does not burn, is a conductor of heat. So, under similar circumstances, papers would be charred more quickly in a steel cabinet.

Judging from this information alone, the principal advantage of wood over steel office equipment is that
   (A) in case of fire, papers will not be destroyed in a wooden cabinet.
   (B) wooden equipment is cheaper to replace.
   (C) steel does not resist fire as well as wood.
   (D) steel equipment is heavy and cannot be moved about very easily.

7. The total number of errors made during the month, or another period studied, indicates, in a general way, whether the work has been performed with reasonable accuracy. However, this is not in itself a true measure but must be considered in relation to the total volume of work produced.

On the basis of this statement, the accuracy of work performed in a certain stenographic unit is most truly measured by the
   (A) total number of errors made during a specified period.
   (B) comparison of the number of errors made during one month with the number made during the preceding month.
   (C) ratio between the number of errors made and the quantity of work produced during a specified period.
   (D) average amount of work produced by the unit during each month or other designated period of time.

8. "When an employee is encouraged by his supervisor to think of new ideas in connection with his or her work, the habit of improving work methods is fostered."

Of the following, the one that is the most valid implication of this quotation is that
   (A) the improvement of work methods should be the concern not only of the supervisor, but of the employee as well.
   (B) an employee without initiative cannot perform his job well.
   (C) an employee may waste too much time in experimenting with new work methods.
   (D) an improved method for performing a task should not be used without the approval of the supervisor.

9. "Persons in the employ of a public agency generally come into contact with many people outside of working hours. In these contacts, the government employee represents to the public the quality, competence, and stature of public employees as a group."

Of the following statements, the one that is the most valid implication of this quotation is that
   (A) the responsibilities of a public employee cease after office hours.
   (B) government employees who come into contact with the public during working hours should be more efficient than those who have no contact with the public.
   (C) public employees, by their behavior during social activities, can raise the prestige of public employment.
   (D) employees of a private company have greater responsibilities during office hours than employees of a public agency.

10. During the past few years, business has made rapid strides in applying to the field of office management the same fundamental principles of procedure and method that have been successful for years in production work. Present-day competition, resulting in smaller margins of profit, has made it essential to give careful attention to the efficient organization and management of internal administrative affairs so that individual productivity may be increased and unit costs reduced.

According to this paragraph,

(A) office management always lags behind production work.

(B) present-day competition has increased individual productivity.

(C) efficient office management seeks to reduce gross costs.

(D) the margin of profits widens as individual productivity is increased.

Practice Test 2

Directions: Answer each question on the basis of the information stated or implied in the accompanying reading passage. The answer sheet is on page 50.

Questions 1 to 3 refer to this passage:

In order to organize records properly, it is necessary to start from the very beginning and to trace each copy of the record to find out how it is used, how long it is used, and what may finally be done with it. Although several copies of the record are made, one copy should be marked as the copy of record. This is the formal legal copy, held to meet the requirements of the law. The other copies may be retained for brief periods for reference purposes, but these copies should not be kept after their usefulness as references end. There is another reason for tracing records through the office, and that is to determine how long it takes the copy of record to reach the central file. The copy of record must not be kept longer than necessary by the section of the office that has prepared it, but it should be sent to the central file as soon as possible so that it can be available to the various sections of the office. The central file can make the copy of record available to the various sections of the office at an early date only if it arrives at the central file as quickly as possible. Just as soon as its immediate or active service period has ended, the copy of record should be removed from the central file and put into the inactive file in the office to be stored for whatever length of time may be necessary to meet legal requirements, and then destroyed.

1. According to this paragraph, a reason for tracing records through an office is to
   (A) determine how long the central file must keep the records.
   (B) organize records properly.
   (C) find out how many copies of each record are required.
   (D) identify the copy of record.

2. According to this paragraph, in order for the central file to have the copy of record available as soon as possible for the various sections of the office, it is most important that the
   (A) copy of record to be sent to the central file meets the requirements of the law.
   (B) copy of record is not kept in the inactive file too long.
   (C) section preparing the copy of record does not unduly delay in sending it to the central file.
   (D) central file does not keep the copy of record beyond its active service period.

3. According to this paragraph, the length of time a copy of a record is kept in the inactive file of an office depends chiefly on the
   (A) requirements of the law.
   (B) length of time that is required to trace the copy of record through the office.
   (C) use that is made of the copy of record.
   (D) length of the period that the copy of record is used for reference purposes.

Questions 4 to 6 refer to this passage:

The most important unit of the mimeograph machine is a perforated metal drum over which is stretched a cloth ink pad. A reservoir inside the drum contains the ink that flows through the perforations and saturates the ink pad. To operate the machine, the operator first removes the protective sheet from the machine, which keeps the ink from drying while the machine is not in use. He then hooks the stencil face down on the drum, draws the stencil smoothly over the drum, and fastens the stencil at the bottom. The speed with which the drum turns determines the blackness of the copies printed. Slow turning gives heavy, black copies; fast turning gives light, clear-cut reproductions. If reproductions are run on other than porous paper, slip-sheeting is necessary to prevent smearing. Often the printed copy fails to drop readily as it comes from the machine. This may be due to static electricity. To remedy this difficulty, the operator fastens a strip of tinsel from side to side near the impression roller so that the printed copy just touches the soft stems of the tinsel as it is ejected from the machine, thus grounding the static electricity to the frame of the machine.

4. According to this paragraph,
   (A) turning the drum fast produces light copies.
   (B) stencils should be placed face up on the drum.
   (C) ink pads should be changed daily.
   (D) slip-sheeting is necessary when porous paper is being used.

5. According to this paragraph, when a mimeograph machine is not in use,
   (A) the ink should he drained from the drum.
   (B) the ink pad should be removed.
   (C) the machine should be covered with a protective sheet.
   (D) the counter should be set to zero.

6. According to this paragraph, static electricity is grounded to the frame of the mimeograph machine by means of
   (A) a slip-sheeting device.
   (B) a strip of tinsel.
   (C) an impression roller.
   (D) hooks located at the top of the drum.

Questions 7 and 8 refer to this passage:

The proofreading of material typed from copy is performed more accurately and more speedily when two persons perform this work as a team. The person who did not do the typing should read aloud the original copy while the person who did the typing should check the reading against the typed copy. The reader should speak slowly and distinctly. When reading figures, the reader should speak very slowly and repeat the figures, using a different grouping of numbers when repeating the figures. For example, in reading 1954, the reader may say "one-nine-five-four" on first reading the figure and "nineteen fifty-four" on repeating the figure. The reader should read all punctuation marks, taking nothing for granted. Since mistakes can occur anywhere, everything typed should be proofread. To avoid confusion, the proofreading team should use the standard proofreading marks, which are given in most dictionaries.

7. According to this paragraph,
   (A) the person who holds the typed copy is called the reader.
   (B) the two members of a proofreading team should take turns in reading the typed copy aloud.
   (C) the typed copy should he checked by the person who did the typing.
   (D) the person who did not do the typing should read aloud from the typed copy.

8. According to this paragraph,
   (A) it is unnecessary to read the period at the end of the sentence.
   (B) typographical errors should be noted on the original copy.
   (C) each person should develop his own set of proofreading marks.
   (D) figures should be read twice.

Questions 9 and 10 refer to this passage:

Forms are printed sheets of paper on which information is to be entered. While what is printed on the form is most important, the kind of paper used in making the form is also important. The kind of paper should be selected with regard to the use to which the form will be subjected. Printing a form on an unnecessarily expensive grade of paper is wasteful. On the other hand, using too cheap or flimsy a form can materially interfere with satisfactory performance of the work the form is being planned to do. Thus, a form printed on both sides normally requires a heavier paper than a form printed only on one side. Forms to be used as permanent records, or that are expected to have a very long life in files, require a quality of paper that will not disintegrate or discolor with age. A form that will go through a great deal of handling requires a strong, tough paper, while thinness is a necessary qualification when the making of several carbon copies of a form will be required.

9. According to this paragraph, the type of paper used for making forms
   (A) should be chosen in accordance with the use to which the form will be put.
   (B) should be chosen before the type of printing to be used has been decided upon.
   (C) is as important as the information that is printed on it.
   (D) should be strong enough to be used for any purpose.

10. According to this paragraph, forms that are
    (A) printed on both sides are usually economical and desirable.
    (B) to be filed permanently should not deteriorate as time goes on.
    (C) expected to last for a long time should be handled carefully.
    (D) to be filed should not be printed on inexpensive paper.

Practice Test 3

Directions: *Answer each question on the basis of the information stated or implied in the accompanying reading passage. The answer sheet is on page 50.*

Questions 1 to 6 refer to this passage:

A folder is made of a sheet of heavy paper (manila, kraft, pressboard, or red rope stock) that has been folded once so that the back is about one-half inch higher than the front. Folders are larger than the papers they contain in order to protect them. Two standard folder sizes are "letter size" for papers that are $8\frac{1}{2}$ inches $\times$ 11 inches, and "legal cap" for papers that are $8\frac{1}{2}$ inches $\times$ 13 inches.

Folders are cut across the top in two ways: so that the back is straight (straight-cut), or so that the back has a tab that projects above the top of the folder. Such tabs bear captions that identify the contents of each folder. Tabs vary in width and position. The tabs of a set of folders that are "one-half cut" are half the width of the folder and have only two positions.

"One-third cut" folders have three positions, with each tab occupying a third of the width of the folder. Another standard tabbing is "one-fifth cut," which has five positions. There are also folders with "two-fifths cut," with the tabs in the third and fourth, or fourth and fifth, positions.

1. Of the following, the best title for this passage is
    (A) "Filing Folders."
    (B) "Standard Folder Sizes."
    (C) "The Uses of the Folder."
    (D) "The Use of Tabs."

2. According to this passage, one of the standard folder sizes is called
    (A) kraft cut.
    (B) legal cap.
    (C) one-half cut.
    (D) straight-cut.

3. According to this passage, tabs generally are placed along the
    (A) back of the folder.
    (B) front of the folder.
    (C) left side of the folder.
    (D) right side of the folder.

4. According to this passage, a tab is generally used to
    (A) distinguish between standard folder sizes.
    (B) identify the contents of a folder.
    (C) increase the size of the folder.
    (D) protect the papers within the folder.

5. According to this passage, a folder that is two-fifths cut has
    (A) no tabs.
    (B) two tabs.
    (C) three tabs.
    (D) five tabs.

6. According to this passage, one reason for making folders larger than the papers they contain is that
    (A) only a certain size folder can be made from heavy paper.
    (B) they will protect the papers.
    (C) they will aid in setting up a tab system.
    (D) the back of the folder must be higher than the front.

Questions 7 to 10 refer to this passage:

Typed pages can reflect the simplicity of modern art in a machine age. Lightness and evenness can be achieved by proper layout and balance of typed lines and white space. Instead of solid, cramped masses of uneven, crowded typing, there should be a pleasing balance up and down as well as horizontally.

To have real balance, your page must have a center. The eyes see the center of the sheet slightly above the real center. This is the way both you and the reader see it. Try imagining a line down the center of the page that divides the paper in equal halves. On either side of your paper, white space and blocks of typing need to be similar in size and shape. Although left and right margins should be equal, top and bottom margins need not be as exact. It looks better to hold a bottom border wider than a top margin so that your typing rests upon a cushion of white space. To add interest to the appearance of the page, try making one paragraph between one-half and two-thirds the size of an adjacent paragraph.

Thus, by taking full advantage of your typewriter, the pages that you type will not only be accurate, but will also be attractive.

7. It can be inferred from the passage that the basic importance of proper balancing on a typed page is that proper balancing

(A) makes a typed page a work of modern art.
(B) provides exercise in proper positioning of a typewriter.
(C) increases the amount of typed copy on the paper.
(D) draws greater attention and interest to the page.

8. A reader will tend to see the center of a typed page
(A) somewhat higher than the true center.
(B) somewhat lower than the true center.
(C) on either side of the true center.
(D) about two-thirds of an inch above the true center.

9. Which of the following suggestions is *not* given by the passage?
(A) Bottom margins may be wider than top borders.
(B) Keep all paragraphs approximately the same size.
(C) Divide your page with an imaginary line down the middle.
(D) Side margins should be equalized.

10. Of the following, the best title for this passage is
(A) "Increasing the Accuracy of the Typed Page."
(B) "Determination of Margins for Typed Copy."
(C) "Layout and Balance of the Typed Page."
(D) "How to Take Full Advantage of the Typewriter."

Practice Test 4

Directions: *Answer each question on the basis of the information stated or implied in the accompanying reading passage. The answer sheet is on page 50.*

1. The modern conception of the economic role of the public sector (government), as distinct from the private sector, is that every level of government is a link in the economic process. Government's contribution to political and economic welfare, however, must be evaluated not merely in terms of its technical efficiency, but also in light of its acceptability to a particular society at a particular state of political and economic development. Even in a dictatorship, this principle is formally observed, although the authorities usually destroy the substance by presuming to interpret to the public its collective desires.

   The paragraph best supports the statement that
   (A) it is not true that some levels of government are not links in the economic process.
   (B) all dictatorships observe the same economic principles as other governments.
   (C) all links in the economic process are levels of government.
   (D) the contributions of some levels of government do not need to be evaluated for technical efficiency and acceptability to society.
   (E) no links in the economic process are institutions other than levels of government.

2. All property is classified as either personal property or real property, but not both. In general, if something is classified as personal property, it is transient and transportable in nature, while real property is not. Things such as leaseholds, animals, money, and intangible and other moveable goods are examples of personal property. Permanent buildings and land, on the other hand, are fixed in nature and are not transportable.

   The paragraph best supports the statement that
   (A) if something is classified as personal property, it is not transient and transportable in nature.
   (B) some forms of property are considered to be both personal property and real property.
   (C) permanent buildings and land are real property.
   (D) permanent buildings and land are personal property.
   (E) tangible goods are considered to be real property.

3. The Supreme Court's power to invalidate legislation that violates the Constitution is a strong restriction on the powers of Congress. If an Act of Congress is deemed unconstitutional by the Supreme Court, then the Act is voided. Unlike a presidential veto, which can be overridden by a two-thirds vote of the House and the Senate, a constitutional ruling by the Supreme Court must be accepted by the Congress.

   The paragraph best supports the statement that
   (A) if an Act of Congress is voided, then it has been deemed unconstitutional by the Supreme Court.
   (B) if an Act of Congress has not been voided, then it has not been deemed unconstitutional by the Supreme Court.
   (C) if an Act of Congress has not been deemed unconstitutional by the Supreme Court, then it is voided.
   (D) if an Act of Congress is deemed unconstitutional by the Supreme Court, then it is not voided.
   (E) if an Act of Congress has not been voided, then it has been deemed unconstitutional by the Supreme Court.

4. All child-welfare agencies are organizations that seek to promote the healthy growth and development of children. Supplying or supplementing family income so that parents can maintain a home for their children is usually the first such service to be provided. In addition to programs of general family relief, some special programs for broken families are offered when parental care is temporarily or permanently unavailable.

The paragraph best supports the statement that

(A) it is not true that some organizations that seek to promote the healthy growth and development of children are child-welfare agencies.

(B) some programs offered when parental care is temporarily or permanently unavailable are not special programs for broken families.

(C) it is not true that no special programs for broken families are offered when temporary or permanent parental care is unavailable.

(D) all programs offered when parental care is temporarily or permanently unavailable are special programs for broken families.

(E) some organizations that seek to promote the healthy growth and development of children are not child-welfare agencies.

5. A sanitizer is an agent, usually chemical in nature, that is used in hospitals to reduce the number of microorganisms to a level that has been officially approved as safe. Frequently hospitals use stronger antimicrobial agents to ensure that stringent health standards are met. However, if no dangerous microorganisms that must be destroyed are known to be present in a given environment, then sanitizers are used.

The paragraph best supports the statement that, in a given hospital environment,

(A) if dangerous microorganisms that must be destroyed are known to be present, then sanitizers are used.

(B) if sanitizers are used, then some dangerous microorganisms that must be destroyed are known to be present.

(C) if sanitizers are not used, then no dangerous microorganisms that must be destroyed are known to be present.

(D) if only some dangerous microorganisms are known not to be present, then sanitizers are used.

(E) if sanitizers are not used, then dangerous microorganisms that must be destroyed are known to be present.

6. Explosives are substances or devices capable of producing a volume of rapidly expanding gases that exert a sudden pressure on their surroundings. Chemical explosives are the most commonly used, although there are mechanical and nuclear explosives. All mechanical explosives are devices in which a physical reaction is produced, such as that caused by overloading a container with compressed air. While nuclear explosives are by far the most powerful, all nuclear explosives have been restricted to military weapons.

The paragraph best supports the statement that

(A) all explosives that have been restricted to military weapons are nuclear explosives.

(B) no mechanical explosives are devices in which a physical reaction is produced, such as that caused by overloading a container with compressed air.

(C) some nuclear explosives have not been restricted to military weapons.

(D) all mechanical explosives have been restricted to military weapons.

(E) some devices in which a physical reaction is produced, such as that caused by overloading a container with compressed air, are mechanical explosives.

ANSWER KEY TO PRACTICE TESTS

Reading Test 1

1. **D**
2. **D**
3. **B**
4. **C**
5. **D**

6. **A**
7. **C**
8. **A**
9. **C**
10. **D**

Reading Test 2

1. **B**
2. **C**
3. **A**
4. **A**
5. **C**

6. **B**
7. **C**
8. **D**
9. **A**
10. **B**

Reading Test 3

1. **A**
2. **B**
3. **A**
4. **B**
5. **B**

6. **B**
7. **D**
8. **A**
9. **B**
10. **C**

Reading Test 4

1. **(A)** This answer can be inferred from the first sentence of the paragraph, which states that *every level of government is a link in the economic process.* It can be deduced that its contradictory statement, *some levels of government are not links in the economic process,* cannot be true.

    Response B is not supported by the paragraph because it goes beyond the information given. The third sentence of the paragraph states that a dictatorship observes (at least formally) *one* of the same principles as other governments. It cannot be concluded from this that dictatorships observe more than this one principle in common with other governments.

    Responses C and E represent incorrect interpretations of the information given in the first sentence, which states that *every level of government is a link in the economic process.* It cannot be inferred from this statement that *all links in the economic process are levels of government,* only that some are. We know that the category "all levels of government" is contained in the category "links in the economic process," but we do not know whether other links in the economic process exist that are not levels of government. In regard to response E, it cannot be inferred that *no links in the economic process are institutions other than levels of government,* because that would be the same as saying that all links in the economic process are levels of government.

    Response D is not supported by the passage because the second sentence implies that the contributions of *all* levels of government must be evaluated for technical efficiency and acceptability to society. There is nothing to suggest that the contributions of some levels of society do *not* need to be evaluated.

2. **(C)** The answer can be inferred from information contained in the first, second, and fourth sentences. The first sentence is a disjunction—that is, it presents two mutually exclusive alternatives: *All property is classified as either personal property or real property, but not both*. The second sentence states that *if something is classified as personal property, it is transient and transportable in nature*. The fourth sentence states that *permanent buildings and land … are fixed in nature and are not transportable*. From this it can be concluded that, because permanent buildings and land are not transient and transportable in nature, they are not personal property. In view of the disjunction in the first sentence, it can be seen that they must be real property.

Response A is incorrect because it contradicts the information presented in the second sentence of the paragraph.

Response B is incorrect because it contradicts the first sentence, which states that *all property is classified as either personal property or real property, but not both*.

Response D contradicts the information presented in the second and fourth sentences. The second sentence states that if something is classified as personal property, it is transient and transportable in nature. The fourth sentence indicates that permanent buildings and land do not have these qualities. Therefore, it can be concluded that they are not personal property.

Response E seems to be derived from the third sentence, which says that intangible goods are real property. In fact, the third sentence gives examples of tangible goods that are personal property.

3. **(B)** The essential information from which the answer is to be inferred is contained in the second sentence, which states that if an Act of Congress has been deemed unconstitutional, then it is voided. In response B, we are told that an Act of Congress is not voided; therefore, we can conclude that *it has not been deemed unconstitutional by the Supreme Court*.

Response A is not supported by the paragraph because the paragraph does not indicate whether an Act of Congress is voided *only* when it has been deemed unconstitutional or if it could be voided for other reasons.

Response C, like response A, cannot be inferred from the paragraph because the paragraph does not indicate whether an Act of Congress would be voided if the Supreme Court did not declare it to be unconstitutional.

Responses D and E are incorrect because they both contradict the paragraph.

4. **(C)** The answer can be inferred from the last sentence in the paragraph, which states that *some special programs for broken families are offered when parental care is temporarily or permanently unavailable*. If this statement is true, then its negation, *no special programs for broken families are offered when temporary or permanent parental care is unavailable,* cannot be true.

Response A is incorrect because it contradicts the first sentence of the paragraph.

Responses B and D cannot be validly inferred because the paragraph does not provide sufficient information to support the inferences made. Specifically, for response B, there is insufficient information to determine whether some programs offered when parental care is temporarily or permanently unavailable are *not* special programs for families. As far as response D is concerned, the paragraph does not state that *all* programs offered when parental care is temporarily or permanently unavailable are special programs for broken families.

Response E is wrong because the paragraph states that *all child-welfare agencies are organizations that seek to promote the healthy growth and development of children*. There is no way of knowing from this statement whether there are organizations other than child-welfare agencies that seek to promote the healthy growth and welfare of children.

5. **(E)** The essential information from which the answer can be inferred is contained in the third sentence of the paragraph. An analysis of this sentence reveals that response E is validly inferable because if it were not true that *dangerous microorganisms that must be destroyed are known to be present*, then sanitizers would be used. In response E, we are told that *sanitizers are not used*; therefore, we can conclude that *dangerous microorganisms that must be destroyed are known to be present*.

    Response A is wrong because the paragraph does not definitely state what is done if dangerous microorganisms that must be destroyed are known to be present. It may be that, in such cases, only stronger antimicrobial agents are used.

    Responses B and C are wrong because they run contrary to the information given in the paragraph to the effect that sanitizers are used if no dangerous microorganisms are known to be present.

    Response D is wrong because the information in the paragraph provides no evidence whatsoever about what measures would be adopted if only some (presumably specific) dangerous microorganisms are known not to be present.

6. **(E)** The answer can be validly inferred from the third sentence in the paragraph. This sentence states that *all mechanical explosives are devices in which a physical reaction is produced, such as that caused by overloading a container with compressed air*. From this, we can safely conclude that some devices in which a physical reaction is produced, such as that caused by overloading a container with compressed air, are mechanical explosives.

    Response A cannot be inferred because the paragraph does not provide sufficient information to draw the conclusion that all explosives that have been restricted to military weapons are nuclear weapons. It may be that other explosives that are not nuclear weapons also have been restricted to military weapons.

    Responses B and C are incorrect because they contradict the paragraph.

    Response D is wrong because the paragraph provides no information at all about whether mechanical explosives are restricted to military weapons.

EFFECTIVE EXPRESSION

Because language is a living, active thing, your grasp of correct and effective expression is best measured by a type of question that tests a multitude of grammatical skills. That's why these questions are so very important and useful to you: They draw upon your practical ability to discern and correct errors in grammar, much like those designed to trick you on civil service examinations.

Directions: *In each of the following passages, some portions are underlined and numbered. Corresponding to each numbered portion are three different ways of saying the same thing. Read through each passage quickly to determine the sense of the passage, and then return to the underlined portions. If you feel that an underlined portion is correct and is stated as well as possible, mark letter A, NO CHANGE. If you feel that there is an error in grammar, sentence structure, punctuation, or word usage, choose the correct answer. If an underlined portion appears to be correct, but you believe that one of the alternatives would be more effective, mark that choice. Remember, you are to choose the best answer. The answer sheet to this test is found at the beginning of this chapter.*

Sample Exercise

If a <u>person were to try</u> stripping the disguises from
                    1
actors while they play a scene upon the stage, showing to the

1. A. NO CHANGE
   B. Person were to try
   C. Person was to try
   D. person was to try

audience <u>there real looks</u> and the faces they were
                      2

2. A. NO CHANGE
   B. their real looks
   C. there Real Looks
   D. their "real looks"

<u>born with. Would</u> not such a one spoil the whole play?
        3

3. A. NO CHANGE
   B. born to—would
   C. born. Would
   D. born with, would

Destroy the illusion and <u>any play was ruined.</u>
                          4

4. A. NO CHANGE
   B. any Play was ruined
   C. any play is ruined?
   D. any play is ruined.

Sample Exercise Answer Key

1. **(A)** The passage is correct as shown, and therefore NO CHANGE is the best selection.
2. **(B)** The possessive pronoun is spelled *their*.
3. **(D)** The comma corrects the sentence fragment.
4. **(D)** The present tense *is* is consistent with the present tense *destroy*.

Passage 1

The standardized educational or psychological tests,
<u>that are</u> widely used to aid in selecting, classifying, assign-
 —
1
ing, or <u>promoting students,</u> employees, and military person-
2
nel have been the target of recent attacks in books, maga-
zines, and <u>newspapers that are printed every day.</u> The tar-
3
get is wrong, for in attacking the tests, critics <u>revert atten-</u>
4
<u>tion from</u> the fault that <u>lays with illinformed</u> or incompetent
4   5
users. The tests themselves are merely <u>tools; with</u> character-
6
istics that can be <u>assessed reasonably precise</u> under specified
7
conditions. Whether the results will be valuable, meaning-
less, or even misleading <u>are dependent partly upon</u> the tool
8
itself but largely upon the user.

1. A. NO CHANGE
    B. tests that are
    C. tests, which are
    D. tests; which are

2. A. NO CHANGE
    B. promoting of students
    C. promotion of students
    D. promotion for students

3. A. NO CHANGE
    B. the daily press
    C. newspapers that are published
        daily
    D. the daily newspaper press

4. A. NO CHANGE
    B. revert attention to
    C. divert attention from
    D. avert attention from

5. A. NO CHANGE
    B. lies with poorly-informed
    C. lays with poor-informed
    D. lies with ill-informed

6. A. NO CHANGE
    B. tools with
    C. tools, possessed of
    D. tools; whose

7. A. NO CHANGE
    B. assessed as to its reasonable
        precision
    C. assessed reasonably and with
        precision
    D. assessed with reasonable
        precision

8. A. NO CHANGE
    B. is dependant partly upon
    C. depend partly upon
    D. depends partly upon

Passage 2

The forces that generate conditions conducive to crime and <u>riots, are stronger</u> in urban communities <u>then in rural</u>
        9   10

<u>areas.</u> Urban living is more anonymous <u>living, it</u> often
 10   11
releases the individual from community restraints more com-

mon in <u>tradition, oriented societies</u> <u>But</u> more freedom
               12   13
from constraints and controls also provides greater freedom

to deviate. In the more impersonalized, <u>formally, controlled</u>
                                       14
urban society regulatory orders of conduct are often directed by distant bureaucrats. The police are strangers

<u>which execute</u> these prescriptions on, at worst, an alien sub-
 15

community and, at best, an <u>anonymous and unknown</u> set of
                              16
subjects. Minor offenses in a small town or village are often

handled <u>without resort to</u> official police action. As disput-
         17

able as such action may seem to be, <u>you will find it results</u>
                                18
in fewer recorded violations of the law compared to the city.

9. A. NO CHANGE
   B. rioting, are stronger
   C. riots are more strong
   D. riots are stronger

10. A. NO CHANGE
   B. then in rural communities
   C. than in rural areas
   D. then they are in the country

11. A. NO CHANGE
   B. living. It
   C. living; which
   D. living. Because it

12. A. NO CHANGE
   B. traditional oriented societies
   C. traditionally, oriented societies
   D. tradition-oriented societies

13. A. NO CHANGE
   B. Moreover
   C. Therefore
   D. Besides

14. A. NO CHANGE
   B. formally controlled
   C. formalized controlled
   D. formally-controlled

15. A. NO CHANGE
   B. they execute
   C. executing
   D. who conduct executions of

16. A. NO CHANGE
   B. anonymously unknown
   C. Anonymous
   D. anonymous, unknown

17. A. NO CHANGE
   B. without their having to resort to
   C. without needing
   D. outside the limits of

18. A. NO CHANGE
   B. they say it results
   C. you will say, "It results
   D. it nonetheless results

Passage 3

Human beings are born with a desire to <u>communicate</u>
                                                           19
<u>with</u> other human <u>beings, they</u> satisfy this desire in many
 19   20

ways. A smile communicates <u>a friendly feeling,</u> a clenched
                                          21

<u>fist anger</u>; tears, sorrow. From the first days of life, <u>pain</u>
 22   23
<u>and hunger are expressed by baby's</u> by cries and actions.
                     23

Gradually they add expressions of pleasure and <u>smiling</u> for
                                                        24

a familiar face. Soon they begin to reach out <u>for picking up.</u>
                                                      25

<u>Those people who are human beings</u> also use words to com-
                    26

---

19. A. NO CHANGE
     B. communicate to
     C. communicate about
     D. communicate

20. A. NO CHANGE
     B. beings. They
     C. beings, who
     D. beings which

21. A. NO CHANGE
     B. a friendly, feeling;
     C. friendship,
     D. a friendly feeling;

22. A. NO CHANGE
     B. fist an angry feeling,
     C. fist, anger;
     D. fist, angriness,

23. A. NO CHANGE
     B. babies express pain or hunger
     C. a baby's pain or hunger are expressed
     D. pain and hunger is expressed by babies

24. A. NO CHANGE
     B. smiled
     C. smiles
     D. he may smile

25. A. NO CHANGE
     B. to pick up
     C. and pick up
     D. to be picked up

26. A. NO CHANGE
     B. (BEGIN new paragraph)
        Those people who are human beings
     C. (BEGIN new paragraph)
        Human being babies
     D. (BEGIN new paragraph)
        Human beings

municate. Babies eventually learn the language of <u>there</u>
27
parents. If the parents speak English, the baby will learn

to speak English. If the parents speak Spanish, <u>a Spanish-</u>
28
<u>speaking baby will result.</u> An <u>American baby</u> who is taken
2829
from his natural parents and brought up by foster parents
who speak Chinese, Urdu, Swahili, or any other language

<u>will talk</u> the language of the people around <u>them</u> instead of
3031
English.

Words are important tools of learning. <u>It enables, chil-</u>
32
<u>dren</u> to ask questions and understand the answers; they can
32

tell about their discoveries and <u>to express</u> their likes and
33
dislikes.

Passage 4

A high school diploma by itself is not sufficient preparation for many occupations. <u>But neither is a college degree.</u>
34
Different fields of work require different types of
training. Just as there are occupations that require college

degrees, <u>so to there are</u> occupations for which technical
35

---

27. A.   NO CHANGE
    B.   their
    C.   they're
    D.   OMIT

28. A.   NO CHANGE
    B.   their baby will speak Spanish.
    C.   the baby will learn spanish.
    D.   there baby will speak Spanish.

29. A.   NO CHANGE
    B.   American Baby
    C.   american baby
    D.   american-born baby

30. A.   NO CHANGE
    B.   will be speaking
    C.   will learn
    D.   will talk of

31. A.   NO CHANGE
    B.   him
    C.   themselves
    D.   himself

32. A.   NO CHANGE
    B.   It provides children with the means to
    C.   That makes it possible for children to
    D.   Once children learn to use language they can

33. A.   NO CHANGE
    B.   use it to express
    C.   express
    D.   to talk about

34. A.   NO CHANGE
    B.   Nor a college degree.
    C.   No more a college degree.
    D.   Nor a degree from a four-year college.

35. A.   NO CHANGE
    B.   so to are there
    C.   so too there are
    D.   there are to

training or work experience <u>are the most important</u> entry
                              36
requirement. Employers always wish to hire the best qualified applicants, but this does not mean that the jobs always

go to those applicants <u>which are most educated.</u> The type of
                           37

education and training an individual <u>has had is as important</u>
                                          38
as the amount. For this reason, a vital part of the career

planning process is deciding <u>what kind as well as how much</u>
                                  39
education and training to pursue.

   Persons who have definite career goals may not find this

decision <u>difficult, many</u> occupations have specific edu-
              40
cation requirements. Physicians, for example, must gener-

ally complete at least 3 years of college, <u>4 years of Medical</u>
                                               41
<u>School,</u> and in most states, 1 year of residency. Cosmetolo-
   41
gists are required to complete a state-approved cosmetology
course that generally lasts 18 months. <u>For most people,</u>
                                            42
<u>however,</u> the decision is more difficult. Either they have yet
   42
to choose a field of work, or the field they have selected may
be entered in a variety of ways. Making career decisions
requires not only specific information about the types of
education and training preferred for various occupations,
but also <u>to know one's own</u> abilities and aspirations.
             43

Passage 5

   Everyone has at one time or <u>another</u> felt the need to
                                   44

36. A.   NO CHANGE
    B.   is the most important
    C.   are more important
    D.   are of the utmost importance
         as an

37. A.   NO CHANGE
    B.   that are most educated of all
    C.   that have the most years of
         school
    D.   who have the most education.

38. A.   NO CHANGE
    B.   has had are as important
    C.   have had is important
    D.   had had was as important

39. A.   NO CHANGE
    B.   what kind of as well as how
         much of
    C.   what kind of as well as
         how much
    D.   what and how much

40. A.   NO CHANGE
    B.   difficult. Many
    C.   difficult many
    D.   difficult being that many

41. A.   NO CHANGE
    B.   four years of Medical School
    C.   4 years in Medical School
    D.   4 years of medical school

42. A.   NO CHANGE
    B.   However, for most people
    C.   (Begin new paragraph)
    D.   For most persons, however,

43. A.   NO CHANGE
    B.   a knowledge of one's own
    C.   the knowing of ones' own
    D.   you must know your own

44. A.   NO CHANGE
    B.   the other
    C.   an other
    D.   one other

express <u>himself</u>. What must <u>you</u> do in order to learn to say
     45   46

45. A.   NO CHANGE
     B.   theirself
     C.   themself
     D.   theirselves

46. A.   NO CHANGE
     B.   they
     C.   he
     D.   one

exactly what <u>you want</u> to <u>say.</u> <u>You will have to study</u> <u>very</u>
          47   48   49   50

47. A.   NO CHANGE
     B.   we want
     C.   one wants
     D.   everyone wants

48. A.   NO CHANGE
     B.   say?
     C.   say!
     D.   say:

49. A.   NO CHANGE
     B.   They ought to
     C.   We should
     D.   One must

<u>careful</u> the English language and especially <u>it's</u> <u>grammer.</u>
 50   51   52

50. A.   NO CHANGE
     B.   with care
     C.   carefully (inserted after
         language)
     D.   OMIT

51. A.   NO CHANGE
     B.   its
     C.   its'
     D.   their

52. A.   NO CHANGE
     B.   grammer; some
     C.   grammar. (begin a new
         paragraph with Some)
     D.   grammer. (begin a new
         paragraph with Some)

<u>Some</u> people think that <u>Good English</u> is fancy English, but
 52   53

53. A.   NO CHANGE
     B.   good english
     C.   good English
     D.   English that is good

this contention <u>isnt true</u>. Just because a person uses long
54

words it <u>does not mean that</u> <u>he speaks good</u>. The person
55   56

<u>whom</u> uses simple words and phrases <u>which say</u> exactly
 57   58

what he means is using better English <u>than the</u> individual
                  59

who shows off with <u>hard to understand expressions.</u>
                 60

Passage 6

The <u>most serious threatening</u> to modern <u>human beings it</u>
        61   62
<u>would seem</u> is not physical annihilation but the alleged mean-
 62

54. A. NO CHANGE
    B. isn't true.
    C. aint so.
    D. aren't true.

55. A. NO CHANGE
    B. words, it does not mean that
    C. words, you don't know that
    D. words, he does not necessarily.

56. A. NO CHANGE
    B. he speaks well.
    C. speak correct.
    D. speak well.

57. A. NO CHANGE
    B. who
    C. what
    D. which

58. A. NO CHANGE
    B. what say
    C. which says
    D. who say

59. A. NO CHANGE
    B. from
    C. then
    D. instead of

60. A. NO CHANGE
    B. hard to understand, expressions.
    C. hard-to-understand expressions.
    D. hard-to-understand-expressions.

61. A. NO CHANGE
    B. most seriously threatening
    C. most serious threat
    D. seriously threatening

62. A. NO CHANGE
    B. human beings; it would
         seem that
    C. human beings. It would
         seem that
    D. human beings, it would seem,

inglessness of life. This <u>latent vacuum becomes</u> manifest in
63

a state of boredom. Automation will lead to <u>more and more</u>
64

<u>freer time</u>, and many will not know how to use their <u>liesure</u>
64   65

<u>hours, this</u> is evidenced today by what a prominent psychia-
65

trist refers to as Sunday <u>Neurosis the</u> depression that
66

<u>inflicts people who</u> become conscious of the lack of content
67
in their lives when the rush of the busy week stops. Nothing

in the world helps man to keep healthy <u>so much as the</u>
68

knowledge of a life task. Nietzsche wisely <u>said "he who</u>
69

knows a Why of living <u>surmounts over</u> every How."
70

63. A. NO CHANGE
    B. latent vacuum become
    C. latent vacuum have become
    D. latent vacuole becomes

64. A. NO CHANGE
    B. more freer time
    C. more and more free time
    D. more or less free-time

65. A. NO CHANGE
    B. liesure hours, that
    C. leisure hours, that
    D. leisure hours. This

66. A. NO CHANGE
    B. Neurosis, the
    C. neurosis. The
    D. Neurosis. The

67. A. NO CHANGE
    B. inflicts people whom
    C. afflicts people who
    D. afflicts people whom

68. A. NO CHANGE
    B. so much so
    C. so much that
    D. so much as that

69. A. NO CHANGE
    B. said "He who
    C. said, "he whom
    D. said, "He who

70. A. NO CHANGE
    B. surmounted over
    C. surmounts
    D. surmount

Passage 7

The cynical <u>some times</u> are critical. But <u>I do not know</u>
     71   72

<u>of no more worthy</u> motive or purpose that a <u>human being</u>
   72   73

<u>can have had</u> than <u>to try to lie out</u> as your goal a <u>Program</u>
  73   74   75

<u>that will</u> educate the mind, that will conquer disease <u>in the</u>
  75   76

<u>body. That</u> will permit your children <u>and you're people to</u>
  76   77

live in an atmosphere and <u>an environment of</u> beauty and
            78

culture—and enjoy the better things of life. We cannot

conquer disease, <u>nor we cannot</u> educate all humanity.
       79

71. A. NO CHANGE
  B. some of the times
  C. sometimes
  D. at sometimes

72. A. NO CHANGE
  B. I know of no more worthy
  C. I don't know of no more worthy
  D. I can't know of any more worthy

73. A. NO CHANGE
  B. human being could have had
  C. human being could be going to have
  D. human being can have

74. A. NO CHANGE
  B. to try to layout
  C. trying to lie out
  D. trying to lay out

75. A. NO CHANGE
  B. a "Program" that will
  C. a program, that will
  D. a program that will

76. A. NO CHANGE
  B. in the body; that
  C. in the body, but
  D. in the body, and that

77. A. NO CHANGE
  B. and Your People to
  C. and you are people to
  D. and your people to

78. A. NO CHANGE
  B. environs of
  C. the environs of
  D. environments of

79. A. NO CHANGE
  B. or we cannot
  C. nor we can
  D. nor can we

We can't not have a symphony in every town and we cannot
80   81

80. A. NO CHANGE
     B. We can not
     C. We can't
     D. When can we

81. A. NO CHANGE
     B. symphony in
     C. symphony, in
     D. symphony, in

have a mellon art gallery in every capitol. But we can hope
     82   83   84

82. A. NO CHANGE
     B. a "mellon art gallery"
     C. a Mellon "Art" gallery
     D. a Mellon Art Gallery

83. A. NO CHANGE
     B. every capitol?
     C. every capital.
     D. every capital?

84. A. NO CHANGE
     B. Therefore we
     C. Moreover we
     D. Since we

for these amenities and be working for them, and we can give
                  85

85. A. NO CHANGE
     B. work for them
     C. have them work
     D. keep them working

what we have to them. And we can urge them and provide
         86   87

86. A. NO CHANGE
     B. to them; and we can
     C. to them. We can also
     D. to them. Also we can

87. A. NO CHANGE
     B. encourage them
     C. urge it
     D. encourage development of
          the arts

leadership and ideas and try to move along.
               88

88. A. NO CHANGE
     B. and try to move up.
     C. and try to move them up.
     D. OMIT

Directions: Questions 89 to 100 consist of a single sentence with all or part of the sentence underlined. Following each sentence are four different ways of phrasing the underlined part. Select the one phrasing that makes the sentence both correct and effective. If you feel that there is no error in the original sentence, select NO CHANGE as your answer. Blacken the letter of your choice on the answer sheet.

89. They were very kind to my friend and I.
   A   NO CHANGE
   B.   to my friend and me.
   C.   to me and my friend.
   D.   to both I and my friend.

90. We tried to quickly finish the work.
   A.   NO CHANGE
   B.   We quickly tried to finish the work.
   C.   We tried to finish the work quickly.
   D.   We tried to finish the work quick.

91. People get use to prosperity easily.
   A.   NO CHANGE
   B.   get easily use to prosperity.
   C.   get use to prosperity easy.
   D.   get used to prosperity easily.

92. I saw neither the books or the pencils on the desk.
   A.   NO CHANGE
   B.   I saw neither the books nor the pencils
   C.   I did not see neither the books nor the pencils
   D.   Neither did I see the books or the pencils

93. This is John Smith, the man who I was telling you about yesterday.
   A.   NO CHANGE
   B.   about who I was telling you
   C.   I was telling you about
   D.   about whom I was telling you

94. Is this the book you want me to copy from?
   A.   NO CHANGE
   B.   from what you want me to copy?
   C.   from which you want me to copy?
   D.   from whom you want me to copy?

95. If you disobey traffic regulations, you will loose your driver's license.
   A.   NO CHANGE
   B.   lose your drivers' license.
   C.   lose your driver's license.
   D.   your driver's license lose.

96. The exhausted animal lay there, sick.
   A.   NO CHANGE
   B.   animal lied there,
   C.   animal laid there,
   D.   animal layed there,

97. Was it him that you called yesterday?
   A.   NO CHANGE
   B.   he who you called
   C.   he whom you called
   D.   him who you called

98. I and him went to the football game.
   A.   NO CHANGE
   B.   Him and I went
   C.   He and I went
   D.   He and me went

99. Irregardless of the weather, classes will be held tonight.
   A.   NO CHANGE
   B.   Irregardless what the weather,
   C.   Regardless of the whether,
   D.   Regardless of the weather,

100. Some students believe the sum of the figures should be included in the final averages.
   A.   NO CHANGE
   B.   the some of the figures
   C.   that some of the figures
   D.   that sum of the figures

Answer Key to Practice Test

1. B	21. D	41. D	61. C	81. A
2. A	22. C	42. C	62. D	82. D
3. B	23. B	43. B	63. A	83. C
4. C	24. C	44. A	64. C	84. A
5. D	25. D	45. A	65. D	85. B
6. B	26. D	46. D	66. B	86. C
7. D	27. B	47. C	67. C	87. D
8. D	28. B	48. B	68. A	88. D
9. D	29. A	49. D	69. D	89. B
10. C	30. C	50. D	70. C	90. C
11. B	31. B	51. B	71. C	91. D
12. D	32. D	52. C	72. B	92. B
13. A	33. C	53. C	73. D	93. C
14. B	34. A	54. B	74. D	94. C
15. C	35. C	55. D	75. D	95. C
16. C	36. B	56. D	76. D	96. A
17. A	37. D	57. B	77. D	97. C
18. D	38. A	58. A	78. A	98. C
19. A	39. C	59. A	79. D	99. D
20. B	40. B	60. C	80. C	100. A

Explanatory Answers

1. **(B)** The phrase following *tests* is an essential part of this sentence and should not be set off by commas.

2. **(A)** This is correct.

3. **(B)** The three words *the daily press* say everything that is said by the other, more wordy choices.

4. **(C)** *Divert,* meaning "to turn from one course to another," is the most appropriate choice. *Revert* means "to return," and *avert* means "to turn away or prevent."

5. **(D)** The present tense of the verb *to lie,* meaning "belonging to," is required here.

6. **(B)** It is not necessary to separate the prepositional phrase from the rest of the sentence.

7. **(D)** This is the clearest and least awkward choice.

8. **(D)** The subject of the verb here is implied—the subject is actually the significance of the results. Thus, a singular verb is needed, and choice D gives the only singular verb construction that is spelled correctly.

9. **(D)** Do not use a comma to separate a subject and a verb (except when the subject contains a nonessential clause, an appositive or another phrase that is set off by two commas).

10. **(C)** *Than,* a conjunction, is used after the comparative degree of an adjective or adverb. *Then,* an adverb, means "at that time" or "next."

11. **(B)** To correct this run-on sentence, it is necessary to add a period after *living*. Beginning the next sentence with *Because* creates a sentence fragment rather than a complete sentence.

12. **(D)** Use a hyphen in unit modifiers immediately preceding the word or words modified. *Tradition-oriented* is a unit modifier.

13. **(A)** *But* is correct to indicate a contrasting idea. *Moreover* and *besides* mean "in addition to what has been said." *Therefore* means "for that reason."

14. **(B)** Do not use punctuation between the terms of a unit modifier when the first term is an adverb modifying the second term.

15. **(C)** The participle *executing,* meaning "carrying out," not "putting to death," is the correct word for this sentence. *Which* refers to things, not to people. Choice **(B)** Creates a run-on sentence.

16. **(C)** *Anonymous* means "unknown."

17. **(A)** This is the most concise and correct way to make this statement.

18. **(D)** As written, this sentence illustrates a needless shift in subject (from *action* to *you*), which results in a dangling modifier.

19. **(A)** This is correct.

20. **(B)**   As written, this is a run-on sentence. To correct it, add a period after *beings* and start a new sentence with *They*.

21. **(D)**   Use a semicolon to separate sentence parts of equal rank if one or more of these parts is subdivided by commas.

22. **(C)**   Use a comma to indicate the omission of a word or words. This phrase actually means "a clenched fist (communicates) anger."

23. **(B)**   Avoid the shift from the active to the passive voice. The possessive *baby's* is incorrectly substituted for the plural *babies*.

24. **(C)**   *And* is used to correct similar grammatical elements—in this case, the noun *expressions* and the noun *smiles*.

25. **(D)**   The present infinitive is correct because the action of the infinitive is present or future in relation to the action of the finite verb *begin*.

26. **(D)**   The introduction of a new topic—the use of words to communicate—indicates the need for a new paragraph. *Human beings* are people, so the phrase *Those people who are* is unnecessary.

27. **(B)**   The possessive pronoun needed here is *their*. *There* refers to place, and *they're* is a contraction for *they are*.

28. **(B)**   A comparison is being drawn between English-speaking and Spanish-speaking families. The two sentences that form the comparison should be parallel in structure. *Spanish* is a proper noun and must begin with a capital letter.

29. **(A)**   *American* is a proper noun and should be capitalized; *baby* is merely a noun and, therefore, needs no capital letter.

30. **(C)**   *Talk* means to use *language* for conversing or communicating.

31. **(B)**   The subject of this sentence, which is also the antecedent of the pronoun, is singular (*baby*); therefore, the pronoun must also be singular.

32. **(D)**   Avoid the indefinite use of *it*. In standard written English, *it* requires a stated antecedent for clarity.

33. **(C)**   Items presented in series should be parallel in structure.

34. **(A)**   This is correct.

35. **(C)**   Don't confuse the homonyms *to, two,* and *too*. *To* means "in the direction of." *Two* is the numeral 2. *Too* means "more than" or "also."

36. **(B)**   Use a singular verb (*is*) after two singular subjects (*training, experience*) joined by *or* or *nor*.

37. **(D)**   The relative pronoun *who* refers to persons; *which* refers to animals or things; and *that* refers to persons, animals, or things.

38. **(A)**   This is correct. *Individual* is singular and therefore takes the singular verb form *has had*. *Type* is also singular and therefore takes the singular verb *is*.

39. **(C)**   The preposition *of* is needed after the word *kind*. It is incorrect to say "what kind education."

40. **(B)**   To eliminate the comma splice, add a period after *difficult* and start a new sentence with *Many*. Choice D is incorrect because *being* is a participle, not a conjunction.

41. **(D)**   Capitalize only the name of a specific medical school, not medical schools in general.

42. **(C)**   There is a change in emphasis from people who do not find career decisions difficult to those who do. Such a subject change indicates the need for a new paragraph.

43. **(B)**   The *not only … but also* construction should connect words or phrases of equal rank—in this case, two nouns (*information* and *knowledge*).

44. **(A)**   The idiom is correctly written. *Another* is always one word.

45. **(A)**   *Everyone* is singular; therefore, the pronoun must be singular. Furthermore, none of the incorrect choices is a legitimate word.

46. **(D)**   Avoid use of the word *you* when not addressing a specific person or group of people.

47. **(C)**   As in question 46, avoid the use of *you*.

48. **(B)**   A question must end with a question mark.

49. **(D)**   Again, see question 46.

50. **(D)**   The sentence is incorrect as written because *careful* is an adjective, and an adverb is needed to modify the verb *study*. Choices B and C are correct but awkward. Because studying implies care, no modifying adverb is required.

51. **(B)**   The possessive form of *it* is *its*. *It's* is the contraction for *it is*. *The English language* is singular.

52. **(C)**   The author is introducing a new idea, so a new paragraph is required.

53. **(C)**   *English* is the name of the language, so it must be capitalized. There is no reason to capitalize the adjective *good*. Choice D is verbose.

54. **(B)**   *This contention* is singular, so the singular verb *is* must be used. The correct contraction for *is not* is *isn't*.

55. **(D)**   *It* is an expletive (a pronoun subject with no antecedent). An expletive is always weak, especially when it occurs in the middle of a sentence. Unless a sentence is compound, try to maintain the same subject throughout the sentence, as in choice D.

56. **(D)**   Because the passage continues from choice D of question 55, the subject *he* has already been stated. *Correct* is an adjective and thus cannot modify the verb *speak*.

57. **(B)** *Who* is the subject of the verb *to use. Which* cannot apply to people.

58. **(A)** The subject, *words and phrases,* is plural, requiring use of the plural verb *say. Who* cannot refer to things. *What* is not a relative pronoun.

59. **(A)** *Than* is a pronoun expressing comparison. *Then* is an adverb expressing progression in time.

60. **(C)** *Hard-to-understand* is a made-up adjective, and its parts must be connected by hyphens.

61. **(C)** The noun form needed to serve as the subject of this sentence is *threat,* not *threatening.*

62. **(D)** *It would seem* is used here as a parenthetical expression and thus should be set off from the main part of the sentence by commas.

63. **(A)** This is correct.

64. **(C)** The comparative degree is formed either by adding *-er* to the adjective or by using an expression such as "more and more" before the adjective. Use one of these comparative methods, but not both.

65. **(D)** It is necessary to begin a new sentence after *leisure hours* because a new thought is being introduced.

66. **(B)** A comma is needed to separate the term *Sunday Neurosis* from the appositional phrase that follows. The appositional phrase does not express a complete thought and therefore is not a sentence.

67. **(C)** This sentence requires the verb *afflict,* meaning "to trouble," not *inflict,* which means "to impose." Because *people* is the subject of the verb *become, who,* not *whom,* is correct.

68. **(A)** This is correct.

69. **(D)** When using a direct quotation, use a comma to separate the beginning of the quotation from the preceding phrase. Except in rare cases, the first word of a quotation is capitalized.

70. **(C)** The phrase *surmount over* is repetitive because surmount, means "to overcome." To avoid a switch in verb tense, use the present, *surmounts.*

71. **(C)** *Sometimes* is written as one word.

72. **(B)** All other choices are double negatives.

73. **(D)** All that is needed is a simple present tense.

74. **(D)** The general rule for the verbs *to lie* and *to lay* is this: Use *lay* when you can substitute *put.* One would *put down* a goal.

75. **(D)** No capitalization or punctuation is necessary.

76. **(D)** *That will permit* is the beginning of the final item in a list. *And* precedes the last item in an inclusive list.

77. **(D)** The possessive form of *you* is *your. You're* is the contraction for *you are.* The capital form, as in choice B, is used only when referring to a deity.

78. **(A)** One lives in only one environment.

79. **(D)** Choice D is the correct idiom.

80. **(C)** Choice A constitutes the double negative. *Cannot* would be correct, but it must be written as one word.

81. **(A)** No punctuation or capitalization is necessary.

82. **(D)** Mellon Art Gallery is the name of an art gallery. Each word of a name must begin with a capital letter.

83. **(C)** *The Capitol* is the domed building in Washington, D.C. All other uses of *capital* are spelled *-al.*

84. **(A)** Because this sentence contrasts in tone with the previous sentence, *but* is the correct transition word.

85. **(B)** Choices C and D change the meaning of the sentence. Choice A is verbose.

86. **(C)** Choice A is correct but is confusing in its repeated use of *and.* Choice D would be correct, but a comma would be needed after *also.*

87. **(D)** *Them* refers to *these amenities.* One does not "urge" or "encourage" amenities, nor can one introduce a new pronoun, *it,* without an antecedent. Therefore, choice D is the only correct answer.

88. **(D)** This last clause provides only confusion and verbosity.

89. **(B)** *I* is the nominative case, and the objective case—*me*—is needed.

90. **(C)** The adverb *quickly* should modify the verb *finish,* not the verb *tried.*

91. **(D)** The past participle *used* is required.

92. **(B)** The *neither ... nor* construction is needed.

93. **(C)** Use of a relative pronoun creates wordiness; eliminate this whenever possible.

94. **(C)** Avoid ending sentences with prepositions.

95. **(C)** *Lose* is the correct verb; *loose* means "not tight."

96. **(A)** No change is necessary.

97. **(C)** A predicate nominative *he* is needed after the linking verb *was.*

98. **(C)** The nominative case is needed for a compound subject.

99. **(D)** *Regardless* is correct; *irregardless* is not an accepted word.

100. **(A)** No change is necessary.

VERBAL ANALOGIES

Verbal analogies test your understanding of word meanings and your ability to grasp relationships between words and ideas. There are various classifications of relationships, such as similarity (synonym), opposition (antonym), cause and effect, and sequence. A verbal analogy may be written in mathematical form (CLOCK : TIME :: THERMOMETER : TEMPERATURE) or expressed in words (CLOCK is to TIME as THERMOMETER is to TEMPERATURE).

A verbal analogy has four terms in two pairs. You may be presented with the first complete pair, which establishes the relationship, and the first half of the second pair followed by a list of possible matches. Or, you may be given just the first pair and then a selection of paired terms from which you must find the pair that implies the same relationship as the first pair.

1. Read each question carefully.
2. Establish what the exact relationship is between the two terms in the sample pair.
3. Study the selection of possible answers carefully, and eliminate any pairs that do not share the same relationship as the sample pair.
4. Read the remaining choices through again, this time substituting the key relationship word from the sample pair (for instance, CLOCK *measures* TIME; THERMOMETER *measures* TEMPERATURE).
5. Answer the easy questions first. You can come back to the others later.

Sample Verbal Analogy Questions

WINTER : SUMMER :: COLD : (A) wet (B) future (C) warm (D) freezing

Winter and summer are opposites. Cold and warm are also opposites. Therefore, (C) is correct.
SPELLING : PUNCTUATION :: (A) pajamas : fatigue (B) powder : shaving (C) bandage : cut (D) biology : physics

Spelling and punctuation are parts of the mechanics of English. Biology and physics are parts of the field of science. Therefore, (D) is correct.

Practice Test 1

Directions: In each question, the two capitalized words have a certain relationship to each other. Select the letter of the pair of words that are related in the same way as the two capitalized words. The sample answer sheet is found at the beginning of Part 2.

1. INTIMIDATE : FEAR ::
   (A) maintain : satisfaction
   (B) astonish : wonder
   (C) sooth : concern
   (D) feed : hunger

2. STOVE : KITCHEN ::
   (A) window : bedroom
   (B) sink : bathroom
   (C) television : living room
   (D) trunk : attic

141

3. CELEBRATE : MARRIAGE ::
   (A) announce : birthday
   (B) report : injury
   (C) lament : bereavement
   (D) face : penalty

4. MARGARINE : BUTTER ::
   (A) cream : milk
   (B) lace : cotton
   (C) nylon : silk
   (D) egg : chicken

5. NEGLIGENT : REQUIREMENT ::
   (A) careful : position
   (B) remiss : duty
   (C) cautious : injury
   (D) cogent : task

6. GAZELLE : SWIFT ::
   (A) horse : slow
   (B) wolf : sly
   (C) swan : graceful
   (D) elephant : gray

7. IGNOMINY : DISLOYALTY ::
   (A) fame : heroism
   (B) castigation : praise
   (C) death : victory
   (D) approbation : consecration

8. SATURNINE : MERCURIAL ::
   (A) Saturn : Venus
   (B) Apennines : Alps
   (C) redundant : wordy
   (D) allegro : adagio

9. ORANGE : MARMALADE ::
   (A) potato : vegetable
   (B) jelly : jam
   (C) tomato : ketchup
   (D) cake : picnic

10. BANISH : APOSTATE ::
   (A) reward : traitor
   (B) welcome : ally
   (C) remove : result
   (D) avoid : truce

Practice Test 2

Directions: *In each question, the two capitalized words have a certain relationship to each other. Select the letter of the pair of words that are related in the same way as the two capitalized words. The sample answer sheet is found at the beginning Part 2.*

1. CIRCLE : SPHERE ::
   (A) square : triangle
   (B) balloon : jet plane
   (C) heaven : hell
   (D) wheel : orange

2. OPEN : SECRETIVE ::
   (A) mystery : detective
   (B) tunnel : toll
   (C) forthright : snide
   (D) better : best

3. AFFIRM : HINT ::
   (A) say : deny
   (B) assert : convince
   (C) confirm : reject
   (D) charge : insinuate

4. THROW : BALL ::
   (A) kill : bullet
   (B) shoot : gun
   (C) question : answer
   (D) hit : run

5. SPEEDY : GREYHOUND ::
   (A) innocent : lamb
   (B) animate : animal
   (C) voracious : tiger
   (D) sluggish : sloth

6. TRIANGLE : PYRAMID ::
   (A) cone : circle
   (B) corner : angle
   (C) square : box
   (D) pentagon : quadrilateral

7. IMPEACH : DISMISS ::
- (A) arraign : convict
- (B) exonerate : charge
- (C) imprison : jail
- (D) plant : reap

8. EMULATE : MIMIC ::
- (A) slander : defame
- (B) praise : flatter
- (C) aggravate : promote
- (D) complain : condemn

9. HAND : NAIL ::
- (A) paw : claw
- (B) foot : toe
- (C) head : hair
- (D) ear : nose

10. SQUARE : DIAMOND ::
- (A) cube : sugar
- (B) circle : ellipse
- (C) innocence : jewelry
- (D) pentangle : square

Practice Test 3

Directions: *In each question, the two capitalized words have a certain relationship to each other. Select the letter of the pair of words that are related in the same way as the two capitalized words. The sample answer sheet is found at the beginning of Part 2.*

1. WOODSMAN : AXE ::
- (A) mechanic : wrench
- (B) carpenter : saw
- (C) draftsman : ruler
- (D) doctor : prescription

2. BIGOTRY : HATRED ::
- (A) sweetness : bitterness
- (B) segregation : integration
- (C) fanaticism : intolerance
- (D) sugar : grain

3. ASSIST : SAVE ::
- (A) request : command
- (B) rely : descry
- (C) hurt : aid
- (D) declare : deny

4. 2 : 5 ::
- (A) 5 : 7
- (B) 6 : 17
- (C) 6 : 15
- (D) 5 : 14

5. DOUBLEHEADER : TRIDENT ::
- (A) twins : troika
- (B) ballgame : three bagger
- (C) chewing gum : toothpaste
- (D) freak : zoo

6. BOUQUET : FLOWER ::
- (A) key : door
- (B) air : balloon
- (C) skin : body
- (D) chain : link

7. LETTER : WORD ::
- (A) club : people
- (B) homework : school
- (C) page : book
- (D) product : factory

8. 36 : 4 ::
- (A) 3 : 27
- (B) 9 : 1
- (C) 12 : 4
- (D) 5 : 2

9. GERM : DISEASE ::
- (A) trichinosis : pork
- (B) men : woman
- (C) doctor : medicine
- (D) war : destruction

10. WAVE : CREST ::
- (A) pinnacle : nadir
- (B) mountain : peak
- (C) sea : ocean
- (D) breaker : swimming

Practice Test 4

Directions: In each question, the two capitalized words have a certain relationship to each other. Select the letter of the pair of words that are related in the same way as the two capitalized words. The sample answer sheet is found at the beginning of Part 2.

1. CONTROL : ORDER ::
   (A) joke : clown
   (B) teacher : pupil
   (C) disorder : climax
   (D) anarchy : chaos

2. WOOD : CARVE ::
   (A) trees : sway
   (B) paper : burn
   (C) clay : mold
   (D) pipe : blow

3. STATE : BORDER ::
   (A) nation : state
   (B) property : fence
   (C) Idaho : Montana
   (D) planet : satellite

4. SOLDIER : REGIMENT ::
   (A) navy : army
   (B) lake : river
   (C) star : constellation
   (D) amphibian : frog

5. APOGEE : PERIGEE ::
   (A) dog : pedigree
   (B) opposite : composite
   (C) inappropriate : apposite
   (D) effigy : statue

6. ASYLUM : REFUGEE ::
   (A) flight : escape
   (B) destination : traveler
   (C) lunatic : insanity
   (D) accident : injury

7. WORRIED : HYSTERICAL ::
   (A) hot : cold
   (B) happy : ecstatic
   (C) lonely : crowded
   (D) happy : serious

8. WORD : CHARADE ::
   (A) phrase : act
   (B) idea : philosophy
   (C) fun : party
   (D) message : code

9. PLAYER : TEAM ::
   (A) fawn : doe
   (B) book : story
   (C) ball : bat
   (D) fish : school

10. BANANA : BUNCH ::
   (A) city : state
   (B) world : earth
   (C) president : nation
   (D) people : continent

Practice Test 5

Directions: *In each question, the two capitalized words have a certain relationship to each other. Select the letter of the pair of words that are related in the same way as the two capitalized words. The sample answer sheet is found at the beginning of Part 2.*

1. MOTH : CLOTHING ::
(A) egg : larva
(B) suit : dress
(C) hole : repair
(D) stigma : reputation

2. LINCOLN : NEBRASKA ::
(A) Washington : D.C.
(B) Trenton : New Jersey
(C) New York : U.S.
(D) Chicago : New York

3. BUZZ : HUM ::
(A) noise : explosion
(B) reverberation : peal
(C) tinkle : clang
(D) echo : sound

4. BOXER : GLOVES ::
(A) swimmer : water
(B) bacteriologist : microscope
(C) businessman : bills
(D) fruit : peddler

5. DECISION : CONSIDERATION ::
(A) gift : party
(B) plea : request
(C) fulfillment : wish
(D) conference : constitution

6. ILLUSION : MIRAGE ::
(A) haunter : specter
(B) imagination : concentration
(C) dream : reality
(D) mirror : glass

7. FRANCE : EUROPE ::
(A) Australia : New Zealand
(B) Paris : France
(C) Israel : Egypt
(D) Algeria : Africa

8. INSULT : INVULNERABLE ::
(A) success : capable
(B) poverty : miserable
(C) purchase : refundable
(D) assault : impregnable

9. POISON : DEATH ::
(A) book : pages
(B) music : violin
(C) kindness : cooperation
(D) life : famine

10. ROCK : SLATE ::
(A) wave : sea
(B) boat : kayak
(C) swimmer : male
(D) lifeguard : beach

Answer Key to Practice Tests

Test 1

1. **(B)** To intimidate is to inspire fear; to astonish is to inspire wonder.

2. **(B)** A stove is often part of a kitchen; a sink is often part of a bathroom.

3. **(C)** You happily celebrate a marriage; you sorrowfully lament a bereavement.

4. **(C)** Margarine is a manufactured substitute for butter; nylon is a manufactured substitute for silk.

5. **(B)** A person may be negligent in meeting a requirement; he may similarly be remiss in performing his duty.

6. **(C)** A gazelle is known to be swift; a swan is known to be graceful.

7. **(A)** One falls into ignominy if he shows disloyalty; one gains fame if he shows heroism.

8. **(D)** *Saturnine* and *mercurial* are antonyms; so are *allegro* and *adagio*.

9. **(C)** Marmalade is made from oranges; ketchup is made from tomatoes.

10. **(B)** An apostate is banished (sent away); an ally is welcomed (brought in).

Test 2

1. **(D)** All four are round: circle, sphere, wheel, and orange.

2. **(C)** *Open* is the opposite of *secretive*; *forthright* is the opposite of *snide*.

3. **(D)** When you affirm, you are direct; when you hint, you are indirect. When you charge, you are direct; when you insinuate, you are indirect.

4. **(B)** One throws a ball; one shoots a gun.

5. **(D)** A greyhound is proverbially speedy; on the other hand, a sloth is proverbially sluggish.

6. **(C)** A triangle is a three-sided plane figure; a pyramid is a three-sided solid figure. A square is a four-sided plane figure; a box is a four-sided solid figure.

7. **(A)** To impeach is to charge or challenge; if the impeachment proceedings are successful, the charged person is dismissed. To arraign is to call into court as a result of accusation; if the accusation is proved correct, the arraigned person is convicted.

8. **(B)** To emulate is to imitate another person's good points; to mimic is to imitate everything about another person. To praise is to speak well of another person's good points; to flatter is to praise everything about another person.

9. **(A)** For people, the horny sheaths at the end of the hand are called nails; for animals, the horny sheaths at the end of the paws are called claws.

10. **(B)** A diamond is a partially compressed square; an ellipse is a partially compressed circle.

Test 3

1. **(B)** A woodsman cuts with an axe; a carpenter cuts with a saw.

2. **(C)** Bigotry breeds hatred; fanaticism breeds intolerance.

3. **(A)** When you assist, you help; when you save, you help a great deal. When you request, you ask; when you command, you are very strong in what you ask for.

4. **(C)** $2\frac{1}{2} \times 2 = 5; 2\frac{1}{2} \times 6 = 15$

5. **(A)** A doubleheader has two parts; a trident has three teeth. Twins are two of a kind; a troika is a vehicle drawn by three horses.

6. **(D)** A flower is part of a bouquet; a link is part of a chain.

7. **(C)** Letters make up a word; pages make up a book.

8. **(B)** $36 \div 9 = 4; 9 \div 9 = 1$

9. **(D)** A germ often causes disease; a war often causes destruction.

10. **(B)** The top of the wave is the crest; the top of the mountain is the peak.

Test 4

1. **(D)** Control results in order; anarchy results in chaos.

2. **(C)** One creates something by carving wood; one creates something by molding clay.

3. **(B)** A border separates one state from another; a fence separates one property from another.

4. **(C)** A soldier is part of a regiment; a star is part of a constellation.

5. **(C)** *Apogee* and *perigee* are opposites, as are *inappropriate* and *apposite*.

6. **(B)** A refugee seeks asylum; a traveler seeks a destination.

7. **(B)** One who is greatly worried may become hysterical; one who is very happy may well be ecstatic.

8. **(D)** A word may be disguised by a charade; a message may be disguised by a code.

9. **(D)** A player is part of a team; a fish is part of a school.

10. **(A)** A banana is one of several bananas in a bunch; a city is one of several cities in a state.

Test 5

1. **(D)** A moth will injure clothing; a stigma will injure a reputation.

2. **(B)** Lincoln is the capital of Nebraska; Trenton is the capital of New Jersey.

3. **(C)** The words *buzz* and *hum* are onomatopoetic, as are the words *tinkle* and *clang*.

4. **(B)** A boxer uses gloves in his profession; a bacteriologist uses a microscope in his profession.

5. **(C)** Consideration is a likely preliminary before making a decision; a wish is preliminary to the fulfillment of that wish.

6. **(A)** An illusion is a mirage; a haunter is a specter.

7. **(D)** France is a country in Europe; Algeria is a country in Africa.

8. **(D)** A person who is invulnerable cannot be hurt by an insult; a city that is impregnable cannot be hurt by an assault.

9. **(C)** Poison often results in death; kindness often results in cooperation.

10. **(B)** Slate is a type of rock; a kayak is a type of boat.

THREE

Arithmetic Ability

CONTENTS

Arithmetic Ability Answer Sheet

Fractions

1. Ⓐ Ⓑ Ⓒ Ⓓ	5. Ⓐ Ⓑ Ⓒ Ⓓ	9. Ⓐ Ⓑ Ⓒ Ⓓ	13. Ⓐ Ⓑ Ⓒ Ⓓ	17. Ⓐ Ⓑ Ⓒ Ⓓ
2. Ⓐ Ⓑ Ⓒ Ⓓ	6. Ⓐ Ⓑ Ⓒ Ⓓ	10. Ⓐ Ⓑ Ⓒ Ⓓ	14. Ⓐ Ⓑ Ⓒ Ⓓ	18. Ⓐ Ⓑ Ⓒ Ⓓ
3. Ⓐ Ⓑ Ⓒ Ⓓ	7. Ⓐ Ⓑ Ⓒ Ⓓ	11. Ⓐ Ⓑ Ⓒ Ⓓ	15. Ⓐ Ⓑ Ⓒ Ⓓ	19. Ⓐ Ⓑ Ⓒ Ⓓ
4. Ⓐ Ⓑ Ⓒ Ⓓ	8. Ⓐ Ⓑ Ⓒ Ⓓ	12. Ⓐ Ⓑ Ⓒ Ⓓ	16. Ⓐ Ⓑ Ⓒ Ⓓ	20. Ⓐ Ⓑ Ⓒ Ⓓ

Decimals

1. Ⓐ Ⓑ Ⓒ Ⓓ	4. Ⓐ Ⓑ Ⓒ Ⓓ	7. Ⓐ Ⓑ Ⓒ Ⓓ	10. Ⓐ Ⓑ Ⓒ Ⓓ	13. Ⓐ Ⓑ Ⓒ Ⓓ
2. Ⓐ Ⓑ Ⓒ Ⓓ	5. Ⓐ Ⓑ Ⓒ Ⓓ	8. Ⓐ Ⓑ Ⓒ Ⓓ	11. Ⓐ Ⓑ Ⓒ Ⓓ	14. Ⓐ Ⓑ Ⓒ Ⓓ
3. Ⓐ Ⓑ Ⓒ Ⓓ	6. Ⓐ Ⓑ Ⓒ Ⓓ	9. Ⓐ Ⓑ Ⓒ Ⓓ	12. Ⓐ Ⓑ Ⓒ Ⓓ	15. Ⓐ Ⓑ Ⓒ Ⓓ

Percents

1. Ⓐ Ⓑ Ⓒ Ⓓ	4. Ⓐ Ⓑ Ⓒ Ⓓ	7. Ⓐ Ⓑ Ⓒ Ⓓ	10. Ⓐ Ⓑ Ⓒ Ⓓ	13. Ⓐ Ⓑ Ⓒ Ⓓ
2. Ⓐ Ⓑ Ⓒ Ⓓ	5. Ⓐ Ⓑ Ⓒ Ⓓ	8. Ⓐ Ⓑ Ⓒ Ⓓ	11. Ⓐ Ⓑ Ⓒ Ⓓ	14. Ⓐ Ⓑ Ⓒ Ⓓ
3. Ⓐ Ⓑ Ⓒ Ⓓ	6. Ⓐ Ⓑ Ⓒ Ⓓ	9. Ⓐ Ⓑ Ⓒ Ⓓ	12. Ⓐ Ⓑ Ⓒ Ⓓ	15. Ⓐ Ⓑ Ⓒ Ⓓ

Graphs

1. Ⓐ Ⓑ Ⓒ Ⓓ	4. Ⓐ Ⓑ Ⓒ Ⓓ	7. Ⓐ Ⓑ Ⓒ Ⓓ	10. Ⓐ Ⓑ Ⓒ Ⓓ	13. Ⓐ Ⓑ Ⓒ Ⓓ
2. Ⓐ Ⓑ Ⓒ Ⓓ	5. Ⓐ Ⓑ Ⓒ Ⓓ	8. Ⓐ Ⓑ Ⓒ Ⓓ	11. Ⓐ Ⓑ Ⓒ Ⓓ	14. Ⓐ Ⓑ Ⓒ Ⓓ
3. Ⓐ Ⓑ Ⓒ Ⓓ	6. Ⓐ Ⓑ Ⓒ Ⓓ	9. Ⓐ Ⓑ Ⓒ Ⓓ	12. Ⓐ Ⓑ Ⓒ Ⓓ	15. Ⓐ Ⓑ Ⓒ Ⓓ

Ratio and Proportion

1. Ⓐ Ⓑ Ⓒ Ⓓ	4. Ⓐ Ⓑ Ⓒ Ⓓ	7. Ⓐ Ⓑ Ⓒ Ⓓ	10. Ⓐ Ⓑ Ⓒ Ⓓ	13. Ⓐ Ⓑ Ⓒ Ⓓ
2. Ⓐ Ⓑ Ⓒ Ⓓ	5. Ⓐ Ⓑ Ⓒ Ⓓ	8. Ⓐ Ⓑ Ⓒ Ⓓ	11. Ⓐ Ⓑ Ⓒ Ⓓ	14. Ⓐ Ⓑ Ⓒ Ⓓ
3. Ⓐ Ⓑ Ⓒ Ⓓ	6. Ⓐ Ⓑ Ⓒ Ⓓ	9. Ⓐ Ⓑ Ⓒ Ⓓ	12. Ⓐ Ⓑ Ⓒ Ⓓ	15. Ⓐ Ⓑ Ⓒ Ⓓ

Work Problems

1. Ⓐ Ⓑ Ⓒ Ⓓ	3. Ⓐ Ⓑ Ⓒ Ⓓ	5. Ⓐ Ⓑ Ⓒ Ⓓ	7. Ⓐ Ⓑ Ⓒ Ⓓ	9. Ⓐ Ⓑ Ⓒ Ⓓ
2. Ⓐ Ⓑ Ⓒ Ⓓ	4. Ⓐ Ⓑ Ⓒ Ⓓ	6. Ⓐ Ⓑ Ⓒ Ⓓ	8. Ⓐ Ⓑ Ⓒ Ⓓ	10. Ⓐ Ⓑ Ⓒ Ⓓ

Tabular Completion

1. Ⓐ Ⓑ Ⓒ Ⓓ Ⓔ   6. Ⓐ Ⓑ Ⓒ Ⓓ Ⓔ   11. Ⓐ Ⓑ Ⓒ Ⓓ Ⓔ   16. Ⓐ Ⓑ Ⓒ Ⓓ Ⓔ   21. Ⓐ Ⓑ Ⓒ Ⓓ Ⓔ

2. Ⓐ Ⓑ Ⓒ Ⓓ Ⓔ   7. Ⓐ Ⓑ Ⓒ Ⓓ Ⓔ   12. Ⓐ Ⓑ Ⓒ Ⓓ Ⓔ   17. Ⓐ Ⓑ Ⓒ Ⓓ Ⓔ   22. Ⓐ Ⓑ Ⓒ Ⓓ Ⓔ

3. Ⓐ Ⓑ Ⓒ Ⓓ Ⓔ   8. Ⓐ Ⓑ Ⓒ Ⓓ Ⓔ   13. Ⓐ Ⓑ Ⓒ Ⓓ Ⓔ   18. Ⓐ Ⓑ Ⓒ Ⓓ Ⓔ   23. Ⓐ Ⓑ Ⓒ Ⓓ Ⓔ

4. Ⓐ Ⓑ Ⓒ Ⓓ Ⓔ   9. Ⓐ Ⓑ Ⓒ Ⓓ Ⓔ   14. Ⓐ Ⓑ Ⓒ Ⓓ Ⓔ   19. Ⓐ Ⓑ Ⓒ Ⓓ Ⓔ   24. Ⓐ Ⓑ Ⓒ Ⓓ Ⓔ

5. Ⓐ Ⓑ Ⓒ Ⓓ Ⓔ   10. Ⓐ Ⓑ Ⓒ Ⓓ Ⓔ   15. Ⓐ Ⓑ Ⓒ Ⓓ Ⓔ   20. Ⓐ Ⓑ Ⓒ Ⓓ Ⓔ   25. Ⓐ Ⓑ Ⓒ Ⓓ Ⓔ

Arithmetic Reasoning

1. Ⓐ Ⓑ Ⓒ Ⓓ Ⓔ   3. Ⓐ Ⓑ Ⓒ Ⓓ Ⓔ   5. Ⓐ Ⓑ Ⓒ Ⓓ Ⓔ   7. Ⓐ Ⓑ Ⓒ Ⓓ Ⓔ   9. Ⓐ Ⓑ Ⓒ Ⓓ Ⓔ

2. Ⓐ Ⓑ Ⓒ Ⓓ Ⓔ   4. Ⓐ Ⓑ Ⓒ Ⓓ Ⓔ   6. Ⓐ Ⓑ Ⓒ Ⓓ Ⓔ   8. Ⓐ Ⓑ Ⓒ Ⓓ Ⓔ   10. Ⓐ Ⓑ Ⓒ Ⓓ Ⓔ

FRACTIONS

Fractions and Mixed Numbers

1. A **fraction** is part of a unit.

   a. A fraction has a **numerator** and a **denominator**.

   Example: In the fraction $\frac{3}{4}$, 3 is the numerator and 4 is the denominator.

   b. In any fraction, the numerator is being divided by the denominator.

   Example: The fraction $\frac{2}{7}$ indicates that 2 is being divided by 7.

   c. In a fraction problem, the whole quantity is 1, which may be expressed by a fraction in which the numerator and denominator are the same number.

   Example: If the problem involves $\frac{1}{8}$ of a quantity, then the whole quantity is $\frac{8}{8}$, or 1.

2. A **mixed number** is an integer together with a fraction, such as $2\frac{3}{5}$, $7\frac{3}{8}$, and so on. The integer is the integral part, and the fraction is the fractional part.

3. An **improper fraction** is one in which the numerator is equal to or greater than the denominator, such as $\frac{19}{6}$, $\frac{25}{4}$, or $\frac{10}{10}$.

4. To change a mixed number to an improper fraction:
   a. Multiply the denominator of the fraction by the integer.
   b. Add the numerator to this product.
   c. Place this sum over the denominator of the fraction.

   Illustration: Change $3\frac{4}{7}$ to an improper fraction.

   SOLUTION:
   $$7 \times 3 = 21$$
   $$21 + 4 = 25$$
   $$3\frac{4}{7} = \frac{25}{7}$$

   Answer: $\frac{25}{7}$

5. To change an improper fraction to a mixed number:
   a. Divide the numerator by the denominator. The quotient, disregarding the remainder, is the integral part of the mixed number.
   b. Place the remainder, if any, over the denominator. This is the fractional part of the mixed number.

Illustration: Change $\frac{36}{13}$ to a mixed number.

SOLUTION:

$$
\begin{array}{r}
2 \\
13\,\overline{)\,36} \\
\underline{26} \\
10 \quad \text{remainder}
\end{array}
$$

$$\frac{36}{13} = 2\frac{10}{13}$$

Answer: $2\frac{10}{13}$

6. The numerator and the denominator of a fraction may be changed by multiplying both by the same number, without affecting the value of the fraction.

   Example: The value of the fraction $\frac{2}{5}$ will not be altered if the numerator and the denominator are multiplied by 2, to result in $\frac{4}{10}$.

7. The numerator and the denominator of a fraction may be changed by dividing both by the same number, without affecting the value of the fraction. This process is called **reducing the fraction**. A fraction that has been reduced as much as possible is said to be in **lowest terms**.

   Example: The value of the fraction $\frac{3}{12}$ will not be altered if the numerator and denominator are divided by 3, to result in $\frac{1}{4}$.

   Example: If $\frac{6}{30}$ is reduced to lowest terms (by dividing both numerator and denominator by 6), the result is $\frac{1}{5}$.

8. As a final answer to a problem:
   a. Improper fractions should be changed to mixed numbers.
   b. Fractions should be reduced as far as possible.

Addition of Fractions

9. Fractions cannot be added unless the denominators are all the same.
   a. If the denominators are the same, add all the numerators and place this sum over the common denominator. In the case of mixed numbers, follow the previous rule for the fractions, and then add the integers.

   Example: The sum of $2\frac{3}{8} + 3\frac{1}{8} + \frac{3}{8} = 5\frac{7}{8}$.

   b. If the denominators are not the same, then in order to be added, the fractions must be converted to ones having the same denominator. To do this, it is first necessary to find the lowest common denominator.

10. The **lowest common denominator** (henceforth called the L.C.D.) is the lowest number that can be divided evenly by all the given denominators. If no two of the given denominators can be divided by the same number, then the L.C.D. is the product of all the denominators.

Example: The L.C.D. of $\frac{1}{2}$, $\frac{1}{3}$, and $\frac{1}{5}$ is $2 \times 3 \times 5 = 30$.

11. To find the L.C.D. when two or more of the given denominators can be divided by the same number:
   a.   Write down the denominators, leaving plenty of space between the numbers.
   b.   Select the smallest number (other than 1) by which one or more of the denominators can be divided evenly.
   c.   Divide the denominators by this number, copying down those that cannot be divided evenly. Place this number to one side.
   d.   Repeat this process, placing each divisor to one side until there are no longer any denominators that can be divided evenly by any selected number.
   e.   Multiply all the divisors and find the L.C.D.

Illustration: Find the L.C.D. of $\frac{1}{5}$, $\frac{1}{7}$, $\frac{1}{10}$, and $\frac{1}{14}$.

SOLUTION:

$$
\begin{array}{r|cccc}
2 & 5 & 7 & 10 & 14 \\ \hline
5 & 5 & 7 & 5 & 7 \\ \hline
7 & 1 & 7 & 1 & 7 \\ \hline
  & 1 & 1 & 1 & 1 \\
\end{array}
$$

$7 \times 5 \times 2 = 70$

Answer: The L.C.D. is 70.

12. To add fractions having different denominators:
   a.   Find the L.C.D. of the denominators.
   b.   Change each fraction to an equivalent fraction that has the L.C.D. as its denominator.
   c.   When all the fractions have the same denominator, they may be added, as in the example following item 9a.

Illustration: Add $\frac{1}{4}$, $\frac{3}{10}$, and $\frac{2}{5}$.

SOLUTION: Find the L.C.D.:

$$
\begin{array}{r|ccc}
2 & 4 & 10 & 5 \\ \hline
2 & 2 & 5 & 5 \\ \hline
5 & 1 & 5 & 5 \\ \hline
  & 1 & 1 & 1 \\
\end{array}
$$

L.C.D. $= 2 \times 2 \times 5 = 20$

$$
\begin{array}{rcl}
\frac{1}{4} & = & \frac{5}{20} \\[6pt]
\frac{3}{10} & = & \frac{6}{20} \\[6pt]
+\frac{2}{5} & = & +\frac{8}{20} \\ \hline
 & & \frac{19}{20}
\end{array}
$$

Answer: $\frac{19}{20}$

13. To add mixed numbers in which the fractions have different denominators, add the fractions by following the rules in item 12, and then add the integers.

Illustration: Add $2\frac{5}{7}$, $5\frac{1}{2}$, and 8.

SOLUTION: L.C.D. = 14

$$
\begin{aligned}
2\tfrac{5}{7} &= 2\tfrac{10}{14} \\
5\tfrac{1}{2} &= 5\tfrac{7}{14} \\
+\,8 &= +\,8 \\
\hline
15\tfrac{17}{14} &= 16\tfrac{3}{14}
\end{aligned}
$$

Answer: $16\frac{3}{14}$

Subtraction of Fractions

14. a. Unlike addition, which may involve adding more than two numbers at the same time, subtraction involves only two numbers.

b. In subtraction, as in addition, the denominators must be the same.

15. To subtract fractions:

a. Find the L.C.D.

b. Change both fractions so that each has the L.C.D. as the denominator.

c. Subtract the numerator of the second fraction from the numerator of the first, and place this difference over the L.C.D.

d. Reduce, if possible.

Illustration: Find the difference of $\frac{5}{8}$ and $\frac{1}{4}$.

SOLUTION: L.C.D. = 8

$$
\begin{aligned}
\tfrac{5}{8} &= \tfrac{5}{8} \\
-\,\tfrac{1}{4} &= -\,\tfrac{2}{8} \\
\hline
&\quad\ \tfrac{3}{8}
\end{aligned}
$$

Answer: $\frac{3}{8}$

16. To subtract mixed numbers:

a. It may be necessary to "borrow" so that the fractional part of the first term is larger than the fractional part of the second term.

b. Subtract the fractional parts of the mixed numbers, and reduce.

c. Subtract the integers.

Illustration: Subtract $16\frac{4}{5}$ from $29\frac{1}{3}$.

SOLUTION: L.C.D. = 15

$$29\frac{1}{3} = 29\frac{5}{15}$$

$$-16\frac{4}{5} = -16\frac{12}{15}$$

Note that $\frac{5}{15}$ is less than $\frac{12}{15}$. Borrow 1 from 29, and change to $\frac{15}{15}$.

$$29\frac{5}{15} = 28\frac{20}{15}$$

$$-16\frac{12}{15} = -16\frac{12}{15}$$

$$12\frac{8}{15}$$

Answer: $12\frac{8}{15}$

Multiplication of Fractions

17.   a.   To be multiplied, fractions need not have the same denominators.

       b.   A whole number has the denominator of 1 understood.

18.   To multiply fractions:

       a.   Change the mixed numbers, if any, to improper fractions.

       b.   Multiply all the numerators, and place this product over the product of the denominators.

       c.   Reduce, if possible.

Illustration: Multiply $\frac{2}{3} \times 2\frac{4}{7} \times \frac{5}{9}$.

SOLUTION:

$$2\frac{4}{7} = \frac{18}{7}$$

$$\frac{2}{3} \times \frac{18}{7} \times \frac{5}{9} = \frac{180}{189}$$

$$= \frac{20}{21}$$

Answer: $\frac{20}{21}$

19.   a.   **Cancellation** is a device to facilitate multiplication. To cancel means to divide a numerator and a denominator by the same number in a multiplication problem.

Example: In the problem $\frac{4}{7} \times \frac{5}{6}$, the numerator 4 and the denominator 6 may be divided by 2.

$$\frac{\overset{2}{\cancel{4}}}{7} \times \frac{5}{\underset{3}{\cancel{6}}} = \frac{10}{21}$$

       b.   The word "of" is often used to mean "multiply."

Example: $\frac{1}{2}$ of $\frac{1}{2} = \frac{1}{2} \times \frac{1}{2} = \frac{1}{4}$

20. To multiply a whole number by a mixed number:
   a.   Multiply the whole number by the fractional part of the mixed number.
   b.   Multiply the whole number by the integral part of the mixed number.
   c.   Add both products.

Illustration: Multiply $23\frac{3}{4}$ by 95.

SOLUTION: $\dfrac{95}{1} \times \dfrac{3}{4} = \dfrac{285}{4}$

$$= 71\frac{1}{4}$$

$$95 \times 23 = 2185$$

$$2185 + 71\frac{1}{4} = 2256\frac{1}{4}$$

Answer: $2256\frac{1}{4}$

Division of Fractions

21. The **reciprocal** of a fraction is that fraction inverted.
   a.   When a fraction is inverted, the numerator becomes the denominator, and the denominator becomes the numerator.

   Example: The reciprocal of $\frac{3}{8}$ is $\frac{8}{3}$.

   Example: The reciprocal of $\frac{1}{3}$ is $\frac{3}{1}$, or simply 3.

   b.   Because every whole number has the denominator of 1 understood, the reciprocal of a whole number is a fraction that has 1 as the numerator and the number itself as the denominator.

   Example: The reciprocal of 5 (expressed fractionally as $\frac{5}{1}$) is $\frac{1}{5}$.

22. To divide fractions:
   a.   Change all the mixed numbers, if any, to improper fractions.
   b.   Invert the second fraction and multiply.
   c.   Reduce, if possible.

Illustration: Divide $\frac{2}{3}$ by $2\frac{1}{4}$.

SOLUTION: $2\frac{1}{4} = \dfrac{9}{4}$

$$\dfrac{2}{3} \div \dfrac{9}{4} = \dfrac{2}{3} \times \dfrac{4}{9}$$

$$= \dfrac{8}{27}$$

Answer: $\dfrac{8}{27}$

23. A **complex fraction** is one that has a fraction as the numerator, or as the denominator, or as both.

Example: $\dfrac{\frac{2}{3}}{5}$ is a complex fraction.

24. To clear (simplify) a complex fraction:
   a. Divide the numerator by the denominator.
   b. Reduce, if possible.

Illustration: Clear $\dfrac{\frac{3}{7}}{\frac{5}{14}}$.

SOLUTION: $\quad \dfrac{3}{7} \div \dfrac{5}{14} = \dfrac{3}{7} \times \dfrac{14}{5} = \dfrac{42}{35}$
$$= \dfrac{6}{5}$$
$$= 1\dfrac{1}{5}$$

Answer: $1\dfrac{1}{5}$

Comparing Fractions

25. If two fractions have the same denominator, the one with the larger numerator is the greater fraction.

Example: $\dfrac{3}{7}$ is greater than $\dfrac{2}{7}$.

26. If two fractions have the same numerator, the one with the larger denominator is the smaller fraction.

Example: $\dfrac{5}{12}$ is smaller than $\dfrac{5}{11}$.

27. To compare two fractions having different numerators and different denominators:
   a. Change the fractions to equivalent fractions with their L.C.D. as their new denominator.
   b. Compare, as in the example following item 25.

Illustration: Compare $\dfrac{4}{7}$ and $\dfrac{5}{8}$.

SOLUTION: L.C.D. = $7 \times 8 = 56$

$$\dfrac{4}{7} = \dfrac{32}{56}$$
$$\dfrac{5}{8} = \dfrac{35}{56}$$

Answer: Because $\dfrac{35}{56}$ is larger than $\dfrac{32}{56}$, $\dfrac{5}{8}$ is larger than $\dfrac{4}{7}$.

Fraction Problems

28. Most fraction problems can be arranged in the form: "What fraction of a number is another number?" This form contains three important parts:

*   The fractional part
*   The number following "of"
*   The number following "is"

a.   If the fraction and the "of" number are given, multiply them to find the "is" number.

Illustration: What is $\frac{3}{4}$ of 20?

SOLUTION: Write the question as "$\frac{3}{4}$ of 20 is what number?" Then multiply the fraction $\frac{3}{4}$ by the "of" number, 20:

$$\frac{3}{\underset{1}{\cancel{4}}} \times \overset{5}{\cancel{20}} = 15$$

Answer: 15

b.   If the fractional part and the "is" number are given, divide the "is" number by fraction to find the "of" number.

Illustration: $\frac{4}{5}$ of what number is 40?

SOLUTION: To find the "of" number, divide 40 by $\frac{4}{5}$:

$$40 \div \frac{4}{5} = \frac{\overset{10}{\cancel{40}}}{1} \times \frac{5}{\underset{1}{\cancel{4}}}$$
$$= 50$$

Answer: 50

c.   To find the fractional part when the other two numbers are known, divide the "is" number by the "of" number.

Illustration: What part of 12 is 9?

SOLUTION: $9 \div 12 = \frac{9}{12}$
$$= \frac{3}{4}$$

Answer: $\frac{3}{4}$

Practice Problems Involving Fractions

Directions: Each question has four suggested answers. Select the correct one, and mark it on the answer sheet on page 151.

1.   Reduce to lowest terms: $\frac{60}{108}$.

(A) $\frac{1}{48}$ (C) $\frac{5}{9}$

(B) $\frac{1}{3}$ (D) $\frac{10}{18}$

2.   Change $\frac{27}{7}$ to a mixed number.

(A) $2\frac{1}{7}$ (C) $6\frac{1}{3}$

(B) $3\frac{6}{7}$ (D) $7\frac{1}{2}$

3. Change $4\frac{2}{3}$ to an improper fraction.
   (A) $\frac{10}{3}$ (C) $\frac{14}{3}$
   (B) $\frac{11}{3}$ (D) $\frac{42}{3}$

4. Find the L.C.D. of $\frac{1}{6}$, $\frac{1}{10}$, $\frac{1}{18}$, and $\frac{1}{21}$.
   (A) 160 (C) 630
   (B) 330 (D) 1260

5. Add $16\frac{3}{8}$, $4\frac{4}{5}$, $12\frac{3}{4}$, and $23\frac{5}{6}$.
   (A) $57\frac{91}{120}$ (C) 58
   (B) $57\frac{1}{4}$ (D) 59

6. Subtract $27\frac{5}{14}$ from $43\frac{1}{6}$.
   (A) 15 (C) $15\frac{8}{21}$
   (B) 16 (D) $15\frac{17}{21}$

7. Multiply $17\frac{5}{8}$ by 128.
   (A) 2200 (C) 2356
   (B) 2305 (D) 2256

8. Divide $1\frac{2}{3}$ by $1\frac{1}{9}$.
   (A) $\frac{2}{3}$ (C) $1\frac{23}{27}$
   (B) $1\frac{1}{2}$ (D) 6

9. What is the value of $12\frac{1}{6} - 2\frac{3}{8} - 7\frac{2}{3} + 19\frac{3}{4}$?
   (A) 21 (C) $21\frac{1}{8}$
   (B) $21\frac{7}{8}$ (D) 22

10. Simplify the complex fraction $\frac{\frac{4}{9}}{\frac{2}{5}}$.
    (A) $\frac{1}{2}$ (C) $\frac{2}{5}$
    (B) $\frac{9}{10}$ (D) $1\frac{1}{9}$

11. Which fraction is largest?
    (A) $\frac{9}{16}$ (C) $\frac{5}{8}$
    (B) $\frac{7}{10}$ (D) $\frac{4}{5}$

12. One brass rod measures $3\frac{5}{16}$ inches long, and another brass rod measures $2\frac{3}{4}$ inches long. Together their length is:
    (A) $6\frac{9}{16}$ inches (C) $6\frac{1}{16}$ inches
    (B) $5\frac{1}{8}$ inches (D) $5\frac{1}{16}$ inches

13. The number of half-pound packages of tea that can be weighed out of a box that holds $10\frac{1}{2}$ pounds of tea is:
    (A) 5 (C) $20\frac{1}{2}$
    (B) $10\frac{1}{8}$ (D) 21

14. If each bag of tokens weighs $5\frac{3}{4}$ pounds, how many pounds do 3 bags weigh?
    (A) $7\frac{1}{4}$ (C) $16\frac{1}{2}$
    (B) $15\frac{3}{4}$ (D) $17\frac{1}{4}$

15. During one week, a man traveled $3\frac{1}{2}$, $1\frac{1}{4}$, $1\frac{1}{6}$, and $2\frac{3}{8}$ miles. The next week he traveled $\frac{1}{4}$, $\frac{3}{8}$, $\frac{9}{16}$, $3\frac{1}{16}$, $2\frac{5}{8}$, and $3\frac{3}{16}$ miles. How many more miles did he travel the second week than the first week?
    (A) $1\frac{37}{48}$ (C) $1\frac{3}{4}$
    (B) $1\frac{1}{2}$ (D) 1

16. A certain type of board is sold only in lengths of multiples of 2 feet. The shortest board sold is 6 feet, and the longest is 24 feet. A builder needs a large quantity of this type of board in $5\frac{1}{2}$-foot lengths. For minimum waste, the lengths to be ordered should be:
    (A) 6 feet (C) 22 feet
    (B) 12 feet (D) 24 feet

17. A man spent $\frac{15}{16}$ of his entire fortune in buying a car for $7500. How much money did he possess?
    (A) $6000 (C) $7000
    (B) $6500 (D) $8000

18. The population of a town was 54,000 in the last census. It has increased $\frac{2}{3}$ since then. Its present population is:
    (A) 18,000 (C) 72,000
    (B) 36,000 (D) 90,000

19. If one third of the liquid contents of a can evaporates on the first day and three fourths of the remainder evaporates on the second day, the fractional part of the original contents remaining at the close of the second day is:

(A) $\frac{5}{12}$ (C) $\frac{1}{6}$

(B) $\frac{7}{12}$ (D) $\frac{1}{2}$

20. A car is run until the gas tank is $\frac{1}{8}$ full. The tank is then filled to capacity by putting in 14 gallons. The capacity of the gas tank of the car is:

(A) 14 gallons   (C) 16 gallons

(B) 15 gallons   (D) 17 gallons

Answer Key

1.	**C**	5.	**A**	9.	**B**	13.	**D**	17.	**D**
2.	**B**	6.	**D**	10.	**D**	14.	**D**	18.	**D**
3.	**C**	7.	**D**	11.	**D**	15.	**A**	19.	**C**
4.	**C**	8.	**B**	12.	**C**	16.	**C**	20.	**C**

Solutions

1. Divide the numerator and denominator by 12:

$$\frac{60 \div 12}{108 \div 12} = \frac{5}{9}$$

One alternate method (there are several) is to divide the numerator and denominator by 6 and then by 2:

$$\frac{60 \div 6}{108 \div 6} = \frac{10}{18}$$

$$\frac{10 \div 2}{18 \div 2} = \frac{5}{9}$$

Answer: **(C)** $\frac{5}{9}$

2. Divide the numerator (27) by the denominator (7):

$$\begin{array}{r} 3 \\ 7\overline{)27} \\ \underline{21} \\ 6 \text{ remainder} \end{array}$$

$$\frac{27}{7} = 3\frac{6}{7}$$

Answer: **(B)** $3\frac{6}{7}$

3. $4 \times 3 = 12$

$12 + 2 = 14$

$4\frac{2}{3} = \frac{14}{3}$

Answer: **(C)** $\frac{14}{3}$

4.

$2\,\underline{)\,6 \quad 10 \quad 18 \quad 21}$ (2 is a divisor of 6, 10, and 18)

$3\,\underline{)\,3 \quad 5 \quad 9 \quad 21}$ (3 is a divisor of 3, 9, and 21)

$3\,\underline{)\,1 \quad 5 \quad 3 \quad 7}$ (3 is a divisor of 3)

$5\,\underline{)\,1 \quad 5 \quad 1 \quad 7}$ (5 is a divisor of 5)

$7\,\underline{)\,1 \quad 1 \quad 1 \quad 7}$ (7 is a divisor of 7)

$\quad 1 \quad 1 \quad 1 \quad 1$

L.C.D. $= 2 \times 3 \times 3 \times 5 \times 7 = 630$

Answer: **(C)** 630

5. L.C.D. = 120

$$16\frac{3}{8} = 16\frac{45}{120}$$
$$4\frac{4}{5} = 4\frac{96}{120}$$
$$12\frac{3}{4} = 12\frac{90}{120}$$
$$+23\frac{5}{6} = +23\frac{100}{120}$$
$$\overline{\qquad\qquad} \quad 55\frac{331}{120} = 57\frac{91}{120}$$

Answer: **(A)** $57\frac{91}{120}$

6. L.C.D. = 42

$$43\frac{1}{6} = 43\frac{7}{42} = 42\frac{49}{42}$$
$$-27\frac{5}{14} = -27\frac{15}{42} = -27\frac{15}{42}$$
$$\overline{\qquad\qquad\qquad\qquad} \quad 15\frac{34}{42} = 15\frac{17}{21}$$

Answer: **(D)** $15\frac{17}{21}$

7. $$17\frac{5}{8} = \frac{141}{8}$$

$$\frac{141}{\cancel{8}} \times \frac{\overset{16}{\cancel{128}}}{1} = 2256$$

Answer: **(D)** 2256

8. $$1\frac{2}{3} \div 1\frac{1}{9} = \frac{5}{3} \div \frac{10}{9}$$
$$= \frac{\overset{1}{\cancel{5}}}{\underset{1}{3}} \times \frac{\overset{3}{\cancel{9}}}{\underset{2}{10}}$$
$$= \frac{3}{2}$$
$$= 1\frac{1}{2}$$

Answer: **(B)** $1\frac{1}{2}$

9. L.C.D. = 24

$$12\frac{1}{6} = 12\frac{4}{24} = 11\frac{28}{24}$$
$$-2\frac{3}{8} = -2\frac{9}{24} = -2\frac{9}{24}$$
$$\overline{\qquad\qquad\qquad\qquad} \quad 9\frac{19}{24} = 9\frac{19}{24}$$
$$-7\frac{2}{3} = -7\frac{16}{24}$$
$$\overline{\qquad\qquad\qquad} \quad 2\frac{3}{24} = 2\frac{3}{24}$$
$$+19\frac{3}{4} = +19\frac{18}{24}$$
$$\overline{\qquad\qquad\qquad} \quad 21\frac{21}{24}$$

$$21\frac{21}{24} = 21\frac{7}{8}$$

Answer: **(B)** $21\frac{7}{8}$

10. To simplify a complex fraction, divide the numerator by the denominator:

$$\frac{4}{9} \div \frac{2}{5} = \frac{\overset{2}{\cancel{4}}}{9} \times \frac{5}{\underset{1}{\cancel{2}}}$$
$$= \frac{10}{9}$$
$$= 1\frac{1}{9}$$

Answer: **(D)** $1\frac{1}{9}$

11. Write all the fractions with the same denominator. L.C.D. = 80

$$\frac{9}{16} = \frac{45}{80}$$
$$\frac{7}{10} = \frac{56}{80}$$
$$\frac{5}{8} = \frac{50}{80}$$
$$\frac{4}{5} = \frac{64}{80}$$

Answer: **(D)** $\frac{4}{5}$

12.
$$3\frac{5}{16} = 3\frac{5}{16}$$
$$+2\frac{3}{4} = +2\frac{12}{16}$$
$$\overline{\qquad\qquad} \quad 5\frac{17}{16}$$
$$= 6\frac{1}{16}$$

Answer: **(C)** $6\frac{1}{16}$ inches

13. $$10\frac{1}{2} \div \frac{1}{2} = \frac{21}{2} \div \frac{1}{2}$$
$$= \frac{21}{\underset{1}{\cancel{2}}} \times \frac{\overset{1}{\cancel{2}}}{1}$$
$$= 21$$

Answer: **(D)** 21

14. $$5\frac{3}{4} \times 3 = \frac{23}{4} \times \frac{3}{1}$$
$$= \frac{69}{4}$$
$$= 17\frac{1}{4}$$

Answer: **(D)** $17\frac{1}{4}$

15. First week:

L.C.D. = 24

$$3\frac{1}{2} = 3\frac{12}{24} \text{ miles}$$
$$1\frac{1}{4} = 1\frac{6}{24}$$
$$1\frac{1}{6} = 1\frac{4}{24}$$
$$+2\frac{3}{8} = +2\frac{9}{24}$$

$$7\frac{31}{24} = 8\frac{7}{24} \text{ miles}$$

Second week:

L.C.D. = 16

$$\frac{1}{4} = \frac{4}{16}$$
$$\frac{3}{8} = \frac{6}{16}$$
$$\frac{9}{16} = \frac{9}{16}$$
$$3\frac{1}{16} = 3\frac{1}{16}$$
$$2\frac{5}{8} = 2\frac{10}{16}$$
$$+3\frac{3}{16} = +3\frac{3}{16}$$

$$8\frac{33}{16} = 10\frac{1}{16} \text{ miles}$$

L.C.D. = 48

$$10\frac{1}{16} = 9\frac{51}{48} \text{ miles second week}$$
$$-8\frac{7}{24} = -8\frac{14}{48} \text{ miles first week}$$

$$1\frac{37}{48} \text{ miles more traveled}$$

Answer: **(A)** $1\frac{37}{48}$

16. Consider each choice:

Each 6-foot board yields one $5\frac{1}{2}$-foot board with $\frac{1}{2}$ foot of waste.

Each 12-foot board yields two $5\frac{1}{2}$-foot boards with 1 foot of waste. ($2 \times 5\frac{1}{2} = 11$; $12 - 11 = 1$ foot waste)

Each 24-foot board yields four $5\frac{1}{2}$-foot boards with 2 feet of waste. ($4 \times 5\frac{1}{2} = 22$; $24 - 22 = 2$ feet waste)

Each 22-foot board may be divided into four $5\frac{1}{2}$-foot boards with no waste. ($4 \times 5\frac{1}{2} = 22$ exactly)

Answer: **(C)** 22 feet

17. $\frac{15}{16}$ of the fortune is $7500.

Therefore, his fortune $= 7500 \div \frac{15}{16}$

$$= \frac{\overset{500}{\cancel{7500}}}{1} \times \frac{16}{\underset{1}{\cancel{15}}}$$

$$= 8000$$

Answer: **(D)** $8000

18. $\frac{2}{3}$ of 54,000 = increase

$$\text{Increase} = \frac{2}{\underset{1}{\cancel{3}}} \times \overset{18,000}{\cancel{54,000}}$$

$$= 36,000$$

Present population $= 54,000 + 36,000$
$$= 90,000$$

Answer: **(D)** 90,000

19. First day: $\frac{1}{3}$ evaporates

$\frac{2}{3}$ remains

Second day: $\frac{3}{4}$ of $\frac{2}{3}$ evaporates

$\frac{1}{4}$ of $\frac{2}{3}$ remains

The amount remaining is

$$\frac{1}{\underset{2}{\cancel{4}}} \times \frac{\overset{1}{\cancel{2}}}{3} = \frac{1}{6} \text{ of original contents}$$

Answer: **(C)** $\frac{1}{6}$

20. $\frac{7}{8}$ of capacity $= 14$ gallons

therefore, capacity $= 14 \div \frac{7}{8}$

$$\frac{\overset{2}{\cancel{14}}}{1} \times \frac{8}{\underset{1}{\cancel{7}}}$$

$$= 16 \text{ gallons}$$

Answer: **(C)** 16 gallons

DECIMALS

1. A **decimal,** which is a number with a decimal point (.), is actually a fraction, the denominator of which is understood to be 10 or some power of 10.

    a. The number of digits, or places, after a decimal point determines which power of 10 the denominator is. If there is one digit, the denominator is understood to be 10; if there are two digits, the denominator is understood to be 100, and so on.

    Example: $.3 = \frac{3}{10}, .57 = \frac{57}{100}, .643 = \frac{643}{1000}$

    b. The addition of zeros after a decimal point does not change the value of the decimal. The zeros may be removed without changing the value of the decimal.

    Example: .7 = .70 = .700 and vice versa, .700 = .70 = .7

    c. Because a decimal point is understood to exist after any whole number, the addition of any number of zeros after such a decimal point does not change the value of the number.

    Example: 2 = 2.0 = 2.00 = 2.000

Addition of Decimals

2. Decimals are added in the same way that whole numbers are added, with the provision that the decimal points must be kept in a vertical line, one under the other. This determines the place of the decimal point in the answer.

    Illustration: Add 2.31, .037, 4, and 5.0017

    SOLUTION:
    $$\begin{array}{r} 2.3100 \\ .0370 \\ 4.0000 \\ + 5.0017 \\ \hline 11.3487 \end{array}$$

    Answer: 11.3487

Subtraction of Decimals

3. Decimals are subtracted in the same way that whole numbers are subtracted, with the provision that, as in addition, the decimal points must be kept in a vertical line, one under the other. This determines the place of the decimal point in the answer.

Illustration: Subtract 4.0037 from 15.3

SOLUTION:
$$\begin{array}{r} 15.3000 \\ -\ 4.0037 \\ \hline 11.2963 \end{array}$$

Answer: 11.2963

Multiplication of Decimals

4. Decimals are multiplied in the same way that whole numbers are multiplied.

    a.   The number of decimal places in the product equals the sum of the decimal places in the multiplicand and in the multiplier.

    b.   If there are fewer places in the product than this sum, then a sufficient number of zeros must be added in front of the product to equal the number of places required, and a decimal point is written in front of the zeros.

Illustration: Multiply 2.372 by .012

SOLUTION:

2.372	(3 decimal places)
$\times$ .012	(3 decimal places)
4744	
2372	
.028464	(6 decimal places)

Answer: .028464

5. A decimal can be multiplied by a power of 10 by moving the decimal point to the *right* as many places as indicated by the power. If multiplied by 10, the decimal point is moved one place to the right; if multiplied by 100, the decimal point is moved two places to the right, and so on.

Example: .235 $\times$ 10 = 2.35
                 .235 $\times$ 100 = 23.5
                 .235 $\times$ 1000 = 235

Division of Decimals

6. There are four types of division involving decimals:
- When the dividend only is a decimal
- When the divisor only is a decimal
- When both are decimals
- When neither dividend nor divisor is a decimal

a.   When the dividend only is a decimal, the division is the same as that of whole numbers, except that a decimal point must be placed in the quotient exactly above that in the dividend.

Illustration: Divide 12.864 by 32

$$
\begin{array}{r}
.402 \\
32\,)\overline{12.864} \\
\underline{12\ 8} \\
64 \\
64
\end{array}
$$

SOLUTION:

Answer: .402

b.   When the divisor only is a decimal, the decimal point in the divisor is omitted, and as many zeros are placed to the right of the dividend as there were decimal places in the divisor.

Illustration: Divide 211327 by 6.817

SOLUTION: 211327 ÷ 6.817   =

(3 decimal places)

$$
\begin{array}{r}
31000 \\
6817\,)\overline{211327000} \\
\underline{20451} \quad \text{(3 zeros added)}\\
6817 \\
\underline{6817}
\end{array}
$$

Answer: 31000

c.   When both divisor and dividend are decimals, the decimal point in the divisor is omitted, and the decimal point in the dividend must be moved to the right as many decimal places as there were in the divisor. If there are not enough places in the dividend, zeros must be added to make up the difference.

Illustration: Divide 2.62 by .131

SOLUTION: .131$)\overline{2.62}$ =

$$
\begin{array}{r}
20 \\
131\,)\overline{2620} \\
\underline{262}
\end{array}
$$

Answer: 20

d.   In instances when neither the divisor nor the dividend is a decimal, a problem may still involve decimals. This occurs in two cases: when the dividend is a smaller number than the divisor, and when it is required to work out a division to a certain number of decimal places. In either case, write in a decimal point after the dividend, add as many zeros as necessary, and place a decimal point in the quotient above that in the dividend.

Illustration: Divide 7 by 50.

$$
\begin{array}{r}
.14 \\
50\overline{)7.00} \\
5\,0 \\
\hline
2\,00 \\
2\,00 \\
\hline
\end{array}
$$

SOLUTION:

Answer: .14

Illustration: How much is 155 divided by 40, carried out to 3 decimal places?

$$
\begin{array}{r}
3.875 \\
40\overline{)155.000} \\
120 \\
\hline
350 \\
320 \\
\hline
300 \\
280 \\
\hline
200 \\
\end{array}
$$

SOLUTION:

Answer: 3.875

7.   A decimal can be divided by a power of 10 by moving the decimal to the *left* as many places as indicated by the power. If divided by 10, the decimal point is moved one place to the left; if divided by 100, the decimal point is moved two places to the left, and so on. If there are not enough places, add zeros in front of the number to make up the difference, and add a decimal point.

Example: .4 divided by 10 = .04
.4 divided by 100 = .004

Rounding Decimals

8.   To round a number to a given decimal place:

a.   Locate the given place.

b.   If the digit to the right is less than 5, omit all digits following the given place.

c.   If the digit to the right is 5 or more, raise the given place by 1 and omit all digits following the given place.

Examples: 4.27 = 4.3 to the nearest tenth
.71345 = .713 to the nearest thousandth

9. In problems involving money, answers usually are rounded to the nearest cent.

Conversion of Fractions to Decimals

10. A fraction can be changed to a decimal by dividing the numerator by the denominator and working out the division to as many decimal places as required.

Illustration: Change $\frac{5}{11}$ to a decimal of 2 places.

SOLUTION: $\frac{5}{11} = 11\overline{)5.00}$
$$
\begin{array}{r}
.45\frac{5}{11} \\
11\overline{)5.00} \\
4.44 \\
\hline
60 \\
55 \\
\hline
5
\end{array}
$$

Answer: $.45\frac{5}{11}$

11. To clear fractions containing a decimal in either the numerator or the denominator, or in both, divide the numerator by the denominator.

Illustration: What is the value of $\frac{2.34}{.6}$?

SOLUTION: $\frac{2.34}{.6} = .6\overline{)2.34} = 6\overline{)23.4}$
$$
\begin{array}{r}
3.9 \\
6\overline{)23.4} \\
18 \\
\hline
54 \\
54 \\
\hline
\end{array}
$$

Answer: 3.9

Conversion of Decimals to Fractions

12. Because a decimal point indicates a number having a denominator that is a power of 10, a decimal can be expressed as a fraction, the numerator of which is the number itself and the denominator of which is the power indicated by the number of decimal places in the decimal.

Example: $.3 = \frac{3}{10}$, $.47 = \frac{47}{100}$

13. When the decimal is a mixed number, divide by the power of 10 indicated by its number of decimal places. The fraction does not count as a decimal place.

Illustration: Change $.25\frac{1}{3}$ to a fraction.

SOLUTION: $.25\frac{1}{3} = 25\frac{1}{3} \div 100$

$$= \frac{76}{3} \times \frac{1}{100}$$

$$= \frac{76}{300} = \frac{19}{75}$$

Answer: $\frac{19}{75}$

14. When to change decimals to fractions:

a.   When dealing with whole numbers, do not change the decimal.

Example: In the problem $12 \times .14$, it is better to keep the decimal:

$$12 \times .14 = 1.68$$

b.   When dealing with fractions, change the decimal to a fraction.

Example: In the problem $\frac{3}{5} \times .17$, it is best to change the decimal to a fraction:

$$\frac{3}{5} \times .17 = \frac{3}{5} \times \frac{17}{100} = \frac{51}{500}$$

15. Because decimal equivalents of fractions are often used, it is helpful to be familiar with the most common conversions.

$\frac{1}{2} = .5$	$\frac{1}{3} = .3333$
$\frac{1}{4} = .25$	$\frac{2}{3} = .6667$
$\frac{3}{4} = .75$	$\frac{1}{6} = .1667$
$\frac{1}{5} = .2$	$\frac{1}{7} = .1429$
$\frac{1}{8} = .125$	$\frac{1}{9} = .1111$
$\frac{1}{16} = .0625$	$\frac{1}{12} = .0833$

Note that the left column contains exact values. The values in the fight column have been rounded to the nearest ten-thousandth.

Practice Problems Involving Decimals

Directions: Each question has four suggested answers. Select the correct one and mark it on the answer sheet on page 151.

1. Add 37.03, 11.5627, 3.4005, 3423, and 1.141.

   (A) 3476.1342   (C) 3524.4322
   (B) 3500   (D) 3424.1342

2. Subtract 4.64324 from 7.

   (A) 3.35676   (C) 2.45676
   (B) 2.35676   (D) 2.36676

3. Multiply 27.34 by 16.943.

   (A) 463.22162   (C) 462.52162
   (B) 453.52162   (D) 462.53162

4. How much is 19.6 divided by 3.2, carried out to 3 decimal places?

   (A) 6.125   (C) 6.123
   (B) 6.124   (D) 5.123

5. What is $\frac{5}{11}$ in decimal form (to the nearest hundredth)?

   (A) .44   (C) .40
   (B) .55   (D) .45

6. What is $.64\frac{2}{3}$ in fraction form?

   (A) $\frac{97}{120}$ (C) $\frac{97}{130}$
   (B) $\frac{97}{150}$ (D) $\frac{98}{130}$

7. What is the difference between $\frac{3}{5}$ and $\frac{9}{8}$ expressed decimally?

   (A) .525   (C) .520
   (B) .425   (D) .500

8. A boy saved up $4.56 the first month, $3.82 the second month, and $5.06 the third month. How much did he save altogether?

   (A) $12.56   (C) $13.44
   (B) $13.28   (D) $14.02

9. The diameter of a certain rod is required to be 1.51 +/- .015 inches. The rod would not be acceptable if the diameter measured:

   (A) 1.490 inches   (C) 1.510 inches
   (B) 1.500 inches   (D) 1.525 inches

10. After an employer figures out an employee's salary of $190.57, he deducts $3.05 for social security and $5.68 for pension. What is the amount of the check after these deductions?

    (A) $181.84   (C) $181.93
    (B) $181.92   (D) $181.99

11. If the outer diameter of a metal pipe is 2.84 inches and the inner diameter is 1.94 inches, the thickness of the metal is:

    (A) .45 inches   (C) 1.94 inches
    (B) .90 inches   (D) 2.39 inches

12. A boy earns $20.56 on Monday, $32.90 on Tuesday, and $20.78 on Wednesday. He spends half of all that he earned during the three days. How much has he left?

    (A) $29.19   (C) $34.27
    (B) $31.23   (D) $37.12

13. The total cost of $3\frac{1}{2}$ pounds of meat at $1.69 a pound, and 20 lemons at $.60 a dozen will be:

(A) $6.00   (C) $6.52

(B) $6.40   (D) $6.92

14. A reel of cable weighs 1279 pounds. If the empty reel weighs 285 pounds and the cable weighs 7.1 pounds per foot, the number of feet of cable on the reel is:

(A) 220   (C) 140

(B) 180   (D) 100

15. 345 fasteners at $4.15 per hundred will cost:

(A) $.1432   (C) $14.32

(B) $1.4320   (D) $143.20

Answer Key

1. **A**	6. **B**	11. **A**
2. **B**	7. **A**	12. **D**
3. **A**	8. **C**	13. **D**
4. **A**	9. **A**	14. **C**
5. **D**	10. **A**	15. **C**

Solutions

1. Line up all the decimal points one under the other. Then add:

```
  37.03
  11.5627
   3.4005
3423.0000
+  1.141
---------
3476.1342
```

Answer: **(A)** 3476.1342

2. Add a decimal point and five zeros to the 7. Then subtract:

```
 7.00000
-4.64324
--------
 2.35676
```

Answer: **(B)** 2.35676

3. Because there are two decimal places in the multiplicand and three decimal places in the multiplier, there will be $2 + 3 = 5$ decimal places in the product.

```
    27.34
 × 16.943
---------
     8202
   1 0936
  24 606
 164 04
 273 4
---------
463.22162
```

Answer: **(A)** 463.22162

4. Omit the decimal point in the divisor by moving it one place to the right. Move the decimal point in the dividend one place to the right, and add three zeros in order to carry your answer out to three decimal places, as instructed in the problem.

$$
\begin{array}{r}
6.125 \\
3.2\overline{\smash{)}19.6{,}000} \\
\underline{19\ 2} \\
40 \\
\underline{32} \\
80 \\
\underline{64} \\
160 \\
\underline{160}
\end{array}
$$

Answer: (**A**) 6.125

5. To convert a fraction to a decimal, divide the numerator by the denominator:

$$
\begin{array}{r}
.454 \\
11\overline{\smash{)}5.000} \\
\underline{4\ 4} \\
60 \\
\underline{55} \\
50 \\
\underline{44} \\
6
\end{array}
$$

Answer: (**D**) .45 to the nearest hundredth

6. To convert a decimal to a fraction, divide by the power of 10 indicated by the number of decimal places. (The fraction does not count as a decimal place.)

$$
64\tfrac{2}{3} \div 100 = \frac{194}{3} \div \frac{100}{1}
$$
$$
= \frac{194}{3} \times \frac{1}{100}
$$
$$
= \frac{194}{300}
$$
$$
= \frac{97}{150}
$$

Answer: (**B**) $\frac{97}{150}$

7. Convert each fraction to a decimal and subtract to find the difference:

$$\frac{9}{8} = 1.125 \qquad \frac{3}{5} = .60$$

$$
\begin{array}{r}
1.125 \\
\underline{-.60} \\
.525
\end{array}
$$

Answer: (**A**) .525

8. Add the savings for each month:

$$
\begin{array}{r}
\$4.56 \\
3.82 \\
\underline{+\ 5.06} \\
\$13.44
\end{array}
$$

Answer: (**C**) $13.44

9.
$$
\begin{array}{r}
1.51 \\
\underline{+0.015} \\
1.525
\end{array}
\qquad
\begin{array}{r}
1.510 \\
\underline{-\ 0.015} \\
1.495
\end{array}
$$

The rod may have a diameter of 1.495 inches to 1.525 inches inclusive.

Answer: (**A**) 1.490 inches

10. Add to find total deductions:
$$
\begin{array}{r}
\$3.05 \\
\underline{+\ 5.68} \\
\$8.73
\end{array}
$$

Subtract total deductions from the salary to find the amount of the check:
$$
\begin{array}{r}
\$190.57 \\
\underline{-\ 8.73} \\
\$181.84
\end{array}
$$

Answer: (**A**) $181.84

11. The difference of the two diameters equals the total thickness of the metal on both ends of the inner diameter.

2.84   .90 ÷ 2 = .45 = thickness of metal
−1.94
.90

Answer: **(A)** .45 inch

12. Add daily earnings to find total earnings:

$20.56
32.90
+ 20.78
$74.24

Divide total earnings by 2 to find out what he has left:

$37.12
2)$74.24

Answer: **(D)** $37.12

13. Find cost of 3[1/2] pounds of meat:

$1.69
× 3.5
845
5 07
$5.915 = $5.92 to the nearest cent

Find the cost of 20 lemons:

$.60 ÷ 12 = $.05 (for 1 lemon)
$.05 × 20 = $1.00 (for 20 lemons)

Add the cost of the meat and the cost of the lemons:

$5.92
+1.00
$6.92

Answer: **(D)** $6.92

14. Subtract the weight of the empty reel from the total weight to find the weight of the cable:

1279 pounds
− 285 pounds
994 pounds

Each foot of cable weighs 7.1 pounds. Therefore, to find the number of feet of cable on the reel, divide 994 by 7.1:

14 0.
7.1)994.0
71
284
284
0 0

Answer: **(C)** 140

15. Each fastener costs:

$4.15 ÷ 100 = $.0415

345 fasteners cost:

345
× .0415
1725
345
13 80
14.3175

Answer: **(C)** $14.32

PERCENTS

1. The **percent symbol** (%) means "parts of a hundred." Some problems involve expressing a fraction or a decimal as a percent. In other problems, it is necessary to express a percent as a fraction or a decimal in order to perform the calculations.

2. To change a whole number or a decimal to a percent:

    a. Multiply the number by 100.

    b. Affix a % sign.

    Illustration: Change 3 to a percent.

    SOLUTION: $3 \times 100 = 300$
    $$3 = 300\%$$

    Answer: 300%

    Illustration: Change .67 to a percent.

    SOLUTION: $.67 \times 100 = 67$
    $$.67 = 67\%$$

    Answer: 67%

3. To change a fraction or a mixed number to a percent:

    a. Multiply the fraction or mixed number by 100.

    b. Reduce, if possible.

    c. Affix a % sign.

    Illustration: Change $\frac{1}{7}$ to a percent.

    SOLUTION: $\frac{1}{7} \times 100 = \frac{100}{7}$
    $$= 14\frac{2}{7}$$
    $$\frac{1}{7} = 14\frac{2}{7}\%$$

    Answer: $14\frac{2}{7}\%$

Illustration: Change $4\frac{2}{3}$ to a percent.

SOLUTION: $4\frac{2}{3} \times 100 = \frac{14}{3} \times 100 = \frac{1400}{3}$

$$= 466\frac{2}{3}$$

$$4\frac{2}{3} = 466\frac{2}{3}\%$$

Answer: $466\frac{2}{3}\%$

4. To remove a % sign attached to a decimal, divide the decimal by 100. If necessary, the resulting decimal may then be changed to a fraction.

Illustration: Change .5% to a decimal and to a fraction.

SOLUTION: $.5\% = .5 \div 100 = .005$

$$.005 = \frac{5}{1000} = \frac{1}{200}$$

Answer: $.5\% = .005$

$$.5\% = \frac{1}{200}$$

5. To remove a % sign attached to a fraction or a mixed number, divide the fraction or mixed number by 100, and reduce, if possible. If necessary, the resulting fraction may then be changed to a decimal.

Illustration: Change $\frac{3}{4}$ % to a fraction and to a decimal.

SOLUTION: $\frac{3}{4}\% = \frac{3}{4} \div 100 = \frac{3}{4} \times \frac{1}{100}$

$$= \frac{3}{400}$$

$$\frac{3}{400} = 400\overline{)3.0000}\ \ ^{.0075}$$

Answer: $\frac{3}{4}\% = \frac{3}{400}$

$$\frac{3}{4}\% = .0075$$

6. To remove a % sign attached to a decimal that includes a fraction, divide the decimal by 100. If necessary, the resulting number may then be changed to a fraction.

Illustration: Change $.5\frac{1}{3}$% to a fraction.

SOLUTION: $.5\frac{1}{3}\% = .005\frac{1}{3}$

$$= \frac{5\frac{1}{3}}{1000}$$

$$= 5\frac{1}{3} \div 1000$$

$$= \frac{16}{3} \times \frac{1}{1000}$$

$$= \frac{16}{3000}$$

$$= \frac{2}{375}$$

Answer: $.5\frac{1}{3}\% = \frac{2}{375}$

7. Some fraction-percent equivalents are used so frequently that it is helpful to be familiar with them.

$$\frac{1}{25} = 4\%$$

$$\frac{1}{20} = 5\%$$

$$\frac{1}{12} = 8\frac{1}{3}\%$$

$$\frac{1}{10} = 10\%$$

$$\frac{1}{8} = 12\frac{1}{2}\%$$

$$\frac{1}{6} = 16\frac{2}{3}\%$$

$$\frac{1}{5} = 20\%$$

$$\frac{1}{4} = 25\%$$

$$\frac{1}{3} = 33\frac{1}{3}\%$$

$$\frac{1}{2} = 50\%$$

$$\frac{2}{3} = 66\frac{2}{3}\%$$

$$\frac{3}{4} = 75\%$$

Solving Percent Problems

8. Most percent problems involve three quantities:
- The rate, R, which is followed by a % sign.
- The base, B, which follows the word "of."
- The amount or percentage, P, which usually follows the word "is."

a. If the rate (R) and the base (B) are known, then the percentage (P) = R × B.

Illustration: Find 15% of 50.

SOLUTION: Rate = 15%

Base = 50

$$P = R \times B$$
$$P = 15\% \times 50$$
$$= .15 \times 50$$
$$= 7.5$$

Answer: 15% of 50 is 7.5.

b. If the rate (R) and the percentage (P) are known, then the base (B) = $\dfrac{P}{R}$.

Illustration: 7% of what number is 35?

SOLUTION: Rate = 7%

Percentage = 35

$$B = \frac{P}{R}$$
$$B = \frac{35}{7\%}$$
$$= 35 \div .07$$
$$= 500$$

Answer: 7% of 500 is 35.

c. If the percentage (P) and the base (B) are known, the rate (R) = $\dfrac{P}{B}$.

Illustration: There are 96 men in a group of 150 people. What percent of the group are men?

SOLUTION: Base = 150

Percentage (amount) = 96

$$\text{Rate} = \frac{96}{150}$$
$$= .64$$
$$= 64\%$$

Answer: 64% of the group are men.

Illustration: In a tank holding 20 gallons of solution, 1 gallon is alcohol. What is the strength of the solution in percent?

SOLUTION: Percentage (amount) = 1 gallon

Base = 20 gallons

Rate = $\frac{1}{20}$

= .05

= 5%

Answer: The solution is 5% alcohol.

9. In a percent problem, the whole is 100%.

Example: If a problem involves 10% of a quantity, the rest of the quantity is 90%.

Example: If a quantity has been increased by 5%, the new amount is 105% of the original quantity.

Example: If a quantity has been decreased by 15%, the new amount is 85% of the original quantity.

Practice Problems Involving Percents

Directions: *Each question has four suggested answers. Select the correct one, and mark it on the answer sheet on page 151.*

1. 10% written as a decimal is
   (A) 1.0   (C) 0.001
   (B) 0.01   (D) 0.1

2. What is 5.37% in fraction form?
   (A) $\frac{537}{10,000}$ (C) $\frac{537}{1000}$
   (B) $5\frac{37}{10,000}$ (D) $5\frac{37}{100}$

3. What percent of $\frac{5}{6}$ is $\frac{3}{4}$?
   (A) 75%   (C) 80%
   (B) 60%   (D) 90%

4. What percent is 14 of 24?
   (A) $62\frac{1}{4}\%$ (C) $41\frac{2}{3}\%$
   (B) $58\frac{1}{3}\%$ (D) $33\frac{3}{5}\%$

5. 200% of 800 equals
   (A) 2500   (C) 1600
   (B) 16   (D) 4

6. If John must have a mark of 80% to pass a test of 35 items, the number of items he may miss and still pass the test is
   (A) 7   (C) 11
   (B) 8   (D) 28

7. The regular price of a TV set that sold for $118.80 at a 20% reduction sale is
   (A) $148.50   (C) $138.84
   (B) $142.60   (D) $ 95.04

8. A circle graph of a budget shows the expenditure of 26.2% for housing, 28.4% for food, 12% for clothing, 12.7% for taxes, and the balance for miscellaneous items. The percent for miscellaneous items is
   (A) 31.5%   (C) 20.7%
   (B) 79.3%   (D) 68.5%

9. Two dozen shuttlecocks and four badminton rackets are to be purchased for a playground. The shuttlecocks are priced at $.35 each, and the rackets are purchased at $2.75 each. The playground receives a discount of 30% from these prices. The total cost of this equipment is
(A) $ 7.29   (C) $13.58
(B) $11.43   (D) $18.60

10. A piece of wood weighing 10 ounces is found to have a weight of 8 ounces after drying. The moisture content was
(A) 25%   (C) 20%
(B) $33\frac{1}{3}\%$ (D) 40%

11. A bag contains 800 coins. Of these, 10 percent are dimes, 30 percent are nickels, and the rest are quarters. The amount of money in the bag is
(A) less than $150
(B) between $150 and $300
(C) between $301 and $450
(D) more than $450

12. Six quarts of a 20% solution of alcohol in water are mixed with 4 quarts of a 60% solution of alcohol in water. The alcoholic strength of the mixture is
(A) 80%   (C) 36%
(B) 40%   (D) 72%

13. A man insures 80% of his property and pays a $2\frac{1}{2}\%$ premium amounting to $348. What is the total value of his property?
(A) $17,000   (C) $18,400
(B) $18,000   (D) $17,400

14. A clerk divided his 35-hour work week as follows: $\frac{1}{5}$ of his time was spent sorting mail, $\frac{1}{2}$ of his time was spent filing letters, and $\frac{1}{7}$ of his time was spent doing reception work. The rest of his time was devoted to messenger work. The percent of time spent on messenger work by the clerk during the week was most nearly
(A) 6%   (C) 14%
(B) 10%   (D) 16%

15. In a school in which 40% of the enrolled students are boys, 80% of the boys are present on a certain day. If 1152 boys are present, the total school enrollment is
(A) 1440   (C)   3600
(B) 2880   (D)   5400

Answer Key

1. (D)	6. (A)	11. (A)
2. (A)	7. (A)	12. (C)
3. (D)	8. (C)	13. (D)
4. (B)	9. (C)	14. (D)
5. (C)	10. (C)	15. (C)

Solutions

1. $10\% = .10 = .1$
Answer: **(D)** 0.1

2. $5.37\% = .0537 = \frac{537}{10,000}$
Answer: **(A)** $\frac{537}{10,000}$

3. Base (number following "of") $= \frac{5}{6}$

Percentage (number following "is") $= \frac{3}{4}$,

$$\text{Rate} = \frac{\text{Percentage}}{\text{Base}}$$
$$= \text{Percentage} \div \text{Base}$$

$$\text{Rate} = \frac{3}{4} \div \frac{5}{6}$$
$$= \frac{3}{\cancel{4}} \times \frac{\cancel{6}^{\,3}}{5}$$
$$= \frac{9}{10}$$

$\frac{9}{10} = .9 = 90\%$
Answer: **(D)** 90%

4. Base (number following "of") $= 24$
Percentage (number following "is") $= 14$
Rate = Percentage ÷ Base
Rate $= 14 \div 24 = .58\frac{1}{3}$
$= 58\frac{1}{3}\%$
Answer: **(B)** $58\frac{1}{3}\%$

5. 200% of $800 = 2.00 \times 800$
$= 1,600$
Answer: **(C)** 1,600

6. He must answer 80% of 35 correctly.
Therefore, he may miss 20% of 35.
20% of $35 = .20 \times 35$
$= 7$
Answer: **(A)** 7

7. Because $118.80 represents a 20% reduction, $118.80 = 80% of the regular price.

Regular price $= \dfrac{\$118.80}{80\%}$
$= \$118.80 \div .80$
$= \$148.50$
Answer: **(A)** $148.50

8. All the items in a circle graph total 100%. Add the figures given for housing, food, clothing, and taxes:

$$\begin{array}{r} 26.2\% \\ 28.4\% \\ 12\ \ \% \\ \underline{12.7\%} \\ 79.3\% \end{array}$$

Subtract this total from 100% to find the percent for miscellaneous items:

$$\begin{array}{r} 100.0\% \\ \underline{79.3\%} \\ 20.7\% \end{array}$$

Answer: **(C)** 20.7%

9. Price of shuttlecocks $= 24 \times \$.35 = \$\ 8.40$
Price of rackets $= 4 \times \$2.75 = \$11.00$
Total price $= \$19.40$
Discount is 30%, and 100% − 30% = 70%
Actual cost = 70% of 19.40
$= .70 \times 19.40$
$= 13.58$
Answer: **(C)** $13.58

10. Subtract weight of wood after drying from original weight of wood to find amount of moisture in wood:

$$\begin{array}{r} 10 \\ \underline{-8} \\ 2 \end{array}$$ ounces of moisture in wood

Moisture content $= \dfrac{2 \text{ ounces}}{10 \text{ ounces}} = .2 = 20\%$

Answer: **(C)** 20%

11. Find the number of each kind of coin:
    10% of 800 = .10 × 800 = 80 dimes
    30% of 800 = .30 × 800 = 240 nickels
    60% of 800 = .60 × 800 = 480 quarters

    Find the value of the coins:

    $$
    \begin{aligned}
    80 \text{ dimes} &= 80 \times .10 = \$\ 8.00 \\
    240 \text{ nickels} &= 240 \times .05 = \ 12.00 \\
    480 \text{ quarters} &= 480 \times .25 = \underline{\ 120.00} \\
    &\qquad\qquad\qquad \text{Total } \$140.00
    \end{aligned}
    $$

    Answer: **(A)** less than $150

12. The first solution contains 20% of 6 quarts
    of alcohol.
    Alcohol content = .20 × 6
    $\qquad\qquad\qquad$ = 1.2 quarts
    Second solution contains 60% of 4 quarts of
    alcohol.
    Alcohol content = .60 × 4
    $\qquad\qquad\qquad$ = 2.4 quarts
    The mixture contains: 1.2 ⁻ 2.4 = 3.6 quarts
    alcohol

    $$6 \ ^{-}\ 4 = 10 \text{ quarts}$$
    $$\text{liquid}$$

    Alcoholic strength of mixture = $\dfrac{3.6}{10}$ = 36%

    Answer: **(C)** 36%

13. $2\frac{1}{2}$% of insured value = $348
    $\qquad$ Insured value = $\dfrac{348}{2\frac{1}{2}\%}$

    $\qquad\qquad\qquad\quad$ = 348 ÷ .025
    $\qquad\qquad\qquad\quad$ = $13,920
    $13,920 is 80% of total value
    $\qquad$ Total value = $13,920 ÷ 80%
    $\qquad\qquad\qquad\quad$ = $13,920 ÷ .80
    $\qquad\qquad\qquad\quad$ = $17,400

    Answer: **(D)** $17,400

14. $\dfrac{1}{5} \times 35 = 7$ hours sorting mail

    $\dfrac{1}{2} \times 35 = 17\frac{1}{2}$ hours filing

    $\dfrac{1}{7} \times 35 = 5$ hours reception
    $\qquad\qquad\qquad\overline{\qquad\qquad\qquad}$
    $\qquad\qquad 29\frac{1}{2}$ hours accounted for

    $35 - 29\frac{1}{2} = 5\frac{1}{2}$ hours left for

    messenger work:

    $= \dfrac{5\frac{1}{2}}{35}$

    $= 5\frac{1}{2} \div 35$

    $= \dfrac{11}{2} \times \dfrac{1}{35}$

    $= \dfrac{11}{70}$

    $= .15\frac{5}{7}$

    Answer: **(D)** most nearly 16% = $15\frac{5}{7}$

15. $\qquad$ 80% of the boys $\qquad$ = 1,152
    $\qquad$ Number of boys $\qquad$ = 1,152 ÷ 80%
    $\qquad\qquad\qquad\qquad\qquad$ = 1,152 ÷ .80
    $\qquad\qquad\qquad\qquad\qquad$ = 1,440
    $\qquad$ 40% of students = 1,440
    Total number of students = 1,440 ÷ 40%
    $\qquad\qquad\qquad\qquad\qquad$ = 1,440 ÷ .40
    $\qquad\qquad\qquad\qquad\qquad$ = 3,600

    Answer: **(C)** 3600

GRAPHS

1. **Graphs** illustrate comparisons and trends in statistical information. The most commonly used graphs are **bar graphs, line graphs, circle graphs,** and **pictographs**.

Bar Graphs

2. **Bar graphs** are used to compare various quantities. Each bar may represent a single quantity or may be divided to represent several quantities.

3. Bar graphs may have horizontal or vertical bars.

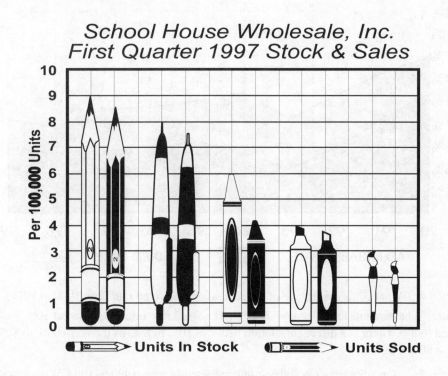

Question 1: What percentage of all units in stock do the paintbrushes comprise?

Answer: Add all the stock together for a total number of units: 900,000 pencils + 800,000 pens + 600,000 crayons + 400,000 markers + 300,000 brushes = 3,000,000 total units. The 3,000,000 units are divided by 300,000 paintbrushes = **10.** The brushes make up 10% of the stock.

Question 2: What is the approximate ratio of sales between the pencils and crayons?

Answer: Pencil sales were a little more than 850,000, and the crayons were about 425,000. The 850,000 pencils are exactly 2 times the 425,000 crayons, making the estimated sales ratio 2 to 1.

Question 3: If at the end of 1996 there were 25,000 pencils still in stock, how many pencils were received within the first quarter of 1997?

Answer: There were 900,000 pencils in stock in the first quarter. The 900,000 units in stock – 25,000 in stock = 875,000 received in the first quarter.

Line Graphs

4. **Line graphs** are used to show trends, often over a period of time.

5. A line graph may include more than one line, with each line representing a different item.

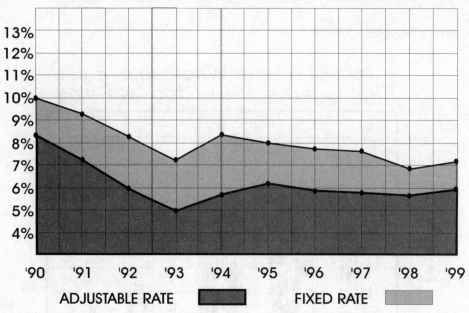

Question 4: What is the percentage of the decrease of the fixed rate from 1990 to 1995?

Answer: The percentage of decrease is 20%. The fixed rate interest started at 10% and was reduced to 8%. There is a direct correlation between 10% to 8%, as there is 100% to 80%. 100% – 80% = 20%.

Question 5: The adjustable rate interest fell consistently from 1990 to 1993. What was the approximate average decrease per year?

Answer: A quick estimate of the average would be slightly more than 1% per year, because 1990 and 1991 fell only a very small amount more than 1%, and 1993 fell exactly 1%.

Question 6: Assuming that the interest rate is going to follow the trend set in 1999, what is the expected range of the rate for the year 2000?

Answer: It would be expected to go up to somewhere in the 6.25% to 6.5% range.

Circle Graphs

6. **Circle graphs** are used to show the relationship of various parts of a quantity to each other and to the whole quantity.

7. Percents are often used in circle graphs. The 360 degrees of the circle represents 100%.

8. Each part of the circle graph is called a **sector**.

The following graph shows the labor force of the United States population.

Labor Force of the United States
Working Population: 137,000,000 (July 1999 Est.)

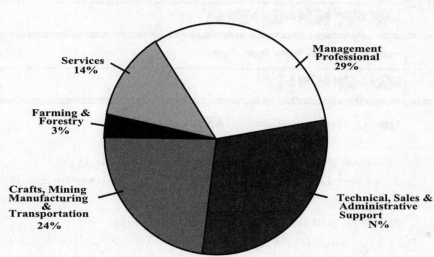

Question 7:   The U.S. labor force has N % involved in the Technical, Sales, and Administration Support categories. What is the value of N?

Answer: There must be a total of 100% in a circle graph. The sum of the other sectors is:

$$14\% + 29\% + 24\% + 3\% = 70\%$$
$$N = 100\% - 70\%$$
$$N = 30\%$$

Question 8:   Out of every hundred working people, how many are involved in the Farming and Forestry category?

Answer: Percentage is expressed as one-hundredth part of the whole. Therefore, 3% represents 3 people out of each 100.

Question 9:   Approximately $\frac{1}{4}$ of the working population is involved in which category of labor?

Answer: The fraction $\frac{1}{4}$ is equal to 25 out of 100, or 25%. The closest category is Crafts, Mining, Manufacturing, and Transportation, which makes up 24% of the United States labor force.

Pictographs

9. **Pictographs** allow comparisons of quantities by using symbols. Each symbol represents a given number of a particular item.

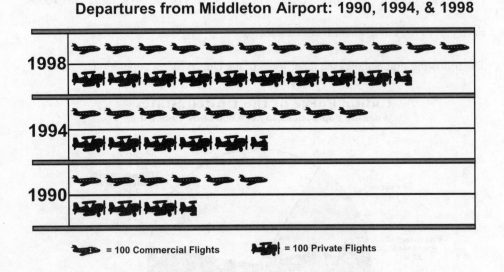

Departures from Middleton Airport: 1990, 1994, & 1998

= 100 Commercial Flights   = 100 Private Flights

Question 10:   How many more commercial flights took off in 1998 than in 1994?

Answer: There are three more symbols for 1998 than for 1994. Each symbol represents 100 departures. Therefore, 300 more flights took off in 1998.

Question 11:   How many more private flights departed in 1998 than 1990?

Answer: There are $9\frac{1}{2}$ symbols in 1998 and $3\frac{1}{2}$ symbols in 1990. $9\frac{1}{2} - 3\frac{1}{2} = 6$ symbols. $6 \times 100 = 600$ more departures that occurred in 1998.

Question 12:   Which year shows half as many flights as another year?

Answer: The 600 commercial flights in 1990 are half as many as the 1,200 commercial flights in 1998.

Practice Problems Involving Graphs

Directions: Each question has four suggested answers. Select the correct one, and mark it on the answer sheet on page 151.

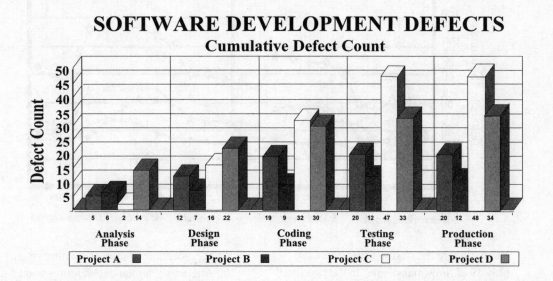

SOFTWARE DEVELOPMENT DEFECTS
Cumulative Defect Count

1. On Project A, what percentage of the defects were identified in the Analysis Phase, compared to the total number identified in all the phases?

   (A) 2%   (C) 40%
   (B) 25%   (D) 15%

2. Which projects were able to overcome their software defects by the Testing Phase?

   (A) Project B and C   (C) Project A and D
   (B) Project B and D   (D) Project A and B

3. Project B concluded with a total defect count of 12, while Project C concluded with a total defect count of 48. What percent greater did Project C have over Project B?

   (A) 75%   (C) 25%
   (B) 300%   (D) 200%

4. What is the average number of defects found in each phase of Project C?

   (A) 3.8   (C) 6.4
   (B) 9.6   (D) 2.6

Questions 5–7 refer to the following graph:

R&D Project Expenditures FY 1997 - 1998

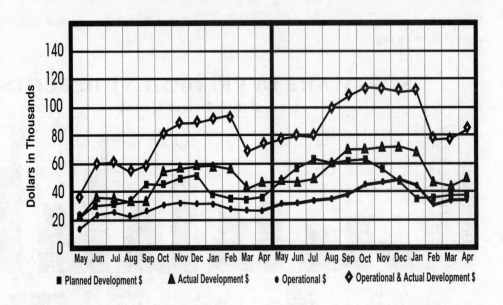

■ Planned Development $ ▲ Actual Development $ ● Operational $ ◆ Operational & Actual Development $

5. Not including the startup expenditures in May 1997, how many times in the two fiscal years (FY) did the Actual R&D Expenditures coincide with the Planned R&D Expenditures?

(A) 1 time (C) 3 times
(B) 6 times (D) 8 times

6. How many months were the total expenditures $100,000 or greater?

(A) 11 months (C) 5 months
(B) 2 months (D) 6 months

7. What percentage of the expenditures from the August 1998 total expenditures went for R&D?

(A) 60% (C) 35%
(B) 100% (D) None of the above

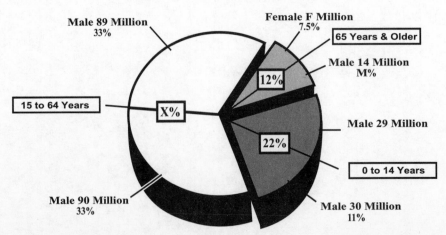

Population of the United States by Age
Population: 272,000,000 (July 1999 Est.)

Questions 8–11 refer to the previous graph:

8. X% represents of the population of the
    United States that is 15 to 64 years old.
    What percent does X represent?
    (A) 27%   (C) 65%
    (B) 33%   (D) 66%

9. How many females (F million) in the United
    States are 65 years or older?
    (A) 24,040,000   (C) 21,004,000
    (B) 22,400,000   (D) 20,400,000

10. What percentage of the population is
    female?
    (A) 51.5%   (C) 49.5%
    (B) 52%   (D) 52.5%

11. Which one of the following Answers is the
    closest to the percentage (M%) of the male
    population 65 years or older?
    (A) 5.5%   (C) 4.5%
    (B) 12%   (D) 33%

Questions 12–15 refer to the following graph:

Great Western Groceries
Fruit Sales for the 1st Six Months of 1998

Each piece of fruit represents 100 bushels

12. What percent of February's total sales were
    pears?
    (A) 22%   (C) 18%
    (B) 25%   (D) 49%

13. What is the total number of bushels sold in
    March?
    (A) 2400 bushels (C) 2000 bushels
    (B) 2600 bushels (D) 2500 bushels

14. How many more bushels were sold in
    January than were sold in April?
    (A) 1000 bushels (C) 250 bushels
    (B) 300 bushels (D) 400 bushels

15. If the average amount received for each
    bushel is $30, how much money was
    received for the fruit sold in June?
    (A) $60,000   (C) $66,000
    (B) $22,000   (D) $56,000

Answer Key

1. **(B)**	6. **(D)**	11. **(C)**
2. **(D)**	7. **(A)**	12. **(B)**
3. **(B)**	8. **(D)**	13. **(D)**
4. **(B)**	9. **(D)**	14. **(B)**
5. **(C)**	10. **(A)**	15. **(C)**

Solutions

1. The percentage is found by dividing the 5 defects found in the Analysis Phase by the 20 found in all the phases: .25 = 25%
   Answer: **(B)** 25%

2. Only Projects A and B had no defects in the Production Phase.
   Answer: **(D)** Project A and B

3. Project B had a total of 12 defects, which is 100% of the defects of that project. Project C had a total of 48 defects, which is 4 times greater than the 100% of Project B.
   $$4 \times 100\% = 400\%$$
   $$400\% - 100\% = 300\%$$
   Answer: **(B)** 300%

4. Project C had a total of 48 defects, as shown in the Production Phase. The total number of defects, 48, divided by 5, the number of phases, equals an average of 9.6 defects found in each phase.
   Answer: **(B)** 9.6 defects

5. The actual and planned expenditures were the same three times: in August 1997, May 1998, and September 1998.
   Answer: **(C)** 3 times

6. In fiscal year 1998, there were six months, from August to January, in which the total expenditures were $100,000 or greater.
   Answer: **(D)** Six months

7. The total amount of the September 1998 expenditures was exactly $100,000 and the amount spent on R&D expenditures was $60,000. Therefore, the correlation to the percentage is directly equal to 60%.
   Answer: **(A)** 60%

8. The percentage is found by combining the 33% of males 15 to 64 years, and the 33% females 15 to 64 years (33% + 33% = 66%).
   Answer: **(D)** 66%

9. The entire population, 272,000,000 is multiplied by the decimal equivalent of 7.5% (.075) to arrive at the answer (.075 × 272,000,000 = 20,400,000).
   Answer: **(D)** 20,400,000

10. The percentages of the females of all ages are added together to arrive at the answer (7.5% + 11% + 33% = 51.5%)
    Answer: **(A)** 51.5%

11. The graph shows that 12% of the population is 65 years and older. Subtract the 7.5% of the females from the 12% to find the percentage of males (12% × 7.5% = 4.5%).
    Answer: **(C)** 4.5%

12. In February, the total number of bushels were 2400. There were 400 bushels of pears sold. 400 ÷ 2400 = .25 = 25%.
    Answer: **(B)** 25%

13. The count of all of the symbols is 25.
    25 × 100 bushels per symbol = 2500 bushels.

    Answer: **(D)** 2500 bushels

14. The count of all the symbols in January
    multiplied by 100 equals 2600 and in April
    equals 2300. 2600 – 2300 = 300 more
    bushels.
    Answer: **(B)** 300 bushels

15. A total of $66,000 was collected. The count
    of all the symbols for June is 22 multiplied
    by 100, or 2200. The 2200 bushels multi-
    plied by the average cost of $30 per bushel
    equals $66,00.
    Answer: **(C)** $66,000

RATIO AND PROPORTION

Ratio

1. A **ratio** expresses the relationship between two (or more) quantities in terms of numbers. The mark used to indicate ratio is the colon (:) and is read "to."

    Example: The ratio 2:3 is read "2 to 3."

2. A ratio also represents division. Therefore, any ratio of two terms may be written as a fraction, and any fraction may be written as a ratio.

    Example: $3:4 = \frac{3}{4}$

    $$\frac{5}{6} = 5:6$$

3. To simplify any complicated ratio of two terms containing fractions, decimals, or percents:

    a.   Divide the first term by the second.

    b.   Write as a fraction in lowest terms.

    c.   Write the fraction as a ratio.

    Illustration: Simplify the ratio $\frac{5}{6} : \frac{7}{8}$

    SOLUTION: $\frac{5}{6} \div \frac{7}{8} = \frac{5}{6} \times \frac{8}{7} = \frac{20}{21}$

    $$\frac{20}{21} = 20:21$$

    Answer: 20:21

4. To solve problems in which the ratio is given:

    a.   Add the terms in the ratio.

    b.   Divide the total amount that is to be put into a ratio by this sum.

    c.   Multiply each term in the ratio by this quotient.

    Illustration: The sum of $360 is to be divided among three people according to the ratio 3:4:5. How much does each one receive?

    SOLUTION: $3 + 4 + 5 = 12$
    $\$360 \div 12 = \$30$
    $\$30 \times 3 = \$90$
    $\$30 \times 4 = \$120$
    $\$30 \times 5 = \$150$

    Answer: The money is divided thus: $90, $120, $150.

Proportion

5. a.   A **proportion** indicates the equality of two ratios.

    Example: 2:4 = 5:10 is a proportion. This is read "2 is to 4 as 5 is to 10."

    b.   In a proportion, the two outside terms are called the **extremes**, and the two inside terms are called the **means**.

    Example: In the proportion 2:4 = 5:10, 2 and 10 are the extremes, and 4 and 5 are the means.

    c.   Proportions are often written in fractional form.

    Example: The proportion 2:4 = 5:10 may be written $\frac{2}{4} = \frac{5}{10}$.

    d.   In any proportion, the product of the means equals the product of the extremes. If the proportion is in fractional form, the products may be found by cross-multiplication.

    Example: In $\frac{2}{4} = \frac{5}{10}$, $4 \times 5 = 2 \times 10$.

    e.   The product of the extremes divided by one mean equals the other mean; the product of the means divided by one extreme equals the other extreme.

6. Many problems in which three terms are given and one term is unknown can be solved by using proportions. To solve such problems:

    a.   Formulate the proportion very carefully according to the facts given. (If any term is misplaced, the solution will be incorrect.) Any symbol may be written in place of the missing term.

    b.   Determine by inspection whether the means or the extremes are known. Multiply the pair that has both terms given.

    c.   Divide this product by the third term given to find the unknown term.

    Illustration: The scale on a map shows that 2 cm represents 30 miles of actual length. What is the actual length of a road that is represented by 7 cm on the map?

    SOLUTION: The map lengths and the actual lengths are in proportion—that is, they have equal ratios. If *m* stands for the unknown length, the proportion is:

$$\frac{2}{7} = \frac{30}{m}$$

As the proportion is written, *m* is an extreme and is equal to the product of the means, divided by the other extreme:

$$m = \frac{7 \times 30}{2}$$

$$m = \frac{210}{2}$$

$$m = 105$$

Answer: 7 cm on the map represents 105 miles.

Illustration: If a money bag containing 500 nickels weighs 6 pounds, how much will a money bag containing 1600 nickels weigh?

SOLUTION: The weights of the bags and the number of coins in them are proportional. Suppose that w represents the unknown weight. Then:

$$\frac{6}{w} = \frac{500}{1,600}$$

The unknown is a mean and is equal to the product of the extremes, divided by the other mean:

$$w = \frac{6 \times 1,600}{500}$$
$$w = 19.2$$

Answer: A bag containing 1600 nickels weighs 19.2 pounds.

Practice Problems Involving Ratio and Proportion

Directions: Each question has four suggested answers. Select the correct one, and mark it on the answer sheet on page 151.

1. The ratio of 24 to 64 is
    (A) 8:3
    (B) 24:100
    (C) 3:8
    (D) 64:100

2. The Baltimore Colts won 8 games and lost **3.** The ratio of games won to games played is
    (A) 8:11
    (B) 3:11
    (C) 8:3
    (D) 3:8

3. The ratio of $\frac{1}{4}$ to $\frac{3}{5}$ is
    (A) 1 to 3
    (B) 3 to 20
    (C) 5 to 12
    (D) 3 to 4

4. If there are 16 boys and 12 girls in a class, the ratio of the number of girls to the number of children in the class is
    (A) 3 to 4
    (B) 3 to 7
    (C) 4 to 7
    (D) 4 to 3

5. 259 is to 37 as
    (A) 5 is to 1
    (B) 63 is to 441
    (C) 84 is to 12
    (D) 130 is to 19

6. Two dozen cans of dog food at the rate of three cans for $1.45 would cost
    (A) $10.05
    (B) $11.20
    (C) $11.60
    (D) $11.75

7. A snapshot measures $2\frac{1}{2}$ inches by $1\frac{7}{8}$ inches. It is to be enlarged so that the longer dimension will be 4 inches. The length of the enlarged shorter dimension will be
    (A) $2\frac{1}{2}$ inches
    (B) 3 inches
    (C) $3\frac{3}{8}$ inches
    (D) none of these

8. Men's white handkerchiefs cost $2.29 for three. The cost per dozen handkerchiefs is
    (A) $27.48
    (B) $13.74
    (C) $9.16
    (D) $6.87

9. A certain pole casts a shadow 24 feet long. At the same time, another pole 3 feet high casts a shadow 4 feet long. How high is the first pole, given that the heights and shadows are in proportion?
    (A) 18 feet
    (B) 19 feet
    (C) 20 feet
    (D) 21 feet

10. The actual length represented by $3\frac{1}{2}$ inches on a drawing having a scale of $\frac{1}{8}$ inch to the foot is
   - (A) 3.75 feet
   - (B) 28 feet
   - (C) 360 feet
   - (D) 120 feet

11. Aluminum bronze consists of copper and aluminum, usually in the ratio of 10:1 by weight. If an object made of this alloy weighs 77 pounds, how many pounds of aluminum does it contain?
   - (A) 7.7
   - (B) 7.0
   - (C) 70.0
   - (D) 62.3

12. It costs 31 cents a square foot to lay vinyl flooring. To lay 180 square feet of flooring, it will cost
   - (A) $16.20
   - (B) $18.60
   - (C) $55.80
   - (D) $62.00

13. If a per diem worker earns $352 in 16 days, the amount that he will earn in 117 days is most nearly
   - (A) $3050
   - (B) $2575
   - (C) $2285
   - (D) $2080

14. Assuming that on a blueprint $\frac{1}{8}$ inch equals 12 inches of actual length, the actual length in inches of a steel bar represented on the blueprint by a line $3\frac{3}{4}$ inches long is
   - (A) $3\frac{3}{4}$
   - (B) 30
   - (C) 450
   - (D) 360

15. A, B, and C invested $9,000, $7,000 and $6,000, respectively. Their profits were to be divided according to the ratio of their investment. If B uses his share of the firm's profit of $825 to pay a personal debt of $230, how much will he have left?
   - (A) $30.50
   - (B) $32.50
   - (C) $34.50
   - (D) $36.50

Answer Key

1. (C)	6. (C)	11. (B)
2. (A)	7. (B)	12. (C)
3. (C)	8. (C)	13. (B)
4. (B)	9. (A)	14. (D)
5. (C)	10. (B)	15. (B)

Solutions

1. The ratio 24 to 64 may be written 24:64 or $\frac{24}{64}$. In fraction form, the ratio can be reduced:
$$\frac{24}{64} = \frac{3}{8} \text{ or } 3:8$$
   Answer: (C) 3:8

2. The number of games played was $3 + 8 = 11$. The ratio of games won to games played is 8:11.
   Answer: (A) 8:11

3. $\frac{1}{4} : \frac{3}{5} = \frac{1}{4} \div \frac{3}{5}$
$$= \frac{1}{4} \times \frac{5}{3}$$
$$= \frac{5}{12}$$
$$= 5:12$$
   Answer: (C) 5 to 12

4. There are $16 + 12 = 28$ children in the class. The ratio of number of girls to number of children is 12:28.

$$\frac{12}{28} = \frac{3}{7}$$

Answer: **(B)** 3 to 7

5. The ratio $\frac{259}{37}$ reduces by 37 to $\frac{7}{1}$. The ratio $\frac{84}{12}$ also reduces to $\frac{7}{1}$. Therefore, $\frac{259}{37} = \frac{84}{12}$ is a proportion.

Answer: **(C)** 84 is to 12

6. The number of cans are proportional to the price. Let p represent the unknown price. Then:

$$\frac{3}{24} = \frac{1.45}{p}$$

$$p = \frac{1.45 \times 24}{3}$$

$$p = \frac{34.80}{3}$$

$$p = \$11.60$$

Answer: **(C)** \$11.60

7. Let s represent the unknown shorter dimension:

$$\frac{2\frac{1}{2}}{4} = \frac{1\frac{7}{8}}{s}$$

$$s = \frac{4 \times 1\frac{7}{8}}{2\frac{1}{2}}$$

$$s = \frac{{}^1\cancel{4} \times \frac{15}{\cancel{8}_2}}{2\frac{1}{2}}$$

$$s = \frac{15}{2} \div 2\frac{1}{2}$$

$$s = \frac{15}{2} \div \frac{5}{2}$$

$$s = \frac{15}{2} \times \frac{2}{5}$$

$$s = 3$$

Answer: **(B)** 3 inches

8. If p is the cost per dozen (12):

$$\frac{3}{12} = \frac{2.29}{p}$$

$$p = \frac{{}^4\cancel{12} \times 2.29}{\cancel{3}_1}$$

$$p = 9.16$$

Answer: **(C)** \$9.16

9. If f is the height of the first pole, the proportion is:

$$\frac{f}{24} = \frac{3}{4}$$

$$f = \frac{{}^6\cancel{24} \times 3}{\cancel{4}_1}$$

$$f = 18$$

Answer: **(A)** 18 feet

10. If y is the unknown length:

$$\frac{3\frac{1}{2}}{\frac{1}{8}} = \frac{y}{1}$$

$$y = \frac{3\frac{1}{2} \times 1}{\frac{1}{8}}$$

$$y = 3\frac{1}{2} \div \frac{1}{8}$$

$$y = \frac{7}{2} \times \frac{8}{1}$$

$$= 28$$

Answer: **(B)** 28 feet

11. Because only two parts of a proportion are known (77 is the total weight), the problem must be solved by the ratio method. The ratio 10:1 means that if the alloy were separated into equal parts, 10 of those parts would be copper and 1 would be aluminum, for a total of $10 + 1 = 11$ parts.

$$77 \div 11 = 7 \text{ pounds per part}$$

The alloy has 1 part aluminum.

$$7 \times 1 = 7 \text{ pounds aluminum}$$

Answer: **(B)** 7.0

12. The cost c is proportional to the number of square feet.

$$\frac{\$.31}{c} = \frac{1}{180}$$

$$c = \frac{\$.31 \times 180}{1}$$

$$c = \$55.80$$

Answer: (**C**) $55.80

13. The amount earned is proportional to the number of days worked. If a is the unknown amount:

$$\frac{\$352}{a} = \frac{16}{117}$$

$$a = \frac{\$352 \times 117}{16}$$

$$a = \$2574$$

Answer: (**B**) $2575

14. If n is the unknown length:

$$\frac{\frac{1}{8}}{3\frac{3}{4}} = \frac{12}{n}$$

$$n = \frac{12 \times 3\frac{3}{4}}{\frac{1}{8}}$$

$$n = \frac{\overset{3}{\cancel{12}} \times \frac{15}{\cancel{4}1}}{\frac{1}{8}}$$

$$n = \frac{45}{\frac{1}{8}}$$

$$n = 45 \div \frac{1}{8}$$

$$n = 45 \times \frac{8}{1}$$

$$n = 360$$

Answer: (**D**) 360

15. The ratio of investment is:

$$9,000:7,000:6,000, \text{ or } 9:7:6$$

$$9 + 7 + 6 = 22$$

$825 ÷ 22 = \$37.50 each share of profit

$7 × \$37.50 = \$262.50 B's share of profit

$$\begin{array}{r} \$262.50 \\ -\ 230.00 \\ \hline \$32.50 \text{ amount B has left} \end{array}$$

Answer: (**B**) $32.50

WORK PROBLEMS

Work Problems

1. a.   In work problems, three items are involved: the number of people working, the time, and the amount of work done.

   b.   The number of people working is directly proportional to the amount of work done—that is, the more people on the job, the more the work that will be done, and vice versa.

   c.   The number of people working is inversely proportional to the time—that is, the more people on the job, the less time it will take to finish it, and vice versa.

   d.   The time expended on a job is directly proportional to the amount of work done—that is, the more time expended on a job, the more work that is done, and vice versa.

Work at Equal Rates

2. a.   When given the time required by a number of people working at equal rates to complete a job, multiply the number of people by their time to find the time required by one person to do the complete job.

   Example: If it takes four people working at equal rates 30 days to finish a job, then one person will take 30×4, or 120 days.

   b.   When given the time required by one person to complete a job, to find the time required by a number of people working at equal rates to complete the same job, divide the time by the number of people.

   Example: If one person can do a job in 20 days, it will take four people working at equal rates $20 \div 4$, or 5 days to finish the job.

3.   To solve problems involving people who work at equal rates:

   a.   Multiply the number of people by their time to find the time required by 1 person.

   b.   Divide this time by the number of people required.

   Illustration: Four workers can do a job in 48 days. How long will it take three workers to finish the same job?

   SOLUTION: One worker can do the job in 48×4, or 192 days.

   Three workers can do the job in $192 \div 3 = 64$ days.

   Answer: It would take three workers 64 days.

4. In some work problems, the rates, though unequal, can be equalized by comparison. To solve such problems:

   a. Determine from the facts given how many equal rates there are.

   b. Multiply the number of equal rates by the time given.

   c. Divide this by the number of equal rates.

   Illustration: Three workers can do a job in 12 days. Two of the workers work twice as fast as the third. How long would it take one of the faster workers to do the job himself?

   SOLUTION: There are two fast workers and one slow worker. Therefore, there are actually five slow workers working at equal rates.

   One slow worker will take 12×5, or 60 days.

   1 fast worker = 2 slow workers; therefore, he will take $60 \div 2$, or 30 days to complete the job.

   Answer: It will take one fast worker 30 days to complete the job.

5. Unit time is time expressed in terms of 1 minute, 1 hour, 1 day, and so on.

6. The rate at which a person works is the amount of work he can do in unit time.

7. If given the time it will take one person to do a job, then the reciprocal of the time is the part done in unit time.

   Example: If a worker can do a job in 6 days, then he can do $\frac{1}{6}$ of the work in 1 day.

8. The reciprocal of the work done in unit time is the time it will take to do the complete job.

   Example: If a worker can do $\frac{3}{7}$ of the work in 1 day, then he can do the whole job in $\frac{7}{3}$, or $2\frac{1}{3}$ days.

9. If given the various times at which each of a number of people can complete a job, to find the time it will take to do the job if all work together:

   a. Invert the time of each to find how much each can do in unit time.

   b. Add these reciprocals to find what part all working together can do in unit time.

   c. Invert this sum to find the time it will take all of them together to do the whole job.

   Illustration: If it takes A 3 days to dig a certain ditch, whereas B can dig it in 6 days, and C in 12, how long would it take all three to do the job?

SOLUTION: A can do it in 3 days; therefore, he can do $\frac{1}{3}$ in one day. B can do it in 6 days; therefore, he can do $\frac{1}{6}$ in one day. C can do it in 12 days; therefore, he can do $\frac{1}{12}$ in one day.

$$\frac{1}{3} + \frac{1}{6} + \frac{1}{12} = \frac{7}{12}$$

A, B, and C can do $\frac{7}{12}$ of the work in one day; therefore, it will take them $\frac{12}{7}$, or $1\frac{5}{7}$ days to complete the job.

Answer: A, B, and C, working together, can complete the job in $1\frac{5}{7}$ days.

10. If given the total time it requires a number of people working together to complete a job, and the times of all but one are known, to find the missing time:

a. Invert the given times to find how much each can do in unit time.

b. Add the reciprocals to find how much is done in unit time by those whose rates are known.

c. Subtract this sum from the reciprocal of the total time to find the missing rate.

d. Invert this rate to find the unknown time.

Illustration: A, B, and C can do a job in 2 days. B can do it in 5 days, and C can do it in 4 days. How long would it take A to do it himself?

SOLUTION: B can do it in 5 days; therefore, he can do $\frac{1}{5}$ in one day. C can do it in 4 days; therefore, he can do $\frac{1}{4}$ in one day. The part that can be done by B and C together in 1 day is:

$$\frac{1}{5} + \frac{1}{4} = \frac{9}{20}$$

The total time is 2 days; therefore, all can do $\frac{1}{2}$ in one day.

$$\frac{1}{2} - \frac{9}{20} = \frac{1}{20}$$

A can do $\frac{1}{20}$ in 1 day; therefore, he can do the whole job in 20 days.

Answer: It would take A 20 days to complete the job himself.

11. In some work problems, certain values are given for the three factors—number of workers, the amount of work done, and the time. It then usually is required to find the changes that occur when one or two of the factors are given different values.

One of the best methods of solving such problems is by directly making the necessary cancellations, divisions and multiplications.

In this problem, it is easily seen that more workers will be required because more houses are to be built in a shorter time.

Illustration: If 60 workers can build 4 houses in 12 months, how many workers would be required to build 6 houses in 4 months?

SOLUTION: To build 6 houses instead of 4 in the same amount of time, we would need $\frac{6}{4}$ of the number of workers.

$$\frac{6}{4} \times 60 = 90$$

Because we now have 4 months where previously we needed 12, we must triple the number of workers.

$$90 \times 3 = 270$$

Answer: 270 workers will be needed to build 6 houses in 4 months.

Work Practice Problems

Directions: Each question has four suggested answers. Select the correct one, and mark it on the answer sheet on page 151.

1. If 314 clerks filed 6594 papers in 10 minutes, what is the number filed per minute by the average clerk?
   (A) 2   (C) 2.1
   (B) 2.4   (D) 2.5

2. Four men working together can dig a ditch in 42 days. They begin, but one man works only half-days. How long will it take to complete the job?
   (A) 48 days   (C) 43 days
   (B) 45 days   (D) 44 days

3. A clerk is requested to file 800 cards. If he can file cards at the rate of 80 cards an hour, the number of cards remaining to be filed after 7 hours of work is:
   (A) 140   (C) 260
   (B) 240   (D) 560

4. If it takes 4 days for 3 machines to do a certain job, it will take 2 machines how long?
   (A) 6 days   (C) 5 days
   (B) $5\frac{1}{2}$ days   (D) $4\frac{1}{2}$ days

5. A stenographer has been assigned to place entries on 500 forms. She places entries on 25 forms by the end of half an hour, when she is joined by another stenographer. The second stenographer places entries at the rate of 45 an hour. Assuming that both stenographers continue to work at their respective rates of speed, the total number of hours required to carry out the entire assignment is:
   (A) 5   (C) $6\frac{1}{2}$
   (B) $5\frac{1}{2}$ (D) 7

6. If in 5 days a clerk can copy 125 pages, 36 lines each, with 11 words to the line, how many pages of 30 lines each and 12 words to the line can he copy in 6 days?
   (A) 145   (C) 160
   (B) 155   (D) 165

7. A and B do a job together in two hours. Working alone, A does the job in 5 hours. How long will it take B to do the job alone?
   (A) $3\frac{1}{3}$ hours   (C) 3 hours
   (B) $2\frac{1}{4}$ hours   (D) 2 hours

8. A stenographer transcribes her notes at the rate of one line typed in 10 seconds. At this rate, how long (in minutes and seconds) will it take her to transcribe notes, which will require seven pages of typing, with 25 lines to the page?
   (A) 29 minutes, 10 seconds
   (B) 17 minutes, 50 seconds
   (C) 40 minutes, 10 seconds
   (D) 20 minutes, 30 seconds

9. A group of five clerks has been assigned to insert 24,000 letters into envelopes. The clerks perform this work at the following rates of speed: Clerk A, 1100 letters an hour; Clerk B, 1450 letters an hour; Clerk C, 1200 letters an hour; Clerk D 1300 letters an hour; Clerk E, 1250 letters an hour. At the end of two hours of work, Clerks C and D are assigned to another task. From the time that Clerks C and D were taken off the assignment, the number of hours required for the remaining clerks to complete this assignment is:
   (A) less than 3 hours
   (B) 3 hours
   (C) more than 3 hours, but less than 4 hours
   (D) more than 4 hours

10. If a certain job can be performed by 18 workers in 26 days, the number of workers needed to perform the job in 12 days is:
    (A) 24   (C) 39
    (B) 30   (D) 52

Answer Key

1. (C)   6. (D)
2. (A)   7. (A)
3. (B)   8. (A)
4. (A)   9. (B)
5. (B)   10. (C)

Solutions

1. 6594 papers ÷ 314 clerks = 21 papers per clerk in 10 minutes
   21 papers ÷ 10 minutes = 2.1 papers per minute filed by average clerk
   Answer: **(C)** 2.1

2. It would take one man $42 \times 4 = 168$ days to complete the job, working alone.
   If $3\frac{1}{2}$ men are working (one man works half-days, and the other 3 work full days), the job would take $168 \div 3\frac{1}{2} = 48$ days.
   Answer: **(A)** 48 days

3. In 7 hours, the clerk files $7 \times 80 = 560$ cards. Because 800 cards must be filed, there are $800 - 560 = 240$ remaining.
   Answer: **(B)** 240

4. It would take one machine $3 \times 4 = 12$ days to do the job. Two machines could do the job in $12 \div 2 = 6$ days.
   Answer: **(A)** 6 days

5. At the end of the first half-hour, there are $500 - 25 = 475$ forms remaining. If the first stenographer completed 25 forms in half an hour, her rate is $25 \times 2 = 50$ forms per hour. The combined rate of the two stenographers is $50 + 45 = 95$ forms per hour. The remaining forms can be completed in $475 \div 95 = 5$ hours. Adding the first half-hour, the entire job requires $5\frac{1}{2}$ hours.

Answer: **(B)** $5\frac{1}{2}$

6. $36 \text{ lines} \times 11 \text{ words} = 396$ words on each page
$125 \text{ pages} \times 396 \text{ words} = 49{,}500$ words in 5 days
$49{,}500 \div 5 = 9900$ words in 1 day
$12 \text{ words} \times 30 \text{ lines} = 360$ words on each page
$9900 \div 360 = 27\frac{1}{2}$ pages in 1 day
$27\frac{1}{2} \times 6 = 165$ pages in 6 days
Answer: **(D)** 165

7. If A can do the job alone in 5 hours, A can do $\frac{1}{5}$ of the job in 1 hour. Working together, A and B can do the job in 2 hours; therefore, in 1 hour they do $\frac{1}{2}$ the job.

In 1 hour, B alone does

$$\frac{1}{2} - \frac{1}{5} = \frac{5}{10} - \frac{2}{10}$$
$$= \frac{3}{10} \text{ of the job.}$$

It would take B $\frac{10}{3}$ hours $= 3\frac{1}{3}$ hours to do the whole job alone.

Answer: **(A)** $3\frac{1}{3}$ hours

8. She must type $7 \times 25 = 175$ lines. At the rate of 1 line per 10 seconds, it will take $175 \times 10 = 1750$ seconds.

1750 seconds $\div 60 = 29\frac{1}{6}$ minutes
$\qquad\qquad\qquad = 29$ minutes,
$\qquad\qquad\qquad\qquad 10$ seconds
Answer: **(A)** 29 minutes, 10 seconds

9.

Clerk	Number of letters per hour
A	1,100
B	1,450
C	1,200
D	1,300
E	+ 1,250
Total =	6,300

All five clerks working together process a total of 6300 letters per hour. After 2 hours, they have processed $6300 \times 2 = 12{,}600$. Of the original 24,000 letters, there are:

$$\begin{array}{r} 24{,}000 \\ -\ 12{,}600 \\ \hline 11{,}400 \end{array}$$ letters remaining.

Clerks A, B, and E working together process a total of 3800 letters per hour. It will take them this long to produce the remaining letters:

$11{,}400 \div 3800 = 3$ hours
Answer: **(B)** 3 hours

10. The job could be performed by 1 worker in 18×26 days $= 468$ days. To perform the job in 12 days would require $468 \div 12 = 39$ workers.
Answer: **(C)** 39

TABULAR COMPLETIONS

Tabular completion questions represent the newest type of arithmetic question to appear on *General Tests*. Numerically, these are among the easiest questions. The arithmetic involved is entirely restricted to addition and subtraction. The numbers may be large, but the process itself is simple.

The difficulty of tabular completion questions lies in choosing which numbers to add or subtract. The tables demand careful reading. In answering these questions, you must first determine which entries combine to create each total and subtotal. If you are unclear as to how a number is arrived at, you may have to look into a completed column to determine how certain figures were determined. Then move over into the column with the unknown you are seeking, and calculate it by combining appropriate entries.

Both the reasoning process involved and the actual calculations are important to successfully answer these questions, but concentration and care should enable you to master them. Practice will help.

Tabular Completion Practice Problems

Directions: These questions are based on information presented in tables. You must calculate the unknown values by using the known values given in the table. In some questions, the exact answer will not be given as one of the response choices. In such cases, you should select response (E), "None of these." Mark your answers on the answer sheet on page 152.

Table for Questions 1–5:

LOCAL GOVERNMENT EXPENDITURES OF FINANCES: 1995 TO 1998

(In Millions of Dollars)

ITEM	1995	1996	1997	1998 TOTAL	1998 PERCENT*
Expenditures	Ⓘ	432,328	485,174	520,966	100.0
Direct General Expenditures ..	326,024	367,340	405,576	Ⓘⱽ	83.2
Utility and Liquor Stores	30,846	Ⓘⓘ	43,016	47,970	9.2
Water and electric	20,734	24,244	28,453	31,499	6.0
Transit and others	10,112	11,947	14,563	16,471	3.2
Insurance Trust Expenditures..	23,504	28,797	36,582	39,466	Ⓥ
Employee retirement	12,273	14,008	Ⓘⓘⓘ	17,835	3.4
Unemployment compensation	11,231	14,789	20,887	21,631	4.2

Hypothetical data.   *Rounded to one decimal place

205

1. What is the value of I in millions of dollars?
   (A) 380,374
   (B) 377,604
   (C) 356,870
   (D) 349,528
   (E) none of these

2. What is the value of II in millions of dollars?
   (A) 338,543
   (B) 64,988
   (C) 53,041
   (D) 40,744
   (E) none of these

3. What is the value of III in millions of dollars?
   (A) 57,469
   (B) 52,277

   (C) 20,887
   (D) 15,695
   (E) none of these

4. What is the value of IV in millions of dollars?
   (A) 472,996
   (B) 433,530
   (C) 425,026
   (D) 134,807
   (E) none of these

5. What is the percent value of V?
   (A) 7.6%
   (B) 7.4%
   (C) 6.7%
   (D) 3.3%
   (E) none of these

Table for Questions 6–10:

REVENUE OF ALL GOVERNMENTS BY SOURCE AND LEVEL OF GOVERNMENT

FISCAL YEAR 1998

(In Millions of Dollars)

SOURCE	TOTAL	FEDERAL	STATE	LOCAL
Total Revenue	1,259,421	660,759	310,828	(V)
Intergovernmental	184,033	1,804	70,786	111,443
From federal government	90,295	—	(III)	22,427
From state or local government	93,738	1,804	2,918	89,016
Revenue from Own Sources	1,075,388	(II)	240,042	176,391
General	820,814	487,706	187,373	145,735
Taxes	(I)	405,714	149,738	94,776
Property	74,969	—	2,949	72,020
Individual and corporate income....	407,257	346,688	55,039	5,530
Sales and gross receipts	134,532	48,561	72,751	13,220
Other	33,470	10,465	18,999	4,006
Charges and miscellaneous	170,586	81,992	37,635	50,959
Utility and liquor stores	29,896	—	4,628	25,268
Insurance trust	224,678	171,249	48,041	5,388
Employee and railroad retirement ...	36,962	6,580	(IV)	5,260
Unemployment compensation	18,733	162	18,443	128
Old age, disability, and health insurance	168,983	164,507	4,476	—

Hypothetical data.

6. What is the value of I in millions of dollars?
   (A) 695,097
   (B) 616,758
   (C) 555,452
   (D) 254,574
   (E) none of these
7. What is the value of II in millions of dollars?
   (A) 835,346
   (B) 662,563
   (C) 658,955
   (D) 417,433
   (E) none of these
8. What is the value of III in millions of dollars?
   (A) 73,704
   (B) 68,868

(C) 67,868
(D) 67,978
(E) none of these

9. What is the value of IV in millions of dollars?
   (A) 43,565
   (B) 29,598
   (C) 25,122
   (D) 22,919
   (E) none of these
10. What is the value of V in millions of dollars?
    (A) 821,567
    (B) 464,175
    (C) 318,490
    (D) 287,834
    (E) none of these

Table for Questions 11–15:

FINANCE COMPANIES—ASSETS AND LIABILITIES: 1993 TO 1999

(In Millions of Dollars)

ITEM	1993	1996	1999
Total Receivables	I	85,994	183,341
Consumer Receivables	31,773	40,814	77,460
Retail passenger car paper and others	11,577	13,399	31,950
Retail consumer goods and loans	20,196	27,415	IV
Business Receivables	22,999	39,286	86,067
Wholesale paper and others	14,084	22,012	48,059
Lease paper and others	8,915	17,274	38,008
Other Receivables	2,341	5,894	19,814
Total Liabilities	60,577	III	175,025
Loans and Notes Payable to Banks	7,551	8,617	15,458
Short-term	II	7,900	7,885
Long-term	969	717	7,573
Commercial Paper	22,073	25,905	52,328
Other Debt	30,953	54,194	V

Hypothetical data.

11. What is the value of I in millions of dollars?
    (A) 54,772
    (B) 57,113
    (C) 63,546
    (D) 68,856
    (E) none of these

12. What is the value of II in millions of dollars?
    (A) 6,582
    (B) 14,522
    (C) 53,026
    (D) 58,236
    (E) none of these

13. What is the value of III in millions of dollars?
    (A) 62,811
    (B) 88,716

    (C) 94,610
    (D) 97,333
    (E) none of these

14. What is the value of IV in millions of dollars?
    (A) 45,610
    (B) 47,610
    (C) 47,611
    (D) 54,117
    (E) none of these

15. What is the value of V in millions of dollars?
    (A) 67,786
    (B) 85,147
    (C) 107,239
    (D) 107,259
    (E) none of these

Table for Questions 16–20:

FEDERAL BUDGET RECEIPTS, OUTLAYS, AND DEBT
FISCAL YEARS 1991 TO 1995

(In Millions of Dollars)

ITEM	FISCAL YEAR				
	1991	1992	1993	1994	1995
Total Receipts	I	298,060	355,559	399,561	463,302
Federal funds	187,505	201,099	241,312	270,490	316,366
Trust funds	116,683	131,750	150,560	165,569	186,988
Interfund transactions	−25,098	−34,789	−36,313	−36,498	−40,052
Total Outlays	324,244	364,473	400,507	448,368	490,997
Federal funds	240,080	269,921	295,757	331,991	362,396
Trust funds	109,262	II	141,063	152,875	168,653
Interfund transactions	−25,098	−34,789	−36,313	−36,498	−40,052
Total Surplus or Deficit (−)	−45,154	−66,413	−44,948	−48,807	V
Federal funds	−52,576	−68,822	−54,444	−61,501	−40,030
Trust funds	7,422	2,409	9,496	12,694	12,336
Gross Federal Debt	544,131	631,866	III	780,425	833,751
Held by government agencies	147,225	151,566	157,295	169,477	189,162
Held by the public	396,906	480,300	551,843	610,948	644,589
Federal Reserve System	84,993	94,714	105,004	IV	115,594
Other	311,913	385,586	446,839	495,468	528,995

Hypothetical data.

16. What is the value of I in millions of dollars?
    (A) 91,585
    (B) 162,407
    ✓(C) 279,090
    (D) 304,188
    (E) none of these

17. What is the value of II in millions of dollars?
    (A) 329,684
    (B) 129,341
    (C) 94,552
    (D) –101,202
    (E) none of these

18. What is the value of III in millions of dollars?
    (A) 709,138
    (B) 814,142

    (C) 1,155,977
    (D) 1,260,981
    (E) none of these

19. What is the value of IV in millions of dollars?
    (A) 115,480
    (B) 244,957
    (C) 325,991
    (D) 441,471
    (E) none of these

20. What is the value of V in millions of dollars?
    (A) –27,694
    (B) –27,716
    (C) –52,388
    (D) 52,388
    (E) none of these

Table for Questions 21–25:

STATE AND LOCAL GOVERNMENT SUMMARY OF FINANCES:
1992 TO 1995

(In Millions of Dollars)

ITEM	1992	1993	1994	1995 TOTAL	1995 PERCENT*
Revenue............................	404,934	451,537	506,728	(IV) 74 89	100.0
From Federal Government .	(I)	83,028	90,295	86,945	15.9
Highways and others.....	41,934	48,335	54,515	54,686	10.0
Employment security administration	1,935	2,056	2,367	2,358	(V) 0.43
Revenue sharing and others	31,295	32,637	33,413	29,901	5.4
From State and Local Sources..................	329,770	368,509	416,433	458,952	84.1
General	268,115	(II)	333,109	369,236	67.6
Taxes	205,514	223,463	244,514	266,299	48.8
Property and other.......	139,196	148,426	(III)	175,554	32.2
Income and others........	66,318	75,037	83,574	90,745	16.6
Charges and miscellaneous................	62,601	75,830	88,595	102,937	18.9

Hypothetical data.   *Rounded to one decimal place.

21. What is the value of I in millions of dollars?
    (A) 287,836
    (B) 75,164
    (C) 73,229
    (D) 43,889
    (E) none of these

22. What is the value of II in millions of dollars?
    (A) 145,046
    (B) 324,853
    (C) 342,949
    (D) 371,889
    (E) none of these

23. What is the value of III in millions of dollars?
    (A) 83,324
    (B) 155,919

    (C) 160,940
    (D) 172,169
    (E) none of these

24. What is the value of IV in millions of dollars?
    (A) 372,007
    (B) 545,897
    (C) 915,133
    (D) 1,181,432
    (E) none of these

25. What is the percent value of V?
    (A) .5%
    (B) 5.9%
    (C) 10.5%
    (D) 15.4%
    (E) none of these

Answer Key

1. **(A)**
2. **(E)**
3. **(D)**
4. **(B)**
5. **(A)**
6. **(E)**
7. **(C)**
8. **(C)**
9. **(C)**
10. **(D)**
11. **(B)**
12. **(A)**
13. **(B)**

14. **(E)**
15. **(C)**
16. **(C)**
17. **(B)**
18. **(A)**
19. **(A)**
20. **(A)**
21. **(B)**
22. **(E)**
23. **(C)**
24. **(B)**
25. **(A)**

Solutions

1. **(A)** To calculate the total 1995 *Expenditures,* add the 1995 values for *Direct General Expenditures, Utility and Liquor Stores*, and *Insurance Trust Expenditure.* Numerically, 326,024 + 30,846 + 23,504 = 380,374.

2. **(E)** The correct value (not given as an answer) is calculated by adding the value for *Water and electric* and the value for *Transit and others.* Numerically, 24,244 + 11,947 = 36,191.

3. **(D)** To calculate the 1997 *Employee retirement* costs, subtract the 1997 value of *Unemployment compensation* from the total *Insurance Trust Expenditure.* Numerically, 36,582 − 20,887 = 15,695.

4. **(B)** To calculate the value of 1998 *Direct General Expenditures,* add the 1998 values of *Utility and Liquor Stores* and *Insurance Trust Expenditure,* and subtract that sum from the total of 1998 *Expenditures.* Numerically, 590,966 − (47,970 + 39,466) = 433,530.

5. **(A)** To calculate the percent of total 1998 *Expenditures* represented by *Insurance Trust Expenditure,* add the percents represented by *Direct General Expenditures* and *Utility and Liquor Stores,* and subtract from 100%. Numerically, 100% (83.2% + 9.25%) = 7.6%. Alternatively, add the two components of *Insurance Trust Expenditure (Employee retirement* and *Unemployment compensation).* Numerically, 3.4% + 4.2% = 7.6%.

6. **(E)** The correct value (not given as an answer) can be calculated by subtracting the value for *Charges and miscellaneous* in the *TOTAL* column from the value for *General* under *Revenue from Own Sources.* Numerically, 820,814 − 170,586 = 650,228.

7. **(C)** *Federal Revenue from Own Sources* can be calculated by subtracting the value for *Intergovernmental* in the *FEDERAL* column from the value for *Total Revenue* in the *FEDERAL* column. Numerically, 660,759 − 1,804 = 658,955.

8. **(C)** Calculate the value of state revenues *From federal government* by subtracting the value of revenues *From state or local government* in the *STATE* column from the value of *Intergovernmental* revenues in the *STATE* column. Numerically, 70,786 − 2,918 = 67,868.

9. **(C)** Calculate the value of state revenues from *Employee and railroad retirement* by subtracting the combined values of *Unemployment compensation* and *Old age, disability, and health insurance* in the *STATE* column from the value of *Insurance trust.* Numerically, 48,041 − (18,443 + 4,476) = 25,122.

10. **(D)** To calculate total local revenue, add together *LOCAL Intergovernmental* revenue and *Revenue from Own Sources* in the *LOCAL* column. Numerically, 111,443 + 176,391 = 287,834.

11. **(B)** *Total 1993 Receivables* can be calculated by adding the values for 1993 *Consumer Receivables, Business Receivables,* and *Other Receivables.* Numerically, 31,773 + 22,999 + 2,341 = 57,113.

12. **(A)** The value of 1993 *Short-term* can be calculated by subtracting the value for *Long-term* from the value for *Loans and Notes Payable to Banks.* Numerically, 7,551 − 969 = 6,582.

13. **(B)** Calculate total 1996 liabilities by adding the value of 1996 *Loans and Notes Payable to Banks, Commercial Paper,* and *Other Debt.* Numerically, 8,617 + 25,905 + 54,194 = 88,716.

14. **(E)** Calculate the value of 1999 *Retail consumer goods and loans* (not given as an answer) by subtracting the value of 1999 *Retail passenger car paper and others* from 1999 *Consumer Receivables.* Numerically, 77,460 − 31,950 = 45,510.

15. **(C)** Calculate the value of 1999 *Other Debt* by subtracting the sum of the values of *Loans and Notes Payable to Banks* and *Commercial Paper* from 1999 *Total Liabilities.* Numerically, 175,025 − (15,458 + 52,328) = 107,239.

16. **(C)** *Total Receipts* for 1991 can be calculated by adding 1999 receipt values for *Federal funds, Trust funds,* and *Interfund transactions.* Numerically, 187,505 + 116,683 + (−25,098) = 279,090.

17. **(B)** The value of outlays for *Trust funds* in 1992 can be calculated by subtracting the outlay values for *Federal funds* and *Interfund transactions* from the value for *Total Outlays.* Numerically, 364,473 − (269,921) — (−34,789) = 129,341.

   Note: This formula is solved as 364,473 − (269,921) + (34,789) = 129,341.

18. **(A)** The value of the 1993 *Gross Federal Debt* can be calculated by adding the values of the 1993 debt *Held by government agencies* and *Held by the public*. Numerically, 157,295 + 551,843 = 709,138.

19. **(A)** The value of the 1994 debt held by the *Federal Reserve System* can be calculated by subtracting all *Other* debt held by the public from the total debt *Held by the public*. Numerically, 610,948 − 495,468 = 115,480.

20. **(A)** The value of the 1995 *Total Surplus or Deficit (−)* can be calculated by adding the 1995 surplus or deficit *Federal funds* and *Trust funds*. Numerically, −40,030 + 12,336 = −27,694.

21. **(B)** The value of 1992 revenue *From Federal Government* can be calculated by subtracting the value for *From State and Local Sources* from the value for *Revenue*. Numerically, 404,934 − 329,770 = 75,164.

22. **(E)** The correct value of *General Revenue from State and Local Sources* in 1993 (not given as an answer) is calculated by adding the value for *Taxes* to the value for *Charges and miscellaneous*. Numerically, 223,463 + 75,830 = 299,293.

23. **(C)** The value of revenue from *State and Local Taxes,* and *Property and others* in 1994 may be calculated by subtracting the value of taxes from *Income and others* from the value of all *Taxes*. Numerically, 244,514 − 83,574 = 160,940.

24. **(B)** The value of all *Revenue* in 1995 may be calculated by adding 1995 revenue collected *From Federal Government* and 1995 revenue collected *From State and Local Sources*. Numerically, 86,945 + 458,952 = 545,897.

25. **(A)** To calculate the percent of 1995 *Revenue* from *Federal Government Employment security administration,* add the percents represented by *Highways and others* and *Revenue sharing and others,* and subtract the sum of those percents from the total percent of revenue *From Federal Government*. Numerically, 15.9% − (10% + 5.4%) = .5%.

ARITHMETIC REASONING PROBLEMS

Directions: *These questions require you to solve problems formulated in both verbal and numeric form. You will have to analyze a paragraph in order to set up the problem and then solve it. If the exact answer is not given as one of the response choices, you should select response (E), "None of these." Mark your answers on the answer sheet on page 152.*

1. An investigator rented a car for four days and was charged $200. The car rental company charged $10 per day plus $.20 per mile driven. How many miles did the investigator drive the car?
    (A) 800
    (B) 950
    (C) 1,000
    (D) 1,200
    (E) none of these

2. In one federal office, $\frac{1}{6}$ of the employees favored abandoning a flexible work schedule system. In a second office that had the same number of employees, $\frac{1}{4}$ of the workers favored abandoning it. What is the average of the fractions of the workers in the two offices who favored abandoning the system?
    (A) $\frac{1}{10}$
    (B) $\frac{1}{5}$
    (C) $\frac{5}{24}$
    (D) $\frac{5}{12}$
    (E) none of these

3. A federal agency had a personal computer repaired at a cost of $49.20. This amount included a charge of $22 per hour for labor and a charge for a new switch that cost $18 before a 10% government discount was applied. How long did the repair job take?
    (A) 1 hour, 6 minutes
    (B) 1 hour, 11 minutes
    (C) 1 hour, 22 minutes
    (D) 1 hour, 30 minutes
    (E) none of these

4. In a large agency where mail is delivered in motorized carts, two tires were replaced on a cart at a cost of $34 per tire. If the agency had expected to pay $80 for a pair of tires, what percent of its expected cost did it save?
    (A) 7.5%
    (B) 17.6%
    (C) 57.5%
    (D) 75.0%
    (E) none of these

5. An interagency task force has representatives from three different agencies. Half of the task force members represent Agency A, one-third represent Agency B, and three represent Agency C. How many people are on the task force?
    (A) 12
    (B) 15
    (C) 18
    (D) 24
    (E) none of these

6. It has been established in recent productivity studies that, on the average, it takes a filing clerk 2 hours and 12 minutes to fill four drawers of a filing cabinet. At this rate, how long would it take two clerks to fill 16 drawers?
    (A) 4 hours
    (B) 4 hours, 20 minutes
    (C) 8 hours
    (D) 8 hours, 40 minutes
    (E) none of these

7. It costs $60,000 per month to maintain a small medical facility. The basic charge per person for

treatment is $40, but 50% of those seeking treatment require laboratory work at an additional average charge of $20 per person. How many patients per month would the facility have to serve in order to cover its costs?

(A) 1,000
(B) 1,200
(C) 1,500
(D) 2,000
(E) none of these

8. An experimental antipollution vehicle powered by electricity traveled 33 kilometers (km) at a constant speed of 110 kilometers per hour (km/h). How many minutes did it take this vehicle to complete its experimental run?

(A) 3
(B) 10
(C) 18
(D) 20
(E) none of these

9. It takes two typists three 8-hour work days to type a report on a word processor. How many typists would be needed to type two reports of the same length in one 8-hour work day?

(A) 4
(B) 6
(C) 8
(D) 12
(E) none of these

10. A clerk is able to process 40 unemployment compensation claims in one hour. After deductions of 18% for benefits and taxes, the clerk's net pay is $6.97 per hour. If the clerk processed 1,200 claims, how much would the government have to pay for the work, based on the clerk's hourly wage *before* deductions?

(A) $278.80
(B) $255.00
(C) $246.74
(D) $209.10
(E) none of these

Answer Key

1. (A)	6. (E)
2. (C)	7. (B)
3. (D)	8. (C)
4. (E)	9. (D)
5. (C)	10. (B)

Solutions

1. **(A)** The investigator rented the car for four days at $10 per day, which is $40; $40 subtracted from the total charge of $200 leaves $160, the portion of the total charge that was expended for the miles driven. This amount divided by the charge per mile (160/.20) gives the number of miles (800) driven by the investigator. The computation is:

    $$4(10) + .20x = 200$$

2. **(C)** Obtain the correct answer by computing the following:

    $$(\frac{1}{6} + \frac{1}{4})/2 = x$$

    This simple arithmetic averaging of two fractions can be accomplished by first finding their lowest common denominator:

    $$\frac{1}{6} = \frac{2}{12} \text{ and } \frac{1}{4} = \frac{3}{12}$$

    The sum of $\frac{2}{12}$ and $\frac{3}{12}$ is $\frac{5}{12}$. This fraction, when multiplied by $\frac{1}{2}$ (which is the same as dividing by 2) gives the correct answer:

    $$\frac{5}{12} \times \frac{1}{2} = \frac{5}{24}$$

3. **(D)** The cost of the switch after the government discount of 10% is applied is $18 - (18 \times .10)$, or $16.20. This amount, when subtracted from the total charge of $49.20, leaves $33, which represents the charge for labor. A charge of $33 at the rate of $22 per hour represents 1.5 hours, or 1 hour and 30 minutes, of work. The computation is:

    $$[49.20 - (18 - (18 \times .10))/22] = x$$

    $$x = \frac{33}{22} = 1.5 \text{ hours or 1 hour, 30 minutes}$$

4. **(E)** The correct answer is not given as one of the response choices.

    The expected $80 cost for a pair of tires would make the cost of a single tire $40. The difference between the actual cost of $34 per tire and the expected cost of $40 per tire is $6, which is 15% of the $40 expected cost. The computation is:

    $$(\frac{80}{2} - 34)/40 = x$$

    $$x = \frac{6}{40} = .15$$

    $$.15 \ x \ 100 = 15\%$$

5. **(C)** Obtain the correct answer by computing the following:

    $$\frac{1}{2}x + \frac{1}{3}x + 3 = x$$

    x is equal to the total number of task force members; $\frac{1}{2}x$ represents the number from Agency A; $\frac{1}{3}x$ represents the number from Agency B; and 3 is the number from Agency C. The first two terms on the left side of the equation can be combined by computing their lowest common denominator, which is 6. Therefore:

    $$\frac{1}{2}x = \frac{3}{6}x \text{ and } \frac{1}{3}x = \frac{2}{6}x$$

    The sum of $\frac{3}{6}x$ and $\frac{2}{6}x$ is $\frac{5}{6}x$, which, when subtracted from x (or $\frac{6}{6}x$), yields the results:

    $$\frac{1}{6}x = 3 \text{ and } x = 3 \times \frac{6}{1}$$

    $$x = 18$$

6. **(E)** The correct answer is not given as one of the response choices. The answer can be obtained by first converting 12 minutes to .2 hour, and then setting up a simple proportion:

$$\frac{2.2}{4} = \frac{x}{16}$$

Solving this proportion, we obtain $4x = 35.2$; $x = 8.8$. However, this is the number of hours that it would take one filing clerk to do the job. If two clerks are filling the 16 drawers, the job would be completed in half that time, or in 4.4 hours, which is 4 hours and 24 minutes.

7. **(B)** The basic charge of $40 applies to *all* patients (x); the additional average charge of $20 applies to only 50% (or one-half) of them (.5x). The combined charges—$40 times the total number of patients (40x), plus $20 times one-half the total number of patients (20[.5x], or 10x)—must equal $60,000, the cost of maintaining the medical facility. Solving for x gives the result of 1,200, the number of patients who must be served per month for the facility to cover its costs. The computation is:

$$40x + 20\,(.5x) = 60,000$$

$$\frac{x = 60,000}{50 = 1,200}$$

8. **(C)** Obtain the correct answer by setting up a simple proportion:

$$\frac{110 \text{ km}}{60 \text{ min}} = \frac{33 \text{ km}}{x \text{ min}}$$

Solving this proportion, we obtain $110x = 1980$; $x = 1980/110 = 18$.

9. **(D)** Obtain the correct answer by computing the following:

$$3 \times 2 \times 2 = x$$

The left side of the equation represents the total number of 8-hour work days of typing required for the two reports: three days times two typists, times two reports equals 12 8-hour work days of typing. If all of this had to be accomplished in one 8-hour work day, 12 typists would be needed to do the job.

10. **(B)** The clerk's net pay of $6.97 per hour represents .82 of the gross pay (100% – 18% = 82%, or .82). We can call the clerk's gross hourly pay S for salary. Then we set up two equations to solve the problem.

First:

$$.82S = 6.97$$

Second:

$$\frac{1,200}{40} \times S = y$$

Solving the first equation, we find that the clerk's hourly salary (S) before deductions is $8.50. Substituting this figure in the second equation, we compute the total number of hours of work involved (1,200 forms divided by 40 forms per hour equals 30 hours of work), and then multiply 30 hours by an hourly wage of $8.50 to get $255.00, the amount that the government would have to pay for the work.

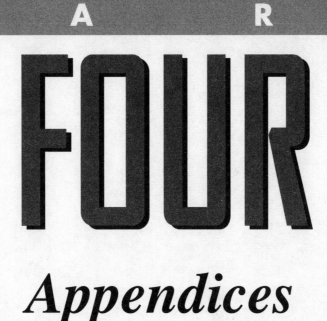

FOUR

Appendices

CONTENTS

IMPORTANT CIVIL SERVICE EMPLOYMENT CONTACTS

Major Federal Agencies Contact Information

Central Intelligence Agency (CIA)
Washington, D.C. 20505
703-482-1100
www.odci.gov

Consumer Product Safety Commission
4330 East-West Highway
Bethesda, MD 20814
301-504-0580
www.cpsc.gov

Environmental Protection Agency
401 M St. SW
Washington, D.C. 20460
202-260-2090
www.epa.gov

Federal Bureau of Investigation (FBI)
935 Pennsylvania Ave. NW
Washington, D.C. 20535
202-324-3000
www.fbi.gov

Federal Communications Commission
1919 M St. NW
Washington, D.C. 20554
202-418-0500
www.fcc.gov

Federal Deposit Insurance Corporation (FDIC)
550 17th St. NW
Washington, D.C. 20429
202-393-8400
www.fdic.gov

Federal Emergency Management Agency
500 C St. SW
Washington, D.C. 20472
202-646-4600
www.fema.gov

Federal Highway Administration
400 7th St. SW
Washington, D.C. 20590
202-366-4000
www.fhwa.dot.gov

Federal Trade Commission
6th St. and Pennsylvania Ave. NW
Washington, D.C. 20580
202-326-2222
www.ftc.gov

Food and Drug Administration
5600 Fishers Lane
Rockville, MD 20857
301-443-1544
www.fda.gov

General Services Administration
18th Street and F Street NW
Washington, D.C. 20405
202-708-5082
www.gsa.gov

Health Resources and Services Administration
5600 Fishers Lane
Rockville, MD 20857
301-443-2086
www.hrsa.dhhs.gov

Immigration and Naturalization Service
425 I St. NW
Washington, D.C. 20530
202-514-2000
www.ins.doj.gov

Library of Congress
1st Street and Independence Ave. SE
Washington, D.C. 20540
202-707-5000
www.lcweb.loc.gov

National Aeronautics and Space Administration
300 E St. SW
Washington, D.C. 20546
202-358-2810
www.nasa.gov

National Science Foundation
4201 Wilson Blvd.
Arlington, VA 22230
703-306-1234
www.nsf.gov

Securities and Exchange Commission
450 5th St. NW
Washington, D.C. 20549
202-942-8088
www.sec.gov

Social Security Administration
6401 Security Blvd.
Baltimore, MD 21235
410-915-8882
www.ssa.gov/ or www.nsf.gov

AUTOMATED TELEPHONE SYSTEM: LOCAL NUMBERS

ALABAMA
Huntsville — 256-837-0894

CALIFORNIA
San Francisco — 415-744-5627

COLORADO
Denver — 303-969-7050

DISTRICT OF COLUMBIA
Washington — 202-606-2700

GEORGIA
Atlanta — 404-331-4315

HAWAII
Honolulu — 808-541-2791

ILLINOIS
Chicago — 312-353-6192

MICHIGAN
Detroit — 313-226-6950

MINNESOTA
Twin Cities — 612-725-3430

MISSOURI
Kansas City — 816-426-5702

NORTH CAROLINA
Raleigh — 919-790-2822

OHIO
Dayton — 937-225-2720

PENNSYLVANIA
Philadelphia — 215-861-3070

PUERTO RICO
San Juan — 787-766-5242

TEXAS
San Antonio — 210-805-2402

VIRGINIA
Norfolk — 757-441-3355

WASHINGTON
Seattle — 206-553-0888

Locations of Federal Job Information "Touch Screen" Computer Kiosks

ALABAMA: Huntsville
520 Wynn Dr., NW

ALASKA: Anchorage
Federal Building
222 W. 7th Ave.
Room 156

ARIZONA: Phoenix
VA Medical Center
650 E. Indian School Rd.
Building 21, Room 141

ARKANSAS: Little Rock
Federal Building
700 W. Capitol
First-floor lobby

CALIFORNIA: Sacramento
801 I St.

COLORADO: Denver
Dept. of Social Services
Employment Center
2200 W. Alameda Ave.
Suite 5B

CONNECTICUT: Hartford
Federal Building
450 Main St.
Lobby

DISTRICT OF COLUMBIA:

Washington, D.C.
Theodore Roosevelt
Federal Building
1900 E St., NW
Room 1416

FLORIDA: Miami
Downtown Jobs and
Benefits Center
Florida Job Service Center
401 NW 2nd Ave.
Suite N-214

Orlando
Florida Job Service Center
1001 Executive Center Dr.
First floor

GEORGIA: Atlanta
Richard B. Russell
Federal Building
75 Spring St., SW
Main lobby, plaza level

HAWAII: Honolulu
Federal Building
300 Ala Moana Blvd.
Room 5316

Fort Shafter
Department of Army,
Army Civilian
Personnel Office,
Army Garrison
Building T-1500

ILLINOIS: Chicago
77 W. Jackson Blvd.
First-floor lobby

INDIANA: Indianapolis
Minton-Capehart
Federal Building
575 N. Pennsylvania St.
Room 339

LOUISIANA: New Orleans
Federal Building
423 Canal St.
First-floor lobby

MAINE: Augusta
Federal Office Building
40 Western Ave.

MARYLAND: Baltimore
George H. Fallon Building
Lombard Street and
Hopkins Plaza
Lobby

MASSACHUSETTS:

Boston
Thomas P. O'Neill, Jr.,
Federal Building
10 Causeway St.
First floor

MICHIGAN: Detroit
477 Michigan Ave.
Room 565

MINNESOTA: Twin Cities
Bishop Henry Whipple
Federal Building
1 Federal Dr.
Room 501
Ft. Snelling

MISSOURI: Kansas City
Federal Building
601 E. 12th St.
Room 134

NEW HAMPSHIRE:

Portsmouth
Thomas McIntyre
Federal Building
80 Daniel St.
First-floor lobby

NEW JERSEY:

Newark
Peter J. Rodino
Federal Building
970 Broad St.
Second floor,
near cafeteria

NEW MEXICO:

Albuquerque
New Mexico State
Job Service
501 Mountain Road NE
Lobby

NEW YORK:

Albany
Leo W. O'Brian
Federal Building
Clinton Avenue and
North Pearl
Basement level

Buffalo
Thaddeus T. Dulski
Federal Building
111 W. Huron St.
Ninth floor

New York City
Jacob K. Javits
Federal Building
26 Federal Plaza
Lobby

New York City
World Trade Center
Cafeteria

Syracuse
James M. Hanley
Federal Building
100 S. Clinton St.

OHIO:

Dayton
Federal Building
200 W. 2nd St.
Room 509

OKLAHOMA:

Oklahoma City
Career Connection Center
7401 NE 23rd St.

OREGON:

Portland
Federal Building
1220 SW Third Ave.
Room 376

Bonneville Power
Administration
905 NE 11th Ave.

Dept. of Army and
Corps of Engineers
Duncan Plaza

PENNSYLVANIA:

Harrisburg
Federal Building
228 Walnut St.
Room 168

Philadelphia
William J. Green, Jr.,
Federal Building
600 Arch St.
Second floor

Pittsburgh
Federal Building
1000 Liberty Ave.
First-floor lobby

Reading
Reading Postal Service
2100 N. 13th St.

PUERTO RICO:

San Juan
U.S. Federal Building
150 Carlos Chardon Ave.
Room 328

RHODE ISLAND:

Providence
380 Westminster
Mall lobby

TENNESSEE:

Memphis
Naval Air Station
Memphis
Transition Assistance
Center
7800 3rd Ave.
Building South 239,
Millington

TEXAS:

Dallas
Federal Building
1100 Commerce St.
First-floor lobby

El Paso
Federal Building
700 E. San Antonio St.
Lobby

Houston
Mickey Leland Federal
Building
1919 Smith St.
First-floor lobby

San Antonio
Federal Building
727 E. Durango
First-floor lobby

UTAH:

Salt Lake City
Utah State Job Service
720 South 2nd East
Reception area

VERMONT:

Burlington
Federal Building
11 Elmwood Ave.
First-floor lobby

VIRGINIA:

Norfolk
Federal Building
200 Granby St.

WASHINGTON:

Seattle
Federal Building
915 Second Ave.
Room 110

WASHINGTON, D.C.:

Theodore Roosevelt
Federal Building
1900 E St., NW
Room 1416

WEBLIOGRAPHY OF FEDERAL EMPLOYMENT WEB SITES

Job Listings

- **Employment Index: Local and State Government Agencies' Job Listings,** www.employmentindex.com/govjob.html—Links to the Web sites of government agencies throughout the United States. Lists public and private sector jobs.

- **Federal Government Job Hotline,** www.unl.edu/careers/jobs/fedhotl.htm—Job hotlines for various federal agencies, from the University of Nebraska-Lincoln.

- **Federal Job Opportunities Bulletin Board,** fjob.opm.gov (Telnet) or ftp.fjob.opm.gov (Transfer Protocol)—Current worldwide federal jobs, many with full announcements, salaries and pay rates, employment information, and other details, from the U.S. Office of Personnel Management. You can record your name and address to have applications mailed to you. Accessible via *dial-up* (912-757-3100).

- **Government and Law Enforcement Jobs,** jobsearch.tqn.com/msubgov.html—An annotated list of Web sites that list jobs with federal, state and local governments, and law enforcement agencies, from the About.com Guide to Job Searching.

- **govtjobs.com,** www.govtjobs.com—A list of jobs in the public sector.

- **HRS Federal Job Search,** www.hrsjobs.com—A subscription job search and e-mail delivery service, which also has a lot of free information.

- **The Internet Job Source,** www.statejobs.com/fed.html—The Federal Jobs section of this site links to job listings at numerous federal agencies and also to online newspapers that list federal job opportunities.

- **Jobs in State Government,** usgovinfo.about.com/blstjobs.htm—An index of state Web sites that list government employment opportunities, with sites ranging from About.com Guide to U.S. Government Info/Resources.

- **U.S. Postal Service: Human Resources,** www.usps.gov/hrisp—A list of vacancies in management, supervisory, administrative, professional, and technical positions only.

- **USAJOBS,** www.usajobs.opm.gov—The official site for worldwide federal employment listings from the U.S. Office of Personnel Management, with full-text job announcements, forms, and answers to frequently asked questions.

Applications and Other Forms

• **Electronic Forms,** www.opm.gov/forms/index.htm—All forms and applications relating to federal employment, from the Office of Personnel Management.

• **The Federal Job Search and Application Form,** usajobs.opm.gov/bla.htm—A description of the federal job search as a three-step process, and three downloadable versions of the OF-612 job application form.

General Information

• **Career City: Government Jobs,** www.careercity.com/content/govcareer/index.asp—A guide to federal and local government employment, with links to job listings.

• **Federal Salaries and Wages,** www.opm.gov/oca/payrates/index.htm—Rates from the U.S. Office of Personnel Management Web site.

• **The Federal Web Locator,** www.vcilp.org/Fed-Agency/fedwebloc.html#toc—Links to agencies in all branches of the federal government, including federal independent establishments and government corporations.

• **Public Service Employees Network,** http://www.pse-net.com/—A guide to government employment, including job listings.

• **The U.S. Office of Personnel Management Web Site,** www.opm.gov—Lots of information on all aspects of federal employment, with an index to make navigation easier.

Online Publications

• **Federal Jobs Digest Online,** www.jobsfed.com—An online version of this well-known publication that provides job listings, federal employment news, and advice on how to get hired.

• **FederalTimes.com,** www.federaltimes.com/—News of interest to those in the federal government.

• **FedForce,** www.clubfed.com/fedforce/fedforce.html—Online service for federal employees, with free registration.

• **GovExec.com,** www.govexec.com—An online publication from *Government Executive Magazine*, bringing news to federal executives and managers.

NOTES

NOTES

NOTES

NOTES

NOTES

NOTES

NOTES

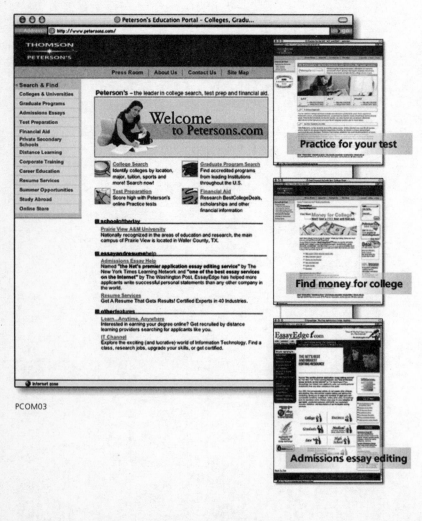